SIDNEY IRONWORKS ACCOUNTS

1541–1573

SIDNEY IRONWORKS ACCOUNTS 1541–1573

edited for the Royal Historical Society

by

D. W. CROSSLEY

B.A.

CAMDEN FOURTH SERIES
VOLUME 15

LONDON
OFFICES OF THE ROYAL HISTORICAL SOCIETY
UNIVERSITY COLLEGE LONDON, GOWER ST., W.C.1
1975

ISBN 0 901050 25 3

Printed in Great Britain by Butler & Tanner Ltd,
Frome and London

CONTENTS

TABLES

FIGURES

INTRODUCTION

I

THE MANUSCRIPTS[1]

The De L'Isle ironworks accounts refer to three undertakings. A forge was operated at Robertsbridge, Sussex, between 1541 and 1573, with two furnaces, one at Robertsbridge between 1541 and 1546, and the other at Panningridge, eight miles away, between 1542 and 1563. Steelworks were in production at Robertsbridge between 1564 and about 1572, and an iron furnace and forge were built in Glamorgan in the early 1560s; these were still in use in 1568. The Robertsbridge and Panningridge ironworks were built by Sir William Sidney, who had purchased Robertsbridge Abbey in 1539, and they passed to his son, Sir Henry, in 1553. It was under the latter that the steelworks and the Glamorgan ironworks were built, and the Robertsbridge ironworks leased out in 1573.

The accounts which have survived are, with one exception, among the De L'Isle and Dudley family papers. Formerly at Penshurst Place, Kent, they were for many years in the care of the Historical Manuscripts Commission for Calendaring, but are now on temporary deposit in the Kent Archives Office, Maidstone. The accounts received a brief indicative treatment in the first volume of the Commission's report, which was sufficient to give an impression of their potential.[2]

The main part of the series is a group of annual summary accounts for the Sussex ironworks between 1541 and 1573, complete except for the years 1550, 1557 and 1561. These summaries are typical of their period, laid out on a charge and discharge system. The charge consisted of the previous year's surplus, small sales of iron, receipts from other estate officials or the Sidneys themselves, and income from rents and agricultural sales. The discharge comprised expenditure on operating the works, but this section also contains household and agricultural items. While these decrease in number over the years 1549–57, there are still some entries in the 1560s which seem irrelevant to ironworking. The main sections are followed by stock accounts and calculations of 'clear gain'.

1 Documents printed in this edition are referred to by bold numbers placed in square brackets in this Introduction, and by the H.M.C. references in italics (see note 5 below).

2 *Report on the Manuscripts of Lord De L'Isle and Dudley*, Historical Manuscripts Commission, (London, 1925), pp. 305–21.

Most of this material derives from the Forge and Furnace books not all of which have survived. All the clerk's receipts were entered in detail in the Forge book, together with payments relating to the forge. It was in this book that expenditure at the original furnace at Robertsbridge was entered. These accounts were probably not the clerk's original working records, for there are a number of fragments, rolls and rough books which have the appearance of preliminary

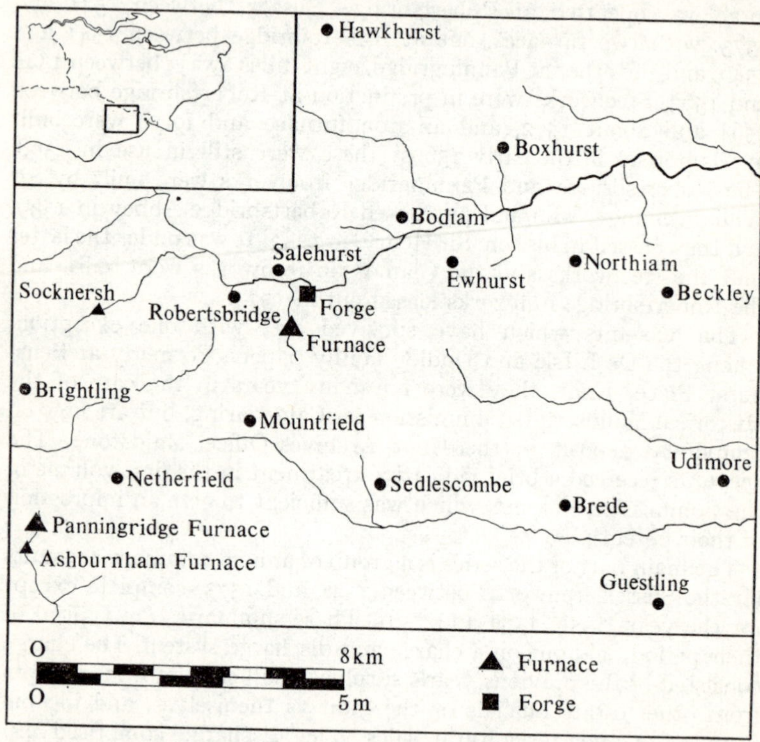

1. Map of Robertsbridge and Panningridge in relation to recorded local markets for iron (*Derived from the Ordnance Survey map of 1878*)

notes, whereas the Forge and Furnace books are well laid out and neatly written. These books contain occasional discrepancies with the summaries, suggesting that the clerk made further checks right up to the presentation of the final accounts.

The surviving material is listed in the Appendix. The fate of the missing items is not known, apart from the Furnace book for 1546.[3]

[3] This Furnace Book passed to the Webster family, who bought the Robertsbridge estate in the 18th century, thence through the Phillips collection, and is

The clerk responsible for the accounts from 1542 until 1549 or 1550 was Henry Westall. He was succeeded by William Blackenall, named in the 1551 account, who continued until 1573. Others involved were Sir John Horrocke, vicar of Salehurst and steward of Sir William Sidney's household, who was responsible for the 1541 accounts (369–70), and John Hawes, the general receiver of the estate, whose name appears on an account lasting from April to August 1542 (372). It is not clear who actually wrote the entries: there is a change of hand in the summaries in 1558, but this does not correspond with the change of clerk.

Apart from the main ironworks papers there are other significant fragments. The first is a sixteenth-century copy of a lease [**1**] of the Panningridge furnace site made by the parson of Penhurst to William Spycer, yeoman, of Dallington, drawn up in 1542, before construction began.[4] The others are for the steelworks [**18–19**] and the Glamorgan ironworks [**20–22**].

Until their arrival in Maidstone the accounts were referred to under a system apparently dating from the original deposit of the entire Penshurst collection with the Historical Manuscripts Commission, in which numbers between 369 and 388 were pencilled on the covers. They are now stored under references corresponding with the normal practice of the Kent Archives Office.[5]

Most of the accounts are written in stitched paper books $12\frac{1}{2}$ in. by 8 in., although the first furnace book [**2**] is 8 in. by 6 in. Some preliminary items are on stitched rolls or written into blank pages of service books from Robertsbridge Abbey. The amount of damage is small; all the summary accounts are legible, but a small proportion of the preliminary material has been affected by damp. One of the steelworks books [**18**] is in places hard to decipher owing to the ink having soaked through the paper to obscure entries on the reverse

---

now in the possession of the Henry E. Huntington Library, San Marino, Calif., whose help in supplying a microfilm copy is acknowledged. A summary and comment is published in E. Straker, 'Westall's Book of Panningridge', *Sussex Archaeological Collections*, lxxii (1931), pp. 253–260 (subsequently cited as Straker, 'Panningridge').

[4] This appears to be a 16th-century copy. It must be assumed that the lease was assigned to Sir William Sidney by Spycer, after a brief interval, this perhaps being the occasion for the making of the copy. The H.M.C. Calendar does not appear to refer to this item. It is uncertain whether the 'Spycer' from whom ore was bought in 1556 was the same man.

[5] In this edition the H.M.C. numbering is placed at the top left of the first page of each item, and the Kent number at the top right. The H.M.C. numbers, being more familiar through their use in the Calendar and by other authors, are used in textual notes and in this introduction, except where ambiguity occurs. (The Kent references use the prefix U 1475.)

sides. The collection was microfilmed under the American Council of Learned Societies' British Manuscripts Project in 1942, the film being held in the Library of Congress, Washington.[6]

While the publication of the entire ironworks accounts would be valuable, their bulk precludes this ideal. It has been decided to include summary accounts which coincide with problems and changes, and those for years whose Forge or Furnace books have survived, enabling detailed information to be added, in footnotes to the texts of the summaries. The Furnace book for 1550 [**7**] has been included, as the only survivor of any kind for that year, and the Forge book for 1555 [**11**] has been taken as a typical example. In addition, the first part of the Panningridge Furnace book for 1543 [**2**] has been printed, to show the building costs of an early blast furnace. With this has been placed the earlier lease for the site [**1**]. The Steelworks and Glamorgan Ironworks accounts [**18–22**] have been reproduced complete.

An Estate survey of 1567–70, detached from the Penshurst collection, is an important topographical source, and is published as *Surveys of the Manors of Robertsbridge . . . .*, ed. R. H. D'Elboux, Sussex Record Society XLVII (1944).

[6] A copy of the microfilm has been consulted during the preparation of this edition. While the photographers excluded certain marginalia, the film has resolved a number of details not now clear to the naked eye on the originals.

II

THE SUSSEX IRONWORKS

In 1540 demand for iron in south-east England was increasing to a significant extent. The growth arose from the development of London, and from the agricultural and constructional needs of the prosperous areas in the south-east which supplied the capital with food. Also there was a fluctuating but significant demand from the dockyards of the Thames and Portsmouth. The response was the introduction of blast furnaces, each of which could provide pig iron with which its forge would produce about 150 tons of bar iron in a year, contrasting with the late medieval water-powered bloomery, whose output was 30–40 tons of bar. Even so, at the beginning of the 1540s the growth in the market for smiths' iron had only recently begun to attract investment on any scale, the earlier furnaces being more closely associated with the arms market. Sir William Sidney was thus taking more of a risk than the numerous landowners who were to build furnaces in the subsequent decades.

In 1539 Sir William had acquired the site, demesnes and certain leased lands of the dissolved Cistercian Abbey of Robertsbridge,[7] an attractive proposition for an office-holder concerned with increasing his income.[8] The *Valor Ecclesiasticus* (1535) shows a compact estate ranging eastwards along the lower Rother,[9] in an area convenient for the dispatch of foodstuffs to the markets of the Cinque Ports and to London. The lands to the south of the river were well wooded, with outcrops of iron ore. While the existing revenues of the estate were no doubt its main attraction, it is likely that the worth of its timber and mineral resources would be appreciated by Sidney. Of the six blast furnaces operating in the Weald by 1540 three were in or near Duchy of Lancaster lands in Ashdown Forest, and, as they supplied the Crown, might well be known to a courtier such as Sir William. Of the rest, two, Darfold and Socknersh, were recently built within four miles of Robertsbridge, using ores similar to those on the Abbey lands[10]. It was, significantly, the Collins, Alexander and

[7] *Letters and Papers Foreign and Domestic, Henry VIII*, xiv, pt. 1, no. 906; xiv, pt. 2, appendix 20; xvi, no. 1056 (77).

[8] H. J. Habakkuk, 'The Market for Monastic Property', *Econ. Hist. Rev.*, 2nd ser., x (1958), pp. 362–80; J. E. Mousley, 'The Fortunes of Some Gentry Families in Elizabethan Sussex', *ibid.*, 2nd ser., xi (1959), pp. 467–83.

[9] *Valor Ecclesiasticus*, Record Commission, i (London 1810), pp. 350–1; *P.R.O. Lists and Indexes (Supplementary Series) III: Lands of the Dissolved Religious Houses*, iv (London 1964), pp. 31–3. D'Elboux, *Surveys*, pp. 180–5.

[10] H. R. Schubert, *A History of the British Iron and Steel Industry . . . to 1775*

John, ironmasters at Socknersh, who supervised construction at Robertsbridge and Panningridge.[11]

Robertsbridge Furnace and Forge

Construction began at the furnace site early in 1541, and smelting was under way late in the summer.[12] The place chosen was on a tributary stream feeding the Rother from the rising ground to the south east (Fig. 2); a dam was built across the tributary valley where it widens into the flood plain, and a pond was formed to the south, to receive water draining from the surrounding woodlands.

The early accounts show no purchases of building materials, suggesting that much stone may have come from the Abbey; they also show a major rebuilding in 1542, when a flood breached the dam and partly demolished the furnace. The equipment of the furnace can be inferred from references to repairs carried out before abandonment in 1546. There were two sets of bellows with iron pipes, indicated by mention in 1542 of re-covering with leather and of smith's work; the type of water-wheel is not known, for no references to repairs to it have survived.

The forge at Robertsbridge was complex and relatively costly to build, because of its siting rather than its equipment. The place chosen was on the southern side of the Rother (Fig. 2) and was fed indirectly from the furnace tributary. There was good reason for the overall layout, for while the furnace was built close to the sources of ore and charcoal, the forge, although near the woodlands to the south, was close to the river and to the landing stage whence bar iron was taken by lighter to Rye. This compromise made water supply difficult, and this accounted for a significant proportion of the cost. The channel that was dug appears to have been a completely new undertaking, suggesting that the forge did not re-use

---

(London 1957), Appendix vi *passim.* (Subsequently cited as 'Schubert, *History*').

[11] For Alexander Collins's later activities see *Tudor Economic Documents* R. H. Tawney and E. Power, ed. (London 1924), i, pp. 237–8.

[12] A single undated sheet (U 1475 E 54/1) in the collection at Maidstone, an item which seems never to have been noted in the Historical Manuscripts Commission Calendar, is worth mentioning. As it refers to Westall and 'the vicar' (Horrocke) it may well have been written by John Hawes, Sir William's steward. It comprises a list of reminders of enquiries to be made at Robertsbridge, which include 'to see what Cattell Remayneth of the olde stock' and instructions over viewing 'all the woods ther'. While it gives the impression of an early stock-taking under new ownership it seems that the furnace works had already been started—'to shewe westall that the vycare dothe charge hym with viii[li] more the was spoken of at his beynge here which he payed for Mynynge'; 'to speke of the settynge of the flasshe over the furnesse pownde'.

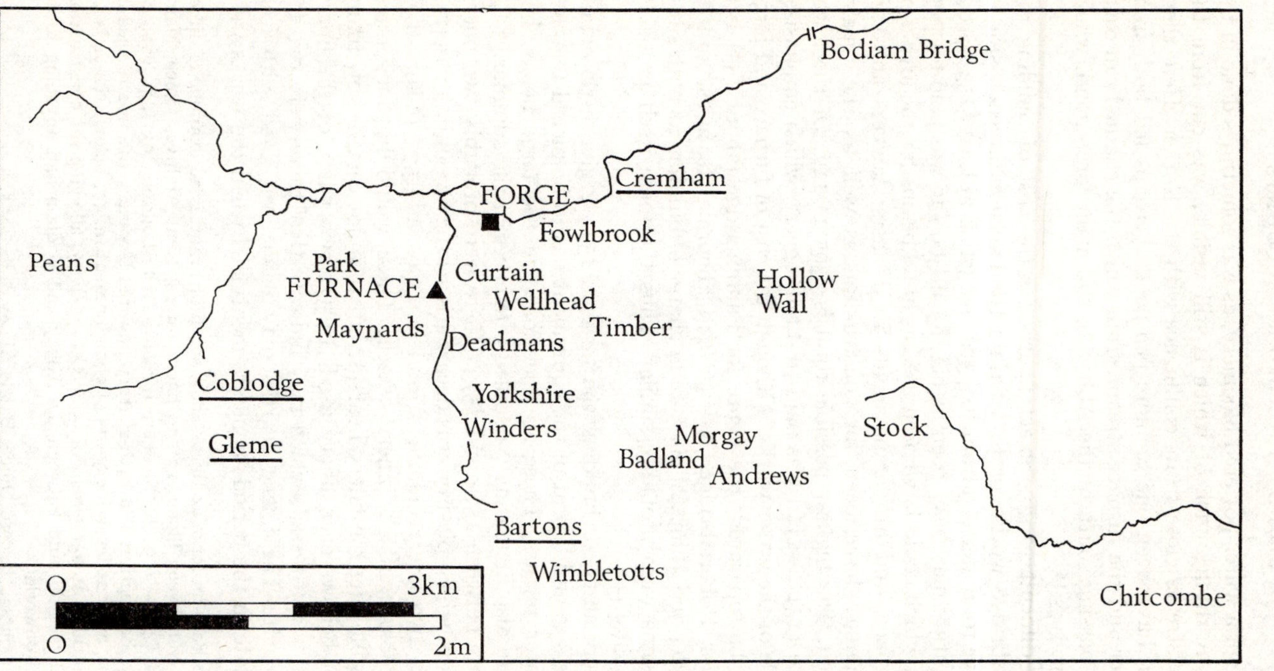

2. **Map of woodlands supplying charcoal to Robertsbridge Forge; place-names underlined have differing modern forms.**
(*Derived from the Ordnance Survey map of 1878*)

the site of a water-powered bloomery, as was sometimes done in the area.[13] A ditch, much of which is still visible, was cut from the furnace stream close to its confluence with the Rother. Here there seem to have been one or more pen-ponds perhaps fed both from the river and the furnace stream, from which the channel ran eastwards, passing south of the Abbey to the main forge pond, whose dam survives.[14]

It is difficult to give exact figures for the cost of building the Robertsbridge works, or to separate the expenses at each site. A tentative total, derived from 369, 372 and 376, is at least £253 14s 8d. Expenditure may have been higher, for in 369 £40 was paid for pigs of iron, which could have been used as lintel beams for the arches of the furnace, and in 372 payments to ditchers, sawyers and carpenters may have been for construction as well as the repairs indicated. The highest possible total is £305 1s 11d. Of the lower estimate £131 9s 11½d was paid to ditch diggers, which emphasises the scale of the water-works. Although the cost of furnace and forge cannot be separated, the figure for Panningridge (about £55) is a guide for Robertsbridge. Neither had abnormal features, and as Alexander and John Collins were in charge of building at both sites, the designs were probably similar. Thus the forge itself probably cost about £65.

The accounts for building the forge in 1541–2 give little detail, and the size and layout of the equipment has to be pieced together from later repairs. These are mentioned in the forge books, but there are also increasingly detailed references in the summaries for the years between 1563 and 1573. There were probably two finery hearths in which pig-iron was decarburised: the accounts for 1541–2 mention two finery chimneys, and in 1556 and 1573 repairs took place to 'one of' the finery wheels. These would have operated bellows blowing the finery hearths, but it is not certain how many pairs of bellows each finery used. In 371 two pairs 'of the finery bellows' were dressed, which may indicate that there were two for each hearth. The finery hearths may have been lined with iron plates late in the period; none are mentioned when the works were

13 The Barham forge at Brooklands, south of Frant, is an example of direct continuity between bloomery and finery forges, Kent Archives Office, Maidstone, U 840/T 109; E. Straker, *Wealden Iron* (London 1931), p. 278. At Chingley, Lamberhurst, a 14th-century powered bloomery site was re-used in the 1580s, after at least 200 years of abandonment (n. 17, below). There is no reason to think an agreement of 1396 (U 1475/E 57) allowing the construction of a mill race on land between the Abbey and Bodiam had anything to do with an ironworks.

14 East Sussex Record Office, Battle Abbey MSS. 4435.

built, but in 1566 the hearths and chimneys were repaired with eleven plates, an early example of a practice well attested from the 1580s onwards.[15] The chimneys, both for the fineries and the chafery, seem to have deteriorated, and after 1555 repairs were frequent; indeed in the 1560s attention was needed in most years. Very little can be gathered about the chafery hearth, used for heating bars being drawn out under the hammer, apart from routine repairs to its chimney, its bellows and its wheel.

The hammer was the most complicated piece of equipment, and would be tripped by cams on the shaft of a water-wheel. Whether it was a tail, belly or nose-helve hammer is uncertain; there are few contemporary illustrations to indicate the type most commonly in use.[16] The wheel required a succession of repairs, particularly new 'arms' (probably spokes) and scoops. Its shaft showed the usual tendency to split, and was bound with iron hoops. There were major repairs to the hammer in 1556 and 1572: taking down the hammer beam and wheel 'and much other' took 20 man-days in 1556, and in 1572 most of the timberwork of the forge was replaced. The hammer head and the anvil were evidently of cast iron: in 1547 the carpenters made a hammer mould; in 1555 moulds for hammer and anvil were carried from Glottenham (two miles south west of Robertsbridge) to Socknersh, and then to Panningridge furnace. Hammer heads were cast—it is not stated where—in 1567, and anvils and heads in 1570. Of some interest are references to the anvil block. This was a heavy piece of timber set below the anvil, and the example recently excavated at Chingley, Kent,[17] was found to be a squared-off length of tree trunk set in a 7-foot-deep pit and braced by radial timbers set against the sides of the pit. The Robertsbridge block was replaced in 1543 and 1551; it was turned in 1553, and perhaps moved again in 1554. Thereafter it appears to have been satisfactory.

In addition storage buildings were required for charcoal and the finished iron, for the latter a substantial tiled structure, perhaps also incorporating the weighing beam carried from London in 1542. There were also three cottages for the forge workers; these are listed in a survey of 1567; the hammerman's house was at the East Gate

[15] P.R.O. Patent Rolls, Elizabeth, 1103: this inventory for St. Leonards Forge, Sussex, is printed in Schubert, *History*, p. 400.

[16] Agricola, surprisingly, only illustrates one complete water-powered hammer; a tail-helve. G. Agricola, *De Re Metallica*, (Basle, 1555), ed. H. and L. Hoover (New York 1950), p. 422. Biringuccio, *De Pirotechnia* (Venice, 1540–9), completely neglects forge hammers.

[17] D. W. Crossley, 'The Ironworks of the Bewl Valley, Kent', Royal Archaeological Institute, Monograph Series, *forthcoming*.

of the Abbey; one finer had a house at the forge itself, and the third was at Courthill.[18]

Panningridge Furnace

In 1542 a furnace was built at Panningridge on land belonging to the parson of Penhurst. In November 1541 a lease, U *1475* E *59* [**1**], had been made to William Spycer, but seems soon to have been transferred to Sir William Sidney. The site was at the eastern end of Panningridge Wood, in the valley of Gifford's Gill between Brightling and Ashburnham; the first Furnace Book, *373* [**2**] shows the work done, and the information can be supplemented from later repair entries.

A detailed appraisal of the structure has already appeared in print, in the report on excavations undertaken at the site in 1964–1970.[19] These made it clear that the furnace bore a general resemblance to those depicted by continental painters of the period.[20]

There remains the more general question of why a second furnace was required. Its construction[21] began so early after smelting started at Robertsbridge that it must be seen as part of an original plan. It may be that prior estimates of furnace production had been pessimistic, and that the pig iron from one site turned out to be sufficient for the forge to refine; for while both operated in 1543–6, Robertsbridge furnace went out of use in the latter year. The choice of Panningridge as the permanent site may appear odd, for its use involved carrying pig iron eight miles to the forge. Indeed Michael Weston, when he leased Robertsbridge in 1573,[22] was prepared to operate the forge and furnace together, so problems of ore or water supply at the latter seem unlikely. Wood supply is perhaps more

[18] This (U 1475 E20/1) is a useful list of the Robertsbridge demesne lands, containing references to many of the woodlands whence charcoal came to the forge. With it should be placed E 20/2, a List of the Sussex Woods of the estate, of much the same period, indicating which were 'appointed to the yron forge'. This, with the Battle Abbey material (n. 14 above) has been of great assistance in compiling *Fig.* 2. See also D'Elboux, *Surveys*, esp. pp. 124ff.

[19] D. W. Crossley, 'A Sixteenth-century Wealden Blast Furnace: a Report on Excavations at Panningridge, Sussex, 1964–70', *Post-Medieval Archaeology* vi (1972), pp. 42–68.

[20] For example: Herri met de Bles, 'Landscape with Ironworks', collection of the Prince of Liechtenstein, in O. Johannsen, *Geschichte des Eisens* [Dusseldorf 1953], opp. p. 144; Bles, 'Landscape with Ironworks and Mines' (Uffizi Gallery, Florence) in Schubert, *History*, frontispiece; Lucas van Valkenborch, 'Rocky Landscape with Huntsman', (Herzog-Anton-Ulrich Museum, Brunswick) in W. Bernt, *The Netherlandish Paintings of the Seventeenth Century* (1970), pl. 1217.

[21] *373*, [2].

[22] p. 43–7 below.

relevant, for while Weston may have been able to get sufficient from the Robertsbridge woods in the 1570s, the situation thirty years before may have been less secure, for the practice of coppicing became more widespread during this period.

III
THE OPERATION OF THE WORKS

(i) RAW MATERIALS

Ore

Little is known of the location or methods of ore-mining for the original furnace at Robertsbridge. Neither an early memorandum, here attributed to Westall,[23] nor the accounts of the years 1541–6 name the land where mining took place; however, the forge book for 1542–3, *379/1* shows that cartage cost 1¾d per load, comparable with the costs at Panningridge from pits a quarter to half a mile away from the furnace there. This corresponds with the geological record, for the base of the Wadhurst clay outcrops in the woods immediately south east and south west of Robertsbridge furnace, and it is at this horizon that the greatest concentration of ore is often found.[24]

The Panningridge accounts are more specific, showing the sources of ore from 1546 until 1556. Originally Panningridge and Haselden woods (Fig. 3) were used, but by the end of the 1540s the area of supply was widening. In 1549 John Cresse's wood appears in the accounts, and was used until 1553. Cresse came from Mountfield, and he was a regular carrier for the works. However, his lands can hardly have been so far from Panningridge, for the ore cost 3d a load to cart, compared with 1½d from Panningridge Wood and 4d or 5d from Haselden. Thus one of the present-day woods on the high ground between Panningridge and Netherfield seems a likely location. From 1554 onwards Snowe's land was used (carriage cost 5d and 6d a load), and from 1556 Spyser's (5d) were used. Walter Snowe appears to have worked occasionally as a carpenter at Panningridge furnace, and was a tenant of John Egleston of Hastings; but neither his holding, nor that of Spyser, have been located, though the last-named may have been the Spycer of Dallington referred to in the Panningridge lease of 1542.

Both the quantity and the quality of the available ore raised problems. The deposits were of nodules scattered in the base of the Wadhurst clay, and mine-pits had a short life, with quantities of

[23] See note 12, above.

[24] H. J. Osborne White, *The Geology of the Country near Lewes* (Geol. Survey, London, 1926), pp. 16–21; *The Geology of the Country near Hastings and Dungeness* (*ibid.*, 1928), pp. 58–69.

clay having to be dug, and backfilled, in the course of extracting the ore. The irregularities in the ground in the woodlands west of Panningridge show the extent of working. Not only was the ore sparse, but competition for it grew, as John Ashburnham's furnace was brought into use half a mile downstream by 1554. In addition, the local ore was peculiar in having its sulphur in the form of calcium sulphate. Normally in the sixteenth century, ore was roasted before smelting to remove the sulphur, and this is referred to in the Glamorgan accounts. But to do this satisfactorily with the Panningridge ores would have required a roasting temperature of 1100°C., which was not possible with the open-hearth roasting of the period.[25] The consequence was that the sulphur content of the iron was high, right through to the finished product, making the Robertsbridge bar of limited use for forging, and suitable only for nail-making and other simple secondary processes. It seems that in some way the problem was recognised, for no roasting was practised at either furnace.

There were also local deposits of a ferruginous limestone: 'shelly' or cyrenae limestone, in appearance a purple conglomerate of shells. This was perhaps thought of as an ore, from its purply rusty colour, and to judge from fragments seen not only at Panningridge but on many other Wealden sites, it was added to the furnace charge.[26] It is not specifically referred to in the accounts, in contrast to the Glamorgan furnace, where limestone was certainly in use, the first documented example in Britain.

Wood and Charcoal (Figs. 2 and 3)

The Forge and Furnace Books show the gradual expansion of the radius of supply. Most of the names of woods near Panningridge have disappeared, apart from Panningridge Wood itself and Haselden Wood, which still form sizeable tracts of coppice, but the relative distances appear from the cartage accounts. Those near Robertsbridge are indicated, where known, on Fig. 2.

The patterns of employment in woodcutting and charcoal burning exhibit seasonal fluctuations. These are clearest in woodcutting, where work was concentrated in the winter months, and in particular in the early spring. Very few payments are recorded between June and October, so probably most of the woodcutters were then occupied in harvest work, either on their own holdings or on those of others. The total number of woodcutters declined at both sites

[25] See note 19, above.

[26] Schubert, *History*, p. 229. For field reports of the material see *Bull. Wealden Iron Research Gp.*, 7 (1974), pp. 12, 20, 21, 26.

during the 1540s; in the early years there were many who were employed on just two or three occasions in a season, but this became less common. The pattern of more regular employment was established rather more quickly at Panningridge than at Robertsbridge, but a seasonal pattern remained at both sites. By the end of the 1540s most wood was being cut by men in regular employment over much of each winter, and who kept to one stretch of woodland until its supplies were used up.

Charcoal-burning employed fewer men than wood-cutting, and here there is also a pattern of reduction in numbers. In the early 1540s numerous colliers provided small quantities, and there were some purchases of charcoal from completely outside sources; but by the end of the decade concentration was obvious. There was also less seasonal burning; by the early 1550s colliers were mostly full-time workers, with less opportunity for harvest work.

Charcoal seems to have been burnt close to where the timber was cut, despite its friability and tendency to reduce to dust in transit; this is inferred from the frequent references to transport of charcoal, but not of wood.

(ii) TRANSPORT

The layout of the ironworks made transport an important factor. The eight-mile journey from Panningridge to Robertsbridge had to be made regularly to prevent costs being inflated by the holding of stocks of pig at the forge.

The details of the ways through Netherfield and Mountfield were examined by Straker;[27] the hilly route must have posed problems in winter, for loads were made up of two pigs together weighing about one ton. However, the accounts show that deliveries were made regularly, so the tracks can rarely have been impassable for long. Each year there were payments for wayleave over the route, showing through whose lands the carts travelled.

Numerous carters appear when rapid repairs were needed. Minor tasks, such as carriage of new anvil blocks from the sawstage in the woods to the Forge were handled by the usual men, but when quantities of building stone or dam material were required there are new names. This is noticeable when the original Robertsbridge furnace was damaged by floods in 1542, and when major repairs were made to the dam at Panningridge in 1555.

Carters were paid in different ways. Regular work was charged

[27] E. Straker, *Wealden Iron* (London, 1931), pp. 363–4 (subsequently cited as 'Straker').

by the load. The standard rate for carriage of sows was 1s 4d per load. Charcoal and ore charges, also by the load, varied by distance, and taking bar from the forge to the quay was on a piece-work basis. Day-rates were paid for repair work and some accounts state whether rates were based on the provision of a cart by the carter. The rate was approximately double that for a man only, 1s 2d–1s 6d for man and cart, rather than 6d–8d.

Water transport was used to take bar iron to Rye. The head of navigation on the Rother appears to have been 'The Oke', probably upstream from Bodiam bridge, and about a mile to the east of Robertsbridge Forge. Lighterage was done at a tonnage rate, and up to six lightermen appear in any one year. The bar was carried to Rye, but the exact size of boat is not clear;[28] John Biddenden, lighterman, was contracted to carry 18 tons in 1542–3 (379/1); the number of journeys involved is not stated. Nor is there any hint as to the means of propulsion, whether horse or sail. At Rye iron was stored in a cellar pending removal, and expenses of transit appear regularly in the forge books under entries such as 'carriage of iron from the wharf to the cellar'. Water transport was also important in the 1560s during the steelworks venture. The plates of cast iron for conversion into steel were brought from Cardiff by sea to Rye, and by lighter to Bodiam.

(iii) CAMPAIGNS AND YIELDS

Some indication of the difficulties experienced in operating the furnace can be seen from the variations in lengths of campaign and in consumption figures. Campaign lengths can usually be derived with fair certainty from the furnace books; for 1546 to 1551, from early in 1553 until late 1556, and for 1558 information is adequate, but as campaigns were usually in progress at the end of each December, the missing accounts for 1552 and 1557 spread uncertainty into adjacent years: it is not clear, to take one example, when the blow ending on 6 April 1558 had begun. The variations in length of operation are very wide (see Table 1); the longest lasted from October 1546 until April 1547, just a week more than six months, and in 1554–5 a campaign ran from October until March. However, there were many examples of two-month campaigns, and some were shorter, particularly when some defect arose. In 1558, for instance, the furnace was blown in on July 1st, to stop on the 9th for the building of a new buttress and hearth. In most cases the furnace was

[28] In 1553 (380/2) a lighter is mentioned as being too large to reach the Oke, and a small boat was used to carry iron as far as Bodiam Bridge.

TABLE 1

Furnace Campaigns

ROBERTSBRIDGE	
1543 (379/1)	March 10–May 13; 12 June→year end. Possible stoppages July 21–6 and Aug. 18–24
PANNINGRIDGE	
1543 (373)	*c.* Jan. 25–Feb. 18 (hearth); Feb. 21–June 12; *c.* June 18–Aug. 7; *c.* Sep. 11–Nov. 5; Dec. 3→
1544–55 *no record*	
1546 (Huntington)	–Feb. 5; *c.* Feb. 15–April 30; May ?–July ?; July 17–Sep. 15; *c.* Oct. 2→April 9 *1547* (Hearth)
1547 (383/1)	May 1–June 17; June 17–Aug 22 (repaired, not relined) Aug. 23–Jan. 9 *1548* (Hearth)
1548 (372A)	Jan. 28–April 11 (Hearth: May 17); Sep. 2–Dec. 18 (Hearth: Dec. 24)
1549 (382/2)	Jan. 23–April 15; *c.* May 30–July 3; Nov. 6–April 30 *1550.*
1550 (*383/3*)[7]	(Hearth: July 11). Aug. 2–*c.* Oct. 21 (Hearth *c.* Nov. 21); *c.* Nov. 25–Jan.25 *1551*
1551 (382/3)	Feb. 21–April 9 (Hearth); April 23–July 25 (Hearth); Sep. 26–Nov. 30; Dec. 7→
1552 *no record*	
1553 (382/4)	?–Feb. 14; March 28–April 28 (Hearth); April 29–June 11; Oct. 23–Nov. 28; Dec. 12–Feb. 12 *1554* (Hearth)
1554 (382/5)	Feb. 16–March 31; Oct. 2–March 3 *1555*
1555 (382/6)	April 17 (casting hammers and anvils only—new hearth); Oct. 1–Nov. 17; Dec. 5–April 18 *1556* (Ref. to new hearth ambiguous: payments on Dec. 26 may refer to Nov. 17–Dec. 5 stoppage). April 18: Hearth.
1556 (382/7)	Dec. 6→
1557 *no record*	
1558 (382/8)	?–April 6; July 1–July 9 (new buttress and hearth): Aug. 10–Oct. 5; Oct. 18→
1559 *no record*	

blown out for the relining of the hearth, but after a short run this seems not always to have been necessary. Indeed some linings, in 1554–5 for example, were remarkably long-lived.

There was some seasonal pattern in operations. Although in some years, for example 1547 and to a lesser degree 1558, there were no long summer breaks in operations, in the middle 1550s these were more pronounced and were presumably due to some combination of slack trade, water shortage or manpower problems.

It is tempting to look for an improvement in yields in those years when long campaigns were achieved. Unfortunately the accounting period ended at the end of December, in the middle of winter campaigns and this dissipated good results into two years' figures.

Further, the yield figures for 1549, important in this context, are of doubtful reliability.

Perhaps the most interesting aspect of consumption figures, both for the furnace and the forge, is the emergence of standardisation, in 1558 for the forge and 1559 for the furnace. From 1558 it was assumed that at the forge 5 loads of charcoal and 30 cwt of pig would be used in producing a ton of bar iron, and these rates were maintained for the next fifteen years, apart from an entirely unexplained figure of 6½ loads of charcoal entered in the 1564 account. At the furnace ore was stated to be used at the rate of 27 loads for a six-day period and charcoal at 22 loads in 1559 and 1560 (the 1561 account is missing), and at 23 loads in 1562.

TABLE 2a

Panningridge Furnace: Ore and Charcoal consumption[1]

	ORE		CHARCOAL			ORE		CHARCOAL	
	per sow	per day	per sow	per day		per sow	per day	per sow	per day
1546	2·7	5·4	2·3	4·5	1554	2·9	5·0	2·6	4·4
1547	2·7	4·6	2·2	3·7	1555	2·5	4·5	3·1	5·6
1548	3·3	3·3	2·3	3·5	1556	3·7	7·5	2·3	4·6
1549	1·8	3·3	2·4	4·4		(2·5	5·1)[2]		
1550	—	—	—	—	1558	—	3·5	2·4	3·7
1551	—	5·0	—	4·5	1559	2·9[3]	4·3	2·4	3·6
1552	3·1	5·8	2·6	4·9	1560	2·8	4·5	2·3	3·7
1553	2·3	4·4	2·2	4·3	1562	—	—	2·4	3·8

1. More reliance should be placed on the 'day' than the 'sow' figures. The latter are derived from cartage payments (from Furnace to Forge) and are thus less direct than desirable. However, while the ore : sow figures fluctuate, those for charcoal : sow, apart from 1555, are encouragingly uniform, suggesting that sow carriage estimates are of some value.
2. The ore figures for 1556 are uncertain. At one point in the account use of 1000 loads is stated, at another, 689: the result of using the latter gives a more convincing result.
3. The actual averages for 1559 onwards fit reasonably with the 'standard' given in the accounts.

Several points of warning should be included here about the reliability of the figures in Tables 2 and 3. In the furnace accounts there is fair certainty about the amounts of charcoal and ore used, as the annual stock figures include these. The number of days for which the furnace ran is usually entered in the main summary

TABLE 2b

Panningridge Furnace: Sows Produced per day

1546	2·0	1552	1·9	1558	1·6
1547	1·7	1553	2·0 (1·95)	1559	1·5
1548	1·5	1554	1·7	1560	1·6
1549	1·8	1555	1·8	1561	—
1550	—	1556	2·1	1562	1·6
1551	—	1557	—		

TABLE 3

Consumption of Charcoal and Pig Iron at Robertsbridge Forge

	Per ton of bar	
	Pig (cwt.)	Charcoal (loads)
1546	33	7·6
1547	27	5·5
1548	28	7·4
1549	33	7·7
1550	—	—
1551	—	6·0
1552	33	6·4
1553	28	7·2
1554	28	6·6
1555	32	5·8
1556	31	7·0
1557	—	—
1558	30[1]	5·0[1]

[1] The standard figures until 1573, except for 1564 (6½ loads of charcoal per ton).

accounts, and some doubts can be resolved from the furnace note-books. For the forge also the charcoal figures seem reliable in most years, as is the final production of bar; there are problems for 1549, when the 'clear gain' calculation has a probably erroneous figure: those from entries under wage payments and stocks make more sense. But the major problem concerns quantities of pig iron. Before 1558 strangely little attention was given by the clerks to these vital figures, and only in 1546 were the numbers of sows made or used included in the stock accounts. It is possible to arrive at a figure by using the stock totals in adjacent years, together with the amount carried from Panningridge to Robertsbridge. The problem lies in the accuracy of the cartage accounts, from which have to be removed stray entries relating to transport of items such as hammers and anvils. This can only be done by using the Furnace Book, or the Forge Books from 1550, when for some reason these figures were transferred thither. We should also be sceptical about the reliability of December stocktakings, for there must have been difficulties about assessing quantities of ore or charcoal, or even pig, when working was in full swing. Further, the central point of the accounts is the working period, the founday. Where standardised consumptions at the furnace are given, charcoal or ore is reckoned not for each sow, or ton of sows, but per founday, as indeed is sow production. Also, pig is reckoned until 1556 by the sow, and there must be some doubt as to whether the 10 cwt sow, carried two to a load, was standard earlier. Most figures fit this assumption, but it is not explicitly stated. In 1568 'at xii^c the sow' is inserted, suggesting that this was a break with normal practice. With these reservations we must examine such figures as we can get.

Overall, at the furnace there does seem to have been a decline in the amount of iron cast in a day. The standardised yield of the final years was 9½ sows per founday (little over 15 cwt per day) but in 1546 and 1556 daily production appears to have reached 1 ton, and was close to that in 1553. While these years' figures may be defective there does appear to have been a decline. Ore and charcoal consumption were steadier, apart from years such as 1549 (ore) and 1555 (charcoal) which may reflect errors in the accounts.

There are fewer problems with the forge figures, which correspond well with those adopted as standard. While there is no great improvement from growing experience, the clerks did seem to be sufficiently confident to set standard yields. What we can see is that the local ores produced a refinable pig, for the 1·5 to 1 yield was a great improvement on the 2 : 1 achieved at Newbridge and compares with the 1·35 : 1 regarded as satisfactory in the 17th century. While it may be that the high sulphur content restricted sales to the lower quality ranges of the market, the actual operation of refining seems not to have been difficult.

(iv) COSTS

Raw Materials

The basic, if not full, costs of charcoal and ore are reasonably accessible when cutting or mining was carried out on ground owned or rented. But when raw materials, particularly standing woods, were purchased there is the problem of knowing how quickly they were cut, carried and used, and whether all their cost should be assigned to smelting or refining in the year of purchase. The stock accounts and on occasion the main accounts provide figures for the amount and cost of wood used, and subject to the proviso above, certain trends are apparent. Further, comparisons may be made between costs and the valuations of stock, assuming the latter approximated to the market price.

The cost of wood depended on its source, and the great variations illustrate the apparent advantage of operating from estate woodland. The great increases in stated costs at Panningridge in 1548, 1551 and 1554 are the result of buying in during that year. At Robertsbridge the difference is equally clear, for after 1558 large quantities were bought. Some can easily be priced, for numbers of cords are stated, but in others only acreages were purchased. It should be noted that wood and ore costs given for Panningridge are slightly on the low side, for they do not take into account the £20 annual rent for Panningridge Wood. This is hard to allocate, for both wood and ore came from this ground; it is perhaps more realistic to enter this rent as an overhead.

These differences between stated costs of estate and bought-out wood, the latter usually but not always purchased standing, underline the inadequacy of contemporary accounting. The estate-grown woods were grossly under-valued, and if bought-in woods and ore, taken at market valuation, had been used consistently, the total cost of making bar iron would at times have closely approached its selling price. To produce bar and sell at this price level indicates either under-pricing, overproduction or a general undervaluation of assets in the industry. Selling wood rather than using it for ironmaking was certainly an alternative, and one which was coming to appear more attractive to the estate in the early 1570s. Essentially the reasons why sites were not leased and ore and charcoal not sold to tenants in the preceding 25 years are twofold. Firstly, that woods were cut for 'great wood' as well as cole-wood; so charcoal could be something of a by-product, or perhaps in occasional cases a bonus from the assarting of land. Secondly the market for small wood was limited, away from the immediate vicinity of towns, until the great expansion in forge and furnace building in the middle of the century. It is when tenant ironmasters appeared in some numbers that estates seemed to retreat from direct operations and sell their wood to the furnaces and forges.

There is an interesting difference between the cost of wood cutting at Panningridge and at Robertsbridge. Rates seem to have been

TABLE 4

Charcoal Costs at Robertsbridge Forge, 1545–73

	Wood: cord	Cords: load of charcoal	Wood cost: load of charcoal	Coaling: load	Carriage: load	Total: load	Price given in stock valuations
	pence		pence	pence	pence	pence	pence
1545	3·0	3·8	11·4	13·5	5·9	30·8	36
1546	3·0	2·7	8·1	13·8	4·1	26·0	36
1547	3·0	2·9	8·7	13·6	3·2	25·5	36
1548	2·9	2·4	6·8	14·7	3·9	25·4	36
1549	3·0	2·3	7·0	14·7	4·7	26·4	40
1550	—	—					—
1551	3·7	3·5	13·0	15·2	6·8	35·0	48
1552	3·8	4·0	15·2	15	5·9	36·1	48
1553	4·0	3·5	14·0	15	4·0	33·0	48
1554	3·5	4·3	15·0	15	6·4	36·0	48
1555	3·6	3·4	11·9	15·2	8·4	35·5	60
1556	3·6	3·0	10·8	*16*	8·6	35·4	60
1557	—	—					—
1558	5·2[1] (3·8)	3·1	16·2	*16*	7·8	40·0	72
1559	14·0[1] (4·0)	*3*	42·0	16·2	8·0	66·2	72
1560	14·0[1] (4·0)	*3*	42·0	16·2	9·0	67·2	72
1561							—
1562	7·3[1] (4·3)	*3*	21·9	18·4	11·9	52·2	80
1563	9·5[1] (4.5)	*3*	28·5	24	6·5	59·0	96
1564	5·4[1] (4·4)	*3·5*	18·8	20	7·6	46·4	96
1565	7·1[1] (4·1)	*4*	28·4	*20*	12·2	60·6	92
1566	7·3[1] (4.3)	*3*	21·9	16	14·6	52·5	96
1567	12·2[1] (4·2)	3·4	41·5	19	15·6	76·1	96
1568	12·2[1] (4.2)	2·7	32·9	20	18·3	71·2	108
1569	4·0	*3·5*	14·0	18·9	18·0	50·9	108
1570	*4*	*4*	16·0	19·5	16·6	52·1	108
1571–2	4·2	*4*	16·8	*19*	11·8	47·6	96
1572–3	4·1	3·5	14·4	*20*	14·2	48·2	—

[1] Wood was bought in these years, and it is assumed here that it was used in the year of purchase. As some was bought standing, both by the (estimated) cord and by acreage, these figures must be taken with caution.

The figures in brackets show the cost of cutting, those in italics are yields and prices stated in the accounts.

TABLE 5

Charcoal Costs at Panningridge Furnace 1545–63

	Wood: cord pence	Cords: load of charcoal	Wood: load of charcoal cost pence	Coaling cost: load pence	Carriage cost: load pence	Total pence	Price given in stock valu-ations pence
1545	2·9	3·3	9·6	14·4	4·3	28·3	36
1546	3·0	2·6	7·7	14·2	4·4	26·3	36
1547	3·2	3·1	9·9	12·8	4·7	27·4	36
1548	8·3[1] (3·0)	4·2	34·8	14·2	5·2	54·2	36
1549	3·6	3·3	11·9	*15*	6·0	32·9	40
1550	—				9·0		
1551	7·7[1] (3·8)	3·4	26·2	*15*	9·6	50·8	48
1552	3·3	3·4	11·2	*16*	10·0	37·2	48
1553	3·7	3·7	13·7	*16*	5·8	35·5	48
1554	5·0[1] (3·4)	3·9	19·4	*15*	8·9	43·3	48
1555	4·0	3·4	13·6	16	9·1	38·7	60
1556	4·6	2·4	11·0	17·2	7·2	35·4	60
1557	—						
1558	4·0	*3*	12·0	16·4	9·5	37·9	72
1559	5·0[2]	*3*[2]	15·0	16·9	12·6	44·5	72
1560	5·5[3]	*3*	16·5	16·6	13·0	46·1	72
1561	—						
1562	5·2	*3·25*	16·9	22·5	15·2	54·6	80[4]
1563	6·3	*3*	18·9	*20*	20·5	59·4	96

1. There were appreciable purchases in these years, and these figures assume that the wood bought was used within the accounting year.
2. This figure is stated in the stock account; 3·5 is given in the main account.
3. This figure is taken from the stock account.
4. This is the valuation for charcoal at Robertsbridge: the Panningridge figure is omitted from the account.

Figures in italics are standard yields and prices stated in the accounts. Figures in brackets refer to the cutting rates in years when wood costs were increased by buying-in.

rather higher at Panningridge after about 1555 but the accounts show no reason for this; and only the relative distances of woodlands from sources of village labour can be suggested.

The total cost of charcoal was influenced by distance from the works, and Table 5 shows how carriage charges at Panningridge rose to equal the cost of charcoal-burning. The tendency can also be seen at Robertsbridge, although somewhat later; in some years in the 1560s cost of carriage virtually equalled coaling, effectively indicating the growing radius of supply. This is emphasised by some of the locations referred to in the 1560s, which show the southward movement in the purchase of standing wood (Fig. 2).

The cost of ore shows less variation. Rates for mining rose by one-third between 1548 and 1552, from 7½d to 10d, before dropping to 9d in 1554 to remain there until 1560. Carriage however shows a

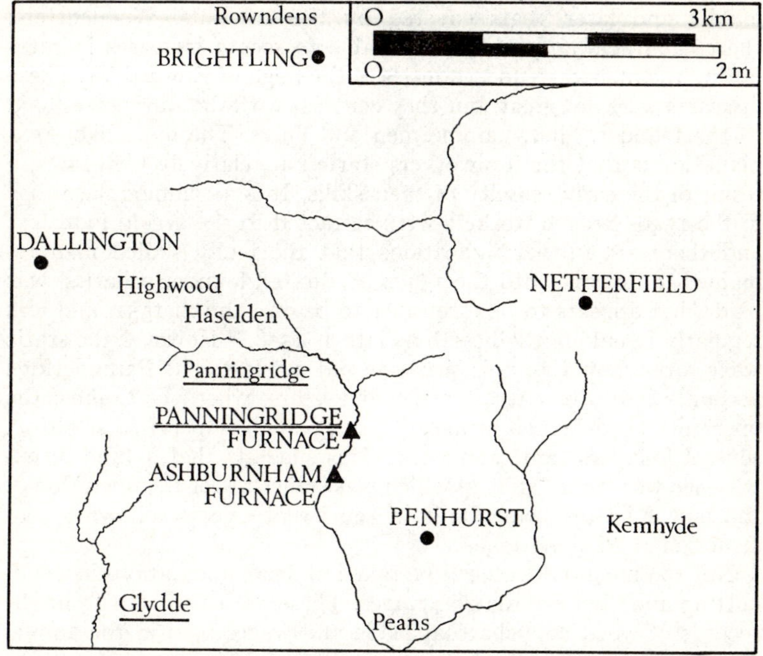

3. Map of woodlands supplying charcoal to Panningridge Furnace; place-names underlined have differing modern forms. (*Derived from the Ordnance Survey map of 1878*)

trend similar to that of charcoal, varying between just under 1d to 1½d a load up to 1548, but rising to 5d for most years in the 1550s, far more than could be explained by any increase in the cost of labour.

Wages

Labour costs at the furnace and the forge remained notably stable. Payment at the furnace was by the 6-day founday and rates remained steady at 8s for the founder and 6s for the filler until 1556; in 1558–60 the filler was paid 6s 8d per founday, and in 1562 the total for both was 15s 8d. At the forge the hammermen and finers received no increase in their rate between 1546, when their total was 13s 4d per ton, and 1560. In 1563 the total was 17s 2d per ton and in 1566 16s 5d. As the old rate of 13s 4d was being paid between 1569 and 1572 the higher figures may be due to the occasional employment of an extra man.

The most striking point is the buoyancy of wages in the woodland occupations, woodcutting, charcoal burning and ore mining in the middle and later years covered by the accounts. Woodcutters, charcoalburners and miners were able to secure increases in rates during the monetary uncertainties of the reign of Edward VI. These increases were not great, but they contrast with the static rates paid to the founder, filler, hammermen and finers. The most likely explanation is that the ironworkers started at relatively high rates, a result of the early scarcity of their skills. It is a commonplace that in the 1540s French workers were attracted to the Weald industry, and there are further indications that the really skilled man remained in demand into the 1550s. A Buxted founder, Charles, was paid what appears to be a retainer to be on hand in 1551, and was regularly remaking the hearth as late as 1558.[29] However the static wage rates show that this situation did not last. The Panningridge accounts indicate that after the first years, when the Collins, the operators of Socknersh furnace (above, p. 5–6), supervised smelting, several founders came and went. This suggests that a fund of experience was being built up which was sufficient for the operation of the new furnaces being built in the twenty years following construction at Panningridge.

Not too much notice need be taken of small fluctuations in woodcutting and charcoal-making wages. These are calculated from the records of wood cut, charcoal made and wages paid in the annual accounts; examination of surviving forge and furnace books shows that in the case of woodcutting, overall rates could be affected by extra payments for cutting old wood, for topping and lopping, or other minor extra work. Similarly the use of two sizes of cart, one about 8% larger than the other, can have a slight effect, not usually identifiable from the consolidated accounts.

[29] P.R.O., E 36/50 (muster rolls: hundred of Netherfield, 1539): 'there be xlix Frenchemen inhabityng in the boroughs and townes aforesaid'. This was before the Sidney works started, but Socknersh would already be in operation. In 1544 the estate paid for Letters Patent for aliens (*375/10*) and the names of five workers were among those granted letters of denization; *Huguenot Society Publications*, viii (Lymington, 1893), *passim*; listed also in Straker, 'Panningridge', p. 260. 'Charles' seems to have been Charles Pulleyn; there are two men of such a name mentioned in the Denization Rolls, both in July 1544. See Schubert, *History*, p. 172, n. 3.

Labourers' wage rates are only available in years for which Furnace and Forge Books survive, and variations are large; in 1548, for instance, day rates varied between 4½d and 8d without clear explanation. Some of the higher rates are occasionally stated as being paid to men 'finding themselves', with the implication that others may have received part-payment in kind, perhaps in food, whose cost is not entered in the accounts.

Overheads

These are perhaps the most difficult costs to assess, particularly at Robertsbridge where so many outside items appear in the accounts, and where some renewals and repairs may have been to buildings away from the forge site. At Panningridge the position was more straightforward, repairs being relatively simple to identify. The rents of the wood have been explained above, leaving miscellaneous items minimal up to 1548, but inflated from 1549 until some months into 1559 by money paid to one Richard Martin, possibly one of the clerk's assistants, whose wages had earlier been entered at Robertsbridge.

(v) THE SALE OF PRODUCTS

Most of the pig iron produced at Panningridge furnace was sent to Robertsbridge for conversion into wrought-iron bars. A small quantity was cast direct into anvils and hammerheads for use at the forge, but this was an insignificant proportion of the total. No guns or ammunition were cast, and references to other goods being cast for sale are very rare.

By far the greatest quantity of wrought iron from the forge was sold in large lots, up to 80 tons, to a limited number of ironmongers. In the 1540s, Webb and Draper were the major buyers, being superseded by Hickeby, Bacon, Golston and Roberts in the 1550s. Roberts was the major buyer throughout the 1560s, although Bacon made sporadic purchases, and Draper, absent since 1553, reappears in 1570. Little information about these buyers emerges from the accounts. Draper and Clarke are described as London men; Edmund Roberts, though described as of Hawkhurst, in fact had considerable interests in London.[30] The concentration on London grew during the 1540s. In the early years sales had been made in Southampton, where delivery had been made to Webb in 1542, although it is not clear whether his subsequent purchases, which end in 1548, were

[30] T. S. Willan, *The Muscovy Merchants of 1555* (London, 1953), pp. 119–20.

also sent there. All the large consignments appear to have been sent to Rye by lighter.

While the large deliveries, for which payment was made direct to the estate's Receiver, are recorded in outline in the annual stock accounts and increasingly noted in the receipts, the small sales are less consistently accessible. The annual accounts only record the total weight thus sold and the money received, and details have to be derived from Forge Books. Here there is sufficient information to show the radius of sales. Smiths from the Rother valley, Rye, Brede, Ewhurst or Nordiam are regularly mentioned and more distant purchasers from Ashford, Farningham, and even Reading, appear on occasion. They bought small quantities, frequently less than 1 cwt at a time. Of particular interest are the small purchases made for the Crown in the 1540s; it is clear from the 1542/3 account 377/1 [**3**] that Camber castle was using Robertsbridge iron at this time. It must be assumed that most of the small purchasers were village smiths who would previously have used bloomery iron. A number can be seen from entries elsewhere in the accounts to have been specialists to some degree. Philpott and Buckett were nail-makers, Philpott perhaps on some scale, to judge from the regularity and size of purchases from him of bellows nails. Another significant purchaser, Slater, a Dallington smith is first mentioned in 1551; it was to him that ironwork, notably fittings and tuyeres for bellows, were taken for repair from Panningridge. It is perhaps worth noting that this specialism was developed by an outside blacksmith rather than within the forge at Robertsbridge.

IV

THE PROFITABILITY OF THE WORKS

Examination of the annual accounts shows that modern concepts of profit and loss measurement are difficult to apply. The form of the records, laid out under charge and discharge, emphasises that medieval accounting was arranged as much to detect fraudulent servants as to render accessible the information from which the success of operations could be gauged. There are essentially three methods which can be used to check on the profits of the works.[31]

(i) THE CALCULATION OF 'CLEAR GAIN'

At the end of each annual account the 'clear gain' was reckoned by totalling the market value of the increases in stocks of raw and semi-finished materials over the previous year, and the market value of the iron produced. From this were deducted all payments, and any reductions in stocks, again at assessed values presumed to be equivalent to market prices. This reckoning could give the clerk a rapid if rather crude view of the year's work; however there are certain shortcomings which are perhaps anachronistic in that they take more variables into account than contemporaries were accustomed to. Most obvious is the tendency in the first decade's accounts to include expenditure not strictly relevant to iron-making. In 1546 for instance, there are payments to farm workers, repairs to marshland property, the purchase of cattle and carriage of rent corn. These would have been better entered elsewhere, but nevertheless the total of expenditure to which they contribute is carried forward for use in the clear gain calculation. Some items may have brought some benefit to the works; fencing, or the provision of foodstuffs for oxen are examples, although the forge books are rarely explicit over this.

After 1550, when William Blackenall probably took over as clerk, fewer outside items appear, but a further weakness remains. The clerk had to be alert to the effects of changes in prices, and thus valuations, for large changes could well affect the clear gain figure. If for instance a large stock of pig iron were in hand and its market value rose, the final figure might, while reflecting the worth of assets, give more cause for satisfaction than could be justified by a closer

[31] For a more detailed discussion see D. W. Crossley, 'The Management of a Sixteenth-Century Ironworks', *Econ. Hist. Rev.*, 2nd ser., *xix* (1966), pp 272–86.

examination of furnace or forge yields. The clerk would also have to watch the state of the bar iron market and his competitive position in it; to take an example, in 1551 there was a high figure for clear gain, inflated by unsold and perhaps unsaleable iron.

(ii) TRANSACTIONS INVOLVING THE GENERAL RECEIVER OF THE ESTATE

One of the peculiarities of these accounts is that the clerk handled only a small proportion of the receipts from sales. Income from large consignments went straight to the estate receiver. Money paid to the clerk by local smiths was insufficient to cover running expenses, and was supplemented by payments from the receiver, from 'my lady' (Lady Sidney), and from Sir William and Sir Henry. In addition some estate rents and receipts from farm sales were diverted to the ironworks in the earlier years. The receiver, if not the clerk, would get some idea of the position of the works by deducting these payments from the totals he received from bulk sales. Such a procedure would also have weaknesses; again, money might have been laid out to build up high stocks of materials, but the receiver would at least calculate partly on the basis of sales that had actually taken place, rather than taking into account only iron made but not necessarily sold, as in the 'clear gain' method.

(iii) CALCULATIONS OF PROFIT DERIVED FROM THE ACCOUNTS

It should be emphasised that the form in which the accounts were drawn up makes it hard to calculate profit from the details of income and expenditure. If the clerk had attempted to do this, it is likely that he would have used a different layout and that some signs of such calculations would have survived.

Nevertheless there is sufficient information in the summary accounts to calculate consumption and costs, despite the omission of figures for pig-iron production, which have to be inferred from the carriage figures. For example in 1548 the cost of producing a ton of bar iron appears to have been £4 4s 5d, compared with the valuation of £7 in the stock accounts. The stock valuation can be taken as approximately the price the market would bear, and in some years this can be checked from the accounts of the estate receiver, who recorded the bulk sales omitted from the ironworks accounts.

The stock valuations can be used at each stage of the process to test whether any operations were endangering profitability and should have been replaced by buying in. By 1558 smelting at the furnace was approaching this point. Pig costs were £1 11s 4d per ton, with the valuation at £1 13s 4d, but in 1559 the figures drifted apart, and the approach to the margin was not repeated. At the forge there was always a comfortable margin between costs and prices: even if charcoal had been bought in, the conversion stage would have remained worthwhile.

V

DIVERSIFICATION AND RETRENCHMENT, 1563–73

The final ten years of the estate's interest in the industry included major changes in the structure of the iron-making operations, the introduction of the steel-making project using iron made on the Glamorgan estate and the final leasing of Robertsbridge Forge in 1573. This was the period in which Sir Henry Sidney was Lord Deputy in Ireland, but his interest in maximising income from his estates did not diminish.

Robertsbridge Iron Works

By 1560 the growth in the number of furnaces in the south-east Weald was at its height; supply radii for charcoal wood were overlapping, and growing output of pig iron was reflected in low prices, made still lower at the end of the 1550s by the Crown's diminished post-war need for cast-iron shot. In the late 1550s Panningridge furnace had been operating at costs approaching the market price of pig, and while there was some recovery, the option of purchasing pig iron was worth considering; also there are archaeological indications that a major rebuilding was necessary at the furnace. Assuming that the 21-year lease of 1542 between the parson of Penhurst and William Spycer had been taken over without alteration, a new agreement would have been required in 1563; this apparently was not made.

From 1561 until 1568 purchases were made from furnaces within about 10 miles of Robertsbridge, mostly in the range of 30–60 tons a year from each. Then in 1568 an arrangement was made with Richard Wekes who ran the 'New Furnace', at Battle Park or Mountfield, for him to supply 210 tons of pig annually, taking in return 70 tons of bar iron, which at the current conversion ratio was half the product of his pig iron.[32] In 1566–7 this was a worthwhile

[32] Relfe and Jefferey in 1563 and 1565, and Relfe alone in 1566 and 1567 sold pig from Panningridge; Collins from Socknersh in each year except 1564, when pig was supplied but not paid for within the year; Wekes from the New Furnace in 1567. Apart from some small suppliers, Barbe, Gardiner, Hervye and Jyles, none otherwise known and none supplying more than 7 tons, the only unknown man is John Morys, from whom 60 tons were purchased in 1563 and 30 tons in 1567. As deliveries did not necessarily take place in the year of payment it is difficult to correlate sellers with their furnaces; in any case the latter are not named in the 1563 and 1564 accounts. Deliveries from Penhurst and Ashburnham in 1565 and Penhurst in 1566 do not fit any of the other suppliers,

scheme from Sidney's point of view, given the relationship between pig and bar prices at the time. Indeed the arrangement gave the forge an incentive to improve its yield, for it had to provide Wekes with a fixed quantity, rather than a proportion of the product from his pig. Improvements were not achieved, and the independent variation of pig and bar prices, noticeable in previous years, went against Sidney. Pig prices declined, which meant that the forge was paying dearly for its supplies.

The arrangement ceased in 1573, when the two Robertsbridge sites were leased to Michael Weston at an annual rent of £200, with a £30 reduction in 1576 as compensation for the poor state of the furnace. The information is insufficient to assess the change. Profits from the forge had been well above this level in each year from 1568, and if there was any advantage it may have been seen in potential sales of timber. However the Rental of 1574 and the Valuation of 1575 both show the ironworks *with* 'the woods on the demeanes' as worth £200, and the Receivers' accounts show no sales of local timber to Weston or anyone else. If this was really so, the arrangement seems unsatisfactory and there must be some suspicion that other factors were involved. It is not clear, for instance, if the demesne woodlands Weston appears to have leased were all of those used for the forge before 1573, or whether there were others which were now required for other purposes, or for recuperation for cutting some years later.

Weston was in a strong position; he was associated with David Willard and Robert Woddy, and together they controlled furnaces and forges over a wide enough area of Kent and Sussex to give them flexibility in their operations. How long the tenancy lasted is not known; sufficiently detailed estate rentals only exist for the years up to 1579. The 1588 list of ironworks is of no help, for the returns for Sussex appear not to have survived.[33]

The later history of the forge and furnace is scanty, but it is

---

and it is just possible that these are attributable to Morys. Whether he was a lessee of Ashburnham furnace and this iron was made there is not clear, so this can only be a tentative suggestion. It is not known when the Mountfield furnace was built; it appears in the 1574 lists (Straker, p. 326). It is closer to Robertsbridge than Wekes' Battle Park furnace. The furnace at Beech (Straker, p. 325) is also a possibility. Schubert (*History*, pp. 367–8) infers, without proof, that Wekes made pig for Robertsbridge here.

[33] Receipts of rents for the ironworks appear in (H.M.C.) 150, 155, 165 and 273. The problem of the acceptability of the returns to the 1588 enquiry into Wealden ironworks is dealt with in C. S. Cattell, 'An Evaluation of the Loseley List of Ironworks within the Weald in the Year 1588', *Archaeologia Cantiana*, lxxxvi (1971), pp. 85–92.

well-established that they continued in use into the 18th century. Only one fragment of later accounts survives, for 1700–2.[34]

The Glamorgan Ironworks

The three surviving accounts comprise Edward Nevet's summary for 1564–5, that of his successor Thomas Danne for 1567–8, and Danne's estimates for the cost of producing pig iron and plates for steelmaking. All three are reproduced in this edition [**20**–**22**], but little external information is available.[35]

Sir Henry Sidney became Lord President of the Council in the Marches of Wales in 1559. He must have become involved in Glamorgan soon after this date, for the 1564 account shows that the works were a going concern. They refer to three co-partners, Sidney, Ralf Knight and Edmund Roberts, the London merchant and iron-monger, purchaser of iron from Robertsbridge forge, and it is not difficult to surmise how the venture began. The estimate of costs [**22**] shows that the furnace and forge sites were rented, but it is not clear from the references to rents in **21** how much land or mining ground was included. **22** (fo. *8v*) refers also to houses and land held in fee simple, but does not identify them.

Although the works are chiefly known for their association with the Robertsbridge steel project, they were in operation before the latter began, producing pig and bar in the normal manner. How soon Edmund Roberts became aware of the potential of the local haematite ores for iron suitable for conversion is not known. In 1564 iron was being sent to Bristol, Gloucester and up the Severn to Bewdley; the total of bar sold, almost 82 tons, indicates a relatively small concern.

The estimate of costs is of particular interest, but Schubert's published comments are based on an inaccurate transcription.[36] The document shows the different quantities of materials used for the two products, but it is not clear whether the plates sent to the steel-makers had a lower carbon content than the furnace's pig iron. One difference was in the amount of limestone and marl used; this must

[34] Schubert, *History*, pp. 192, 229, 233, 385. Fragmentary Accounts for 1700–2 survive in the De L'Isle collection (U 1475 B 18/1–3).

[35] T. Bevan, 'Sussex Ironmasters in Glamorgan', *Trans. Cardiff Naturalists' Soc.*, lxxxvi (1965–7), pp. 5–12, confuses these activities with the Sidneys' interests in the Bridgend area after 1584. W. Llewellin (*Archaeologia Cambrensis*, 3rd ser., ix (1863), pp. 81–119) does not refer to the Sidneys' operations.

[36] Schubert, *History*, p. 319, lists the consumption of raw materials, but transposes the amounts for plates and pig. His suggestion that there was a higher proportion of ore to charcoal in the charge and thus a lower carbon content in the plates therefore seems unsound.

have been dependent on trial and error, and by varying the nature of the slag must have been thought to affect the product. The yields at the Glamorgan forge may have been rather better than at Robertsbridge, for while the 3 : 2 ratio was the aim, the wording in *387* [**21**] 'a lack of weight by a fault in the beam at the furnace' rather suggests that the pigs were 10% lighter than the forgemen had thought.

The location of the furnace and forge are not clear. Schubert suggested that the furnace was at Tongwynlais, about six miles up the River Taff from Cardiff and that the forge was about eight miles east of the furnace, at Rhyd-y-gwern in the Rhymney valley.[37] The carriage costs, 3s 4d per ton from the furnace to Cardiff, 5s between the furnace and the forge and 5s thence to Cardiff correspond with the distances, assuming that each leg was by land. If a boat were used for carrying plates from the furnace at Tongwynlais to Cardiff, the cost might have been expected to be less, but **22** (fo. *1v*) does not make it clear that a boat was being used on the Taff. The entry 'iid the tonne to the bote' could well be from a warehouse in Cardiff to the quay. A house in Cardiff is referred to in **21**.

The Steelworks

Two accounts survive for the steelworks which were set up in 1565 in the buildings of Robertsbridge Abbey and at an unidentified site at Boxhurst, five miles to the north east.[38] The first document [**18**], a general account of expenditure dated 1566 but covering payments from June 1565 and perhaps rather before, is in poor condition, although most of the payments made while the works were being established are legible. The second account [**19**] is a declaration of reckoning for the year beginning in December 1567, although it refers to sales during previous months for which payments were outstanding.

Only a brief note is required here, as these accounts have already been referred to in print.[39] They are significant as the first detailed

[37] Two early furnaces whose sites are noted by D. Morgan Rees in 'Industrial Archaeology in Wales', *Archaeologia Cambrensis*, cxiii (1964), pp. 129–49, are at Cwm Amman (N.G.R. 004992) and Blaincanaid (042048). Both seem too far from Cardiff to correspond with the cost of carriage.

[38] Boxhurst is a farm south east of Sandhurst. It lies about two miles from Bodiam Bridge, where iron plates from Glamorgan and finished steel for London were trans-shipped. No trace of steelworks have been found on the ground. I am grateful to Mr. D. Hemsley for arranging field investigations in this area.

[39] Rhys Jenkins, 'Notes on the Early History of Steelmaking in England', *Trans. Newcomen Society*, iii (1924), pp. 16–40; H. R. Schubert, 'The Economic Aspects of Sir Henry Sidney's Steelworks . . .', *Jnl. Iron and Steel Institute*, clxiv (1950), pp. 278–80; see also Schubert, *History*, pp. 315–21.

record of English steelmaking; indeed this seems to have been the first case in this country of steel being made by the partial decarburisation of pig-iron rather than by a variation of the bloomery process. The Robertsbridge group was made up of Sir Henry Sidney, Ralph Knight and later his widow Joan, the ironmonger Edmund Roberts and David Willard, a prominent ironmaster. They were granted a licence on 8th August 1565[40] to bring aliens to make steel and iron wire, although they were unable to get bills granting monopolies through Parliament. Indeed the monopoly of wire manufacture was gained by William Humphrey, who operated the Tintern wireworks. Before the grant of the licence the group had taken initial steps to seek skilled labour and appropriate materials. The General Account, *384* [**18**] records the payments to John Frolycke and John Bowde for going to Wales in June 1565, presumably to inspect the furnace in Glamorgan which later supplied plates of cast iron for conversion.[41]

A start was made in building forges during the autumn of 1565, and German workmen came between October of that year and May 1566, almost certainly from the Sauerland and Mark, areas whose steel had regularly been sent to England. Production was established by December, and the General Account records considerable sales to London as well as smaller amounts to Coventry, Ipswich, York, Wales and Ireland. Glamorgan iron was used, although in 1565 one load was brought from Chingley furnace, Lamberhurst.

In the period between the two accounts the initial success of the scheme began to wane. Although at first German steel exporters found themselves severely undercut on the London market by the new works, by 1568 cheaper steel from the Baltic in turn undercut the Robertsbridge product, whose sales and price fell between 1566 and 1568 from 169 firkins at £6 10s–£7 to 51 at £6, then to 18½ at £5 in 1570–71, shown in the estate receiver's account for that year. The works were still operating in 1572, but whether for very much longer is in doubt. While the Robertsbridge steelworks appear in an estate survey of 1609, there is no evidence that they were being run.[42]

[40] P.R.O., C66/1052.

[41] Rhys Jenkins, *op. cit.*, pp. 17, 33, states that the steelmakers had been engaged in 1564. Unless the manuscript has deteriorated at a key point this appears to be an error.

[42] Schubert, 'The Economic Aspects of Sir Henry Sidney's Steelworks', pp. 278–80.

VI

EDITORIAL PROCEDURE

In general the guidance given in the 'Report on Editing Historical Documents' in *Bulletin of the Institute of Historical Research*, i (1923), has been followed. In order to save space where preambles and formulae are repeated, the first of a series is underlined and those following are represented by dots. The clerk's working calculations, which occasionally appear in the margins of the original, are omitted when they add nothing to the figures in the main entries.

Obvious contractions are silently expanded; doubtful readings are placed in square brackets. Frequently-repeated contractions of quantities, and contracted proper names whose full spelling is in doubt are not expanded. Certain contracted latin words, whose expanded spellings are doubtful, are also left in their original form. Round brackets enclose material inserted in the text after it was laid out; they are also used to indicate words crossed out in the original, with footnotes for clarification. The form 'ff' is rendered by 'f', '&' by 'and' and 'ye' by 'the'.

Punctuation in the original accounts is irregular; before about 1558 dashes, oblique strokes and spaces are common, but in this edition modern stops are used where clarification is needed in the more complex entries. In the later accounts the original punctuation is mostly in modern form and causes no difficulty.

ACKNOWLEDGMENTS

I am grateful to the Rt. Hon. Viscount De L'Isle for allowing me to study and edit the manuscripts from his archives, to Mr. R. H. Ellis, Secretary of the Royal Commission on Historical Manuscripts and Dr. F. Hull, County Archivist for Kent, for permission to work on the material while in their care, to the Knoop (Economics) Research Fund of Sheffield University for grants in support of research and preparation for this edition, and to Elizabeth Crossley for drawing the maps.

GLOSSARY

Andirons Fire-dogs, commonly made of cast or wrought iron.

Bar Iron A malleable material (wrought iron) with a low carbon content; less than about 0·1%. It was suitable for use by blacksmiths.

Bay Dam.

Blast Furnace The 16th-century blast furnace was a stone tower about 15 feet square and 15–20 feet high. Ore, charcoal and occasionally marl or limestone were charged into the top, the ore was reduced to iron in the shaft and hearth, and liquid iron was cast out of the hearth into moulds. The bellows which blew the furnace were powered by a water wheel.

Bloom Although the term is properly given to the product of the bloomery hearth, it has been borrowed for later processes; in these documents it was used for the lump of wrought iron produced in the finery hearth at the forge, before it was drawn out into bar under the hammer.

Bloomery process The production of wrought iron direct from the ore without the intermediate stage of a high-carbon cast iron, as in the blast furnace. Small bloomery hearths with hand-powered bellows were used from the prehistoric Iron Age onwards, but became larger with the development of water-powered bellows and hammers between 1300 and 1500. See, in particular, R. F. Tylecote, *Metallurgy in Archaeology* (London, 1962), pp. 284–299.

Cast iron (*pig iron*) The alloy of iron and carbon (up to 5%) tapped as a hot liquid from the hearth of the blast furnace, either into plain moulds for pigs (for conversion into wrought iron at the finery forge) or for objects for use (guns, shot, pots, firebacks, hammer heads, etc.).

Chafery *See* Forge.

Finery *See* Forge.

Firkin (*Verken*) A barrel holding 8 or 9 gallons of liquid, or solids. In the steelworks accounts it was referred to as a container for the finished steel, and although apparently used as a standard of measure, it is not clear what weight it represented. Rhys Jenkins suggested about 6 cwt, which Schubert (*History*, p. 317, n. 5) thought too low.

Flash A wooden trough crossing a dam, bringing water to feed a water-wheel.

Forge The term had been used for bloomeries, and in the 16th century could also mean a blacksmith's forge. In these accounts it refers to the finery, hammer and chafery complex, in which pigs or sows of cast iron were converted into wrought iron. The pigs were first melted in oxidising conditions in the finery hearth, to remove most of the carbon, and the resulting blooms hammered out into bar, being re-heated frequently in the chafery hearth. The bellows for the hearths, and the hammer, were all water-powered.

Founday The campaign (the period for which the blast furnace was continuously in operation) was divided for accounting purposes into foundays or 'foundes' usually of 6 days.

Gogyn (*gudgeon*) Bearing for a wheel shaft.

Gut (*jutte*) A channel in the ground. Although there is much uncertainty about 16th-century millwrights' terms, the most likely meaning of this word seems to be the trench in which the wheel-pit was set.

Hammer *See* Forge.

Kilderkin A barrel statutorily containing 18 gallons of beer or 16 gallons of ale.

Mine Ore.

Penstock A gate or shuttle at the end of a flash, regulating the amount of water passing on to a water wheel.

Plates Cast-iron plates for conversion into steel by the reduction of the carbon content to a point rather higher than that of wrought iron.

Shamyons Iron parts in the linkage of water-powered bellows.

Shot *See* Cast Iron.

Slag Silica and other impurities from the ore tapped from the furnace as a hot liquid. On cooling it solidified into a glassy mass; this was broken up on the casting floor of the furnace and removed, sometimes for road metalling. The heaps of slag surrounding 16th-century furnaces usually contain black or dark green material, contrasting with the lighter green common at later sites where more lime was used in the charge. Contemporaries often referred to slag as 'cinders'.

Sows Large pieces of pig-iron, usually cast in moulds (beds) in sand on the casting floor of the furnace. In the 16th century sows were commonly 10 cwt in weight; they were usually 3 to 4 feet long and cast to a square or triangular section perhaps 6–9 inches across.

Tuyere (*Twerne, among various spellings*) The nozzle through which bellows blast reached a hearth.

Whuche The wider meaning is a chest. The term is used at Panningridge in a way that implies a part of the tailrace. This indicates that the length of race immediately downstream from the wheel-pit was led through a culvert in the form of a long timber box with open ends. Although excavations at Panningridge showed that this part of the site had been damaged by a later furnace, an excellent example of the technique has been recorded at Chingley furnace, Lamberhurst, Kent, which was built about 1560.

DOCUMENTS

[1] LEASE OF THE SITE FOR PANNINGRIDGE FURNACE, 1541–2

U 1475 E59

This indenture made the last daye of November the xxiii^th^ yere [of] the reign of our sovereigne lord Kyng Henry the viii bytwene Richard (*blank*) Clarke parson of penhurst in the Countye of Sussex on the oone partye and Wylliam Spycer of dalington in the saide Countye yeoman on the other partye. Wytnesseth that where the saide wylliam is fully myndyd and purposed to erect buyld and sett up a certein furnes to melte in Iron next unto a parcell of Land called Pannyngrege in the parish of Asshbornham in the said Countie Yt is theruppon condescended covenanted grannted and agreed betwene the said persons in maner and fourme following That ys to saye the said Richard hathe dimised grannted to ferme letten and by these presentes dimittith granntith and to ferme lettith unto the saide William Sixe Acres of Lande (with thappurtennants)[1] next adioynyng and lying As the saide landes and woodes called pannyngrege aforesaide that it is to saye oone of the saide vi acres (more or lesse boundying up to the high wey South on the one ende and to a serten hege there now beyng on the Este parte)[2] Wherupon it shall be lyefull to the saide William to erecte or make the wall and to sett the furnes aforesaide and otherwise to use for the necessary and myet Comodyties of the same furnes and the v acres residue of the saide vi acres for and concernyng conveyance of the water and streame miet and necessarye to dryve the whele of the saide furnes with To have and to holde the same vi acres of lande to the saide William Spicer to his executours and assignes from the feaste of Saint Michell Tharchangell next comyng after the date herof unto thende and terme of xxi yeres frome thense next comyng and fully to bee endyd yelding and paying threfore yerely duryng the said terme to the said Richard to his executors and successors[3] xxs sterling at the feaste of thannunciacion of our lady and saint mighell the archangell by evyn porcions to be payd and if yt fortune the said rent to bee [behinde] unpaid in parte or in all after any terme of payment thereof in which it ought to bee paid by the space of xv days[4] that than it shall bee lawful to the saide Richard and his successors yet the premysses[5] to entre and distreyne and the distresses there so taken lawfully from thense to loade dryve and cary

[1] Crossed out.
[2] Inserted between lines.
[3] Substituted for *assigns.*
[4] Substituted for *a quarter of a yere.*
[5] Followed originally by *with appertenances.*

awaye and with theym to retain hold and kepe untyll the said yerely rent together with tharrerages therof be unto the said Richard and his successors fully satisfied contented and paide and the saide Richard for him and his successors covenantith and granntith to and with the saide William his executours and assignes by these presente that the same William his executours and assignes shall from tyme to tyme within thre[6] yeres nexte ensueng after the same furnes shalbe soo erected and sett up (at and uppon suche reasonable price)[7] and price (as the between the said parson and the saide William shalbe concluded agreed)[7] fell cutte downe and carye awaye thorough and over the lande of the saide parsonage all the woodes and underwoodes nowe standing and growing in and uppon all the landes belonging to the saide parsonage except great tymber and suche woode as been growing aboute the saide parsonage and the Barme [ ] (the said William his executors and assignes paying for every lode of Cole iiid and for every lode of mynde the fyrst yere of the foreseid firme id and after the seid fyrst yere for every lode of mynde id ob and unto thend of the foreseid terme and fulfill and make pleyne the mynde pytts of the same)[8] for the defence of theim or of either of theim or of either and also except sowell convenient and miet for thoccupieng of the parsonne ther And also that it shalbe lyefull to the saide wylliam his executors and assignes in all places myet and convenyent by the discrestion of the said wylliam his executors or assignes and upon price aforesaid[9] bytwene the said parties concluded and had to dyg for oore or myne myet and necessarye for the said furnes So that the same wylliam his executors or assignes fyll up agen and make playne the place so dygged at his owne proper costs and charges before he shall breke up any other place Provided always that yf it shall fortune the same water myet for the said furnes not to surrownde or overflowe all the said v acres of lande soo letten by the same parson than yt shall bee liefull to the said parsone and his successors to occupye and manure to his owne propre use and profyt asmoche of the same v acres as shall not bee surrounded or overflowen So that he doo nowe acte upon the same whereby the water myet and necessary for the said furnes shalbe stopped or lett of his [Coste].

6 Originally *foure*, altered to *fyve*, which was in turn amended to *thre*.

7 Passages crossed out.

8 Inserted between the lines.

9 Originally *reasonable*.

[2] THE BUILDING ACCOUNT FOR PANNINGRIDGE FURNACE, 1542–3

373 *U 1475 B9*

[*1r*] *blank*
[*1v*] *blank*
[*2r*] *blank*
[*2v*] *blank*
[*3r*] Allowances Anno xxxvº [1]

The Charges of the fornace edyfyed at panyngredge made yn the xxxiiii yere of the regne of our moost redobted souverane King harry the viii

Dykers first my master barganed wyth Jhon Adams Dyker for the makeng of the wall of the said fornace as it apereth by a byll of Covenantes Indented for the Sume of xxv li

Item the said Jhon Adams had over and above his said Covenantes for the rammyng and of the whuche[2] of the said fornace x s

Item the said Jhon Adams had for rammyng of the flasshe of the fornace ii s viii d

Item the said Jhon had for digyng of the cross trenche of the said flasshe[3] xii d

Item paid unto the said Jhon for ii spades and shovels of him bowght xx d

Carpenters Item my master barganed wyth Jhon Alye and Jhon Bodyll Carpenters for all workes belongeng ther occupacion wyth saweng for the full fynisshyng of the said fornace for the Sume of xi li

Item paid to Jhon Alye and bodyll for makeng of a lodge that the masons might worke drye therin ii s

[*3v*] Item paid unto the said Jhon Alye and bodyll for bordes that the masons had to make their bosses of for saweng of the said borde iiii d

Ironworke[4] Item delyvered unto them for the fornace xlii li of great nayles vi s iiii d

[1] At head of each subsequent page.

[2] The head of the tailrace.

[3] Probably the channel through the top of the dam, containing the trough (flash) to the penstock.

[4] The three items under ironwork appear to be scored out in the *ms*.

D

Item delivered unto them for the said fornace of small nayles liii li ii s iii d

Item delivered unto them for the whele and the pentstock of the said fornace of nayles xi li xix d ob

Helpe to arere the fornace Item paid unto ii Sawers and ii wodde Cutters to helpe for helping to rere the Tymber worke of the said fornace xiiii d

. . . for one barell of bere for suche as dyd helpe to rere the Tymber worke xx d

. . . for brede for them that dyd help to rere the tymber worke of the said fornace vi d

diggers of stone . . . unto them that dygged stones for digging of xi^xx^xviii lodes of stone at iii d the lode for the same fornace lix s vi d

. . . unto Come and his sonne for digyng of Stones vi days ether of them vi d by the daye vi s

. . . unto Robert Dows for iii days digeng of Stones every day vii d xxi d

. . . unto Wyllam fawke for iii days dygyng of stones every day vii d xxi d

. . . to William Spycer at the comanndment of my master for mending ways to cary stone iiii s

[*4^r^*] Diggers of Stone . . . to Wylliam Goldsmyth for ix dayes dygyng of Stone and to Rows at vi d every daye iiii s vi d

Caryers of Stone . . . unto William Spycer for Carage of Stone unto the said fornace xlvi s viii d

. . . unto more of Dalyngton for the Carage of stones ii days every day xviii d iii s

. . . unto Jhon Rabet for vi days Carage of stones every day xvi d viii s

. . . for oone lode of Tyle and for the Carage of the same for the said fornace iii s iiii d

Carage of Sowes . . . unto Jhon Stonestret for Carage of Sowes of Iron for the said fornace xvi d

Carage of Tymber . . . unto Wyllyam Spycer for Carage of Tymber for the said fornace at dyvers tymes as his bill specyfyed xix s

} xx s iiii d

Masons . . . unto Coger the xviii daye of octobre for xi days for hym and his man every daye xv d for them both xiiii s ix d

. . . to birde for iii days every day viii d ii s
. . . unto Wyllyam henly for iii days ii s
. . . to Coverly for iii days worke ii s
. . . to Coger the xv daye of November for ii days every day xv d for hym and his man ii s vi d
. . . to byrde for iiii days every daye viii d ii s vi[ii d]

[*4ᵛ*] . . . to Wylliam henly for iiii days worke ii s viii d
. . . to Coverly for iiii days worke ii s viii d
. . . to iii for serving the masons vii days di every day to ether of them vi d[5] xv s ix d
John and Alexsander Colens barganed wyth the said masons over and above the said summe before written they to have to performe the same fornace agreament vi li xiii s iiii d

Item Dikers . . . to lover and page the xvii day of Decembre for ix days worke in makeng a trench to lay yn the working gutte[6] and ramyng of thsame and fyllyng of the Juttye and makeng a dych to avoyd the water abowt the fornace and for casting owt therth of the same fornace vi d a day ix s

Clensing of the ponde . . . unto the wodde Cutters for the Clensing of the busshys owt of the pond iii s vi d
. . . unto Jhon Rabet for clenseng of busshes and breneng them out of the pond vi d
. . . unto Jhon Robey for clenseng and brennyng of busshes owt of the pond vii d
. . . to Jhon prior and Stephen aselde for breneng busshes and clenseng the ponde xii d
. . . to Jo Sawnder for breneng and clenseng busshes owt of the ponde vi d
. . . to weston for clenseng the pond iiii d

[*5ʳ*] Carage of wodde owt of the ponde . . . to Come longly and his sonne for Carage of Wodde owt of the ponde for safgard thereof from the water which wodde they caryed wyth whyle borows for vii days ether of them vi d a day vii s
. . . to Reynold lyvyatt for Carage wodde owt of the ponde wyth his whyle borow every day vi d for v dayes ii s vi d
. . . to more for Carage of wodde owt of the ponde wyth his wene for i daye xii d

[5] If the wage rate and the total are correct, the working period should perhaps read $10\frac{1}{2}$ days.

[6] *Gutte* and *Juttye* seem to be used for the wheelpit.

. . . to William Spicer for iii days carage yn lyke wise every day xvi d iiii s

Item to James aselde for lyke carage of wodde iii days di every day xvi d iiii s viii d

Necesse for the diggers of stone Item made an yron Sledge iiii yron wedges one pykeaxe to cleve stone wythall xx d
. . . to Jo Colen for a pykeaxe xii d } ii s viii d[7]

Carage of wodde owt of the ponde . . . to Come langly and his sonne for Caryeng of wodde owt of the ponde ii days ether of them vi a day ii s

. . . to Wylliam Spicer and James aselde for Caryeng of wodde out of the ponde v s

. . . to more for i days Carage of the same xii d

[*5v*] The charge of the belows . . . to the Tanner for one bulhide vi s iiii d

. . . to the Curryer for dressing of hym and for dressing of ii hydes of our owne xx d

. . . to bucket for i m of bellows nayles[7] iii s

Item delivered to Alxander Colens ii C i quart of Iron to make pypys for the belows and other necessary thinges for the fornace

[*6r*] . . . for draweng and shettyng of ii yron hopes for the rounde beame of the fornace xii d

. . . to the carpenters for nayles x s ii d ob

Item for instruments to dygge stone iis viii d

Item to buckett for bellowe nayles iii s

The Toles of yron belonging to the fornace . . . for an yron Rake for the Cole viii d

. . . to Alexsander Colens for makeng of dyvers toles for the same fornace vi s viii d

[*6v*] Weanes and gates

xxii December

. . . to Ryc Fyp[ ] and his man for viii days every day xv d to make a Coole weane and ii gates for defense of the grounde where the myne shalbe Caryed x s

. . . for saweng of bordes ii days until William Kenwoode and yis man ii s iiii d

. . . for yron worke of thsame wene ii s iiii d

. . . to the frenchmen for the makyng of a stable bysyde the parson howse v s

[7] Crossed out in *ms.*

. . . to Jo Alye and bodyll for makeng of a trogge to cary tymbre wythall viii d

[7^r] *blank*
[7^v] *blank*
[8^r] *onwards: operating accounts for the furnace.*

[3] SUMMARY ACCOUNT FOR ROBERTSBRIDGE FURNACE AND FORGE AND PANNINGRIDGE FURNACE, 1542–3

377/1 *U 1457 B2/3*

[*1v*] Anno xxxv
[*1v*] *blank*
[*2v*] Robertysbridge

The accompte of henry westall aswell [of all] and singular his receptes as also of all [ ] paymentes as concerned as well the standynge workes and reparacions of the same as also dyverse other Charges that is to saye frome the laste daye of december Anno Regis Henrici viii xxxiiii° unto the same last daye of december Anno Regis predicto xxxv° that is to saye for one hole yere

Recepts

Money Received of my Lady firste the sayd henry Chargyth hymself with money receyvyd at dyverse tymes as hereafter maye appere that is to saye the ii^de daye of february anno xxxiiii° by thandes of John hawes xxli. Item by thandes of John swyfte the xiii^th of february anno predicto xx li. Item by the handes of John hawes the viii^th daye of marche xx li. Item the xxi° daye of Maye by the hands of Barthillmewe Cooke Anno Regis henrici octavi xxxv° xxx li. Item of my ladye the xxx^th daye of July Anno xxxv° ut pr [ ] xx li. Item more of her the xiii^th daye of auguste anno xxxv° liii li. Item by thandes of John hawes the xth daye of december Anno predicto xl li. Item of my lady the xii^th daye of November Anno xxxv° lx li. Item by thands of J. swyfte

[*2v*] the xv^th daye of December Anno xxxv° xl li. Item by thandes of John hawes the xxix^th daye of december Anno xxxv° xl li, which amowntyth unto the sume of iii^C xliii li

Money Received of N. Grene Item he Chargyth hymself with Money by hym receyved of Nycholas Grene aswell by thandes of the sayd Nycholas as also by thandes of dyverse menne for rente and ferme that is to saye at Ester laste paste by the handes of the sayde Nycholas Grene xx li. Item receyvyd by the hands of the sayd Nycolas with vi li x s for the ferme of the parsonage[1] due at the

[1] 379/1 shows this to be Salehurst parsonage, and the payment to have been made by Christopher Symons.

annunciation of our lady laste passed lii li xvi s viii d. Item of hym by thandes of Mr darell[2] for one half yeres ferme of lamberherste due at the sayd feaste of Saynt Mychaell tharchanngell last past vii li xvi d. Item by thandes of John Brycher for Madersham due ut supra vii li. Item of Mr. Sakvyle for fudlands due as before is sayde lxvi s viii d. Item by thandes of Thomas glydde for his di yeres ferme due as before is sayd lxvi s viii d. Item by thandes of William Byne for his di yeres ferme due as before is sayde

[*3*ʳ] xxvi s viii d. Item by thandes of Robert Bullocke for the di yeres ferme of the parsonage of Saleherste due as before is sayde vi li x s. Item by thandes of Edwarde Browne for the di yeres ferme of the parsonage of Udim[ore] due as before is declared liii s iiii d. Item by thandes of Richard Stace als Shether for his di yeres Rent due as before is sayde vi s viii d. Item by thandes of Elwyn for his Rent due ut supra iii s. Item by thandes of Mr Foster for the Rent of playden[3] due ut supra lxiii s x d ob. Item by thandes of Robert padyham uppon his rekninge ix li xiii s iiii d, all which sumes dothe amownte unto Cxvii li viii s ii d ob

Money received of the Tanner Item the sayd henry Chargeth hym self with money receyvyd by hym at dyverse and sondry tymes of the Tanner that is to saye for ix stere hydes at iii s iiii d the pece xxx s. Item for iii Cowe hydes viii s. Item for vi Oxe hydes at iiii s the hyde xxiiii s. Item more for three stere hydes at iii s iiii d the pece

[*3*ᵛ] x s. Item for iiii Mureyne skynnes ix s. Item for xx Calf Skynnes v s iiii d. all which dothe amounte unto the sume of iiii li vi s iiii d

Money Received of the Glover Item he Chargyth hymself with Money Receyvyd by hym of the glover for felles viz for xxxviii felles wherof vi at v d the pece and ii at vi d the pece and xxx at iii d the pece which dothe amounte unto the sume of xi s

Money received for Cattall solde Item he Chargeth hymself with Money by hym receyvyd for Cattell solde viz of James Goodwyn for one Cowe and one Straye haffer price xxx s. Item of Thomas Ewyn for ii Oxen lxxiiii s ii d. Item of a Bocher dwellinge in dertforde for ix Oxen and One stere xvi li vi s viii d. Item for iii shepe solde unto the workemen vi s vii d. Item of R. Covylde for a lame nagge

[2] Thomas Darell (379/1). For Darell's interests in ironworking see Schubert, *History*, pp. 370, 378; Straker, pp. 268, 276.

[3] The lordship of Playden (379/1).

and a mare colt xiis vid. Item for v pygges xixd. All which dothe amounte unto the sume of xxiili xis vid

[*4^r*] Money Received for pannage Item the sayde henry Chargyth hymself with money by hym Received for Mastinge of hogges viz of (*blank*) of hawkherst for iii Shotts xxiiid. of Robert Moone for the mastynge of one sowe and iiii Shotts iiiis vid. Item of Martyn Taylor for ii sows and iii shotts iiis iiiid. of Antony Norman for ii Sowes and iii Shotts iiiis. Item of John Sturdygate for one Sowe and iiii pygges iis iiiid. Item of philpott for one Sowe and v pygges and iii shottes vis viiid. xxiis viiid

Money Received of wooddes and Tymber solde . . . for certeyn woodde and Tymber by hym solde to dyverse Menne as particularly maye appere which dothe amownte unto the sume of lxvili ixs

[*4^v*] Money Received for Beere and Wheatte . . . of Thomas huggens at dyverse tymes as particularly maye appere for whete and bere by hym solde unto the workemen which dothe amounte unto the sume of lxili xs vd ob. Item the sayde henry Chargeth hymself with money by hym receyvyd for bere bruyd for the howsehold and solde unto the workemenne which doth amounte unto vis iiiid lxili xvis ixd ob

Money Received of the profitts of the dayre . . . by hym of the profytts of the dayre whiche dothe amounte unto the sum of xxiiis viid ob

Money Received for herynges solde . . . for herynge solde unto dyverse of the workemenne as particularly maye appere which dothe amounte unto the sume of ixs viid

[*5^r*] Money Received for Iron solde[4] . . . for Iron by hym solde unto dyverse menne viz to John Collyns ii^t^ xii^C^, xiiili ixs. Item more of hym for ii^t^ at Cxvis viiid the tonne xili xiiis iiiid. Item of philpott for i^t^ of Iryn at Cvi^s^ viiid and for xvii^C^ at vis the hundreth Ciis. Item of Thomas Bedle for i^t^ iC at vili the tonne vili vi^s^ Item of Mr Oxenbrydge for one tonne of Iron for the kynges workes at the castell at Cvis viiid. Item of Kensham[5] for v^C^ of Iron at vis the

[4] This list is a condensed version of the entries in 379/1, some of whose items do not appear to be included in this summary. The latter obscures the small deliveries of iron to smiths: Kensham, for instance, took his 5 cwt in five separate lots of 1 cwt each.

[5] Of Fynall (Vinehall); 379/1.

hundreth xxxs. Item of a Smyth of battell for iii^C iiii^xx iiii lib of Iron at vis the hundreth xxis xid. Item of Bradde for di C xxx lib of Iron after vis the hundreth iiiis viiid. Item of peter lawlesse for i^t di at vili the tonne ixli. all which Iron drawyth unto the some of x^t ix^C di iii lib whiche dothe amownte in Money unto the sume of lixli iiid

Item more receyvyd by the sayd henry for Caste Iron for the Castell[6] viili iis iiiid

[5^v] Money Received for Iron Item of Mr Oxenbridge for CCClxxvii^lib of Iron xxiis. Item a Smyth of Ewherst for C of Iron vis iid, which amownteth unto the sume of xxviiis iid Item of henry Shether for di C iiid

sum xxxis iid

Sum Totales Received for Iron lxviili xiiis ixd

Sum Totales Receipt vi^C xxiiili xs iid ob

Wherof

[6^r] payments for the forge workes

hammerman and fyners[7] The sayd henry askyth to be allowed of of Money by hym layde owte and payde unto the hammerman and fyners for hammerynge and fyninge of Cxl t ix^C and iii qrts of Iron the sume of iiii^xx xiiili xis. Item of Money payde unto theym for dressinge of theyr bellowes as may particularly appere, xxis viiid. Item more payd for hepynge of Coles at the forge as lykewyse maye appere viis ixd ob. all which allowances dothe amount unto the sume of iiii^xx xvli vd ob

fownder and fyller[8] Item . . . unto the fownder and fyller as particularly maye appere which dothe ammounte unto the sume of xxviili ixs vid

[6] This appears to correspond with a payment in 379/1 by Mr. Oxenbrydge for 2 t. 13 cwt of cast iron at 4 marks per ton.

[7] 379/1 gives a chronological record of payments from January to March. The hammerman is identified as Bartholomew Collins, and the finers as Carde and Adryan; from the April payment Gwillam was the hammerman, with Carde remaining. Adryan is replaced by Roger Ellis and Alexander (?)Nyntam and his fellow. Identification is less thorough during the autumn, only the hammerman being named. It seems that at the forge, as at the furnaces, the Collins family got operations under way.

[8] Alexander Collins was founder, apart from May and August, when Richard Baker appears in 379/1. Four men worked as fillers at various times during the year.

[6^{v}] Myners[9] Item . . . unto dyverse menne for Myninge . . . xxix li xvii s v d

Wood Cutters Item . . . unto dyverse persons for Cuttinge of woodde as particularly maye appere . . . liiii li iiii s viii d

Colyers[10] Item . . . unto the Colyers for Colinge as lykewyse may appere . . . iiii^{xx}xii li xvii s i d ob

[7^{r}] Caryage of coles and sowes[11] Item . . . for Caryage of Coles Myne and Sowes as particularly may appere . . . vi li vii s ii d ob

Reparacions with neccessaries for the same Item . . . aswell for certeyn thinges bowght for the Reparacions of the sayd workes as also for dyverse mennes labor in Repayringe the same as lykewyes may appere . . .[12] xi li xii s iiii d ob

Charges in delyvery of Iron solde[13] Item . . . for dyverse Caryages and Expences in the delyvery of Iron within the tyme of this Accompte as particularly may appere . . . xii li ii s iii d

[7^{v}] Sum Totales of these payments CCCxxix li

And so the sayd henry owyth CCiiii^{xx}xiii li xix s ii d ob

wherof he askyth to be allowed of money by hym payde for bellowe tymber and Nave tymber with the Charges therunto pertaynynge xxxix s ii d

And yett he owyth CCiiii^{xx}xii li ob

wherof

[8^{r}] *blank*

[8^{v}] *blank*

[9] Six names appear in 379/1, including Roger Ellis (see note 7 above).

[10] Four colliers appear in 379/1.

[11] This is recorded in great detail in 379/1 and shows the use made of casual work, with one exception, Browning. During the year the following were employed:

> John Allyn 48 days (autumn), John Stonestrete 20 days (May, October), Browning 140 days (throughout), William Stonestrete 20 days (May, October), John Jacob 2 days, Thomas Mannser 13 days (January, March) Christopher Symons 108 loads ore (June, July), John Role 2 days.

(The entries mix weeks and days: it is assumed for the above that six-day weeks were worked.)

[12] 379/1 words these items in great detail (fos *24^{r}–25^{v}*); they include dressing bellows, repairs to wheels, bellows, dams, and the hammer, and new cole baskets.

[13] 379/1 gives the cost of lighterage on the Rother, and the details of arranging for delivery of iron at Rye.

[9r] *blank*
[9v] *blank*

[10r] Payments

Oates bowght The seyd henry askyth to be allowyd of money layde owte and payde for fresshe Oates bowght aswell for the fyndinge of the howse in my Masters absens as also at hys repayre unto his sayd howse within the tyme of this accompte as particularly maye appere which dothe amounte unto the sume of xix li v s v d

wheate bowght Item . . . xx qrt of whete with vii s viii d for thepping of the byer and Caryage of the same unto the Oke and with xviii d for Caryage from the Oke home unto the howse which amountyth unto the sume of ix li xv s x d

Malte bowght Item . . . iiii^xx qrt of Malte, viz xx qrt at v s viii d the qrt and xx qrt at vi s iii d ob the qrt, and xl qrt at vi s vi d the qrt, with vi s for thepping of the byer and with xxii s viii d for the Cariage ut supra xxvi li v s

[10v] Ottes bowght Item . . . xxiii semes and xii bushels by hym bowght viz of henry upton iii semes at v s iiii d and iii semes at v s x d. Item lawrens derby viii bushels at iii s iiii d. Item of partryge at Ewherst for xii bushels at v s. Item of J. Clerke of Ewherst viii bushels at iii s iiii d. Item of henry Clerke of Ewherst a seme at vi s viii d and of Xpofer Symon x semes at v s iiii d. vi li vi s vi d

Cattall bowght Item . . . viz of William forest ii steeres price xxxiii s iiii d. Item of Raaffe hope iii shepe and xiii lambes price xxi s viii d. Item of william Stubbes xl wethers price viii li ii s. Item of pelsett of Kent xxx wethers price iiii li. Item xix ewes with the Caryage xxxix s. Item for ii sowes and ii shottes price ix s all which sumes amownte unto xvii li v s

Pease bowght Item . . . of money by hym payde for iii bz of pease price v s vii d

[11r] herynge bowght Item . . . iii barelles of heringe with the Charges of the Caryage at xvi s iiii d and for iii Cads Red herynge with the Charges at viii s the Cade which doth amownte unto the sume of lxxi s

fysshe bowght Item . . . Ciiii Salte fysshes bowght by the vycar of Rykmansworthe with the Caryage of the same fisshe iiii li xvi s iiii d

Item more for a quarterne of smalle salte fysshe iii s ix d

hoppes bowght Item . . . iii^{C}xlv lib of hoppes at xviii s the C lxi s v d and for ii^{C}xxviii lib of hoppes price xxv s x d which dothe amownte with xvi d for caryage unto the sume of iiii li xviii s iiii d

Salte bowght Item . . . viii bz of Salte vii s vii d and for vii bz baye salte price ix s iiii d which amowntyth unto the sume of xvi s xi d

[*11v*] Sum iiii^{xx}xiii li ix s viii d

And yett he owyth Ciiii^{xx}xviii li ix s[14] iiii d ob

whereof

[*12r*] *blank*

[*12v*] *blank*

[*13r*] Laborers in husbondrye . . . unto dyverse persons for theyr labor at dyverse and sondry tymes in husbondrye which doth amounte as particularly maye appere unto the sume ix l ix s iiii d

harvest worke Item . . . for Repynge Mowynge and Makynge of haye . . . iiii li xvii s i d

Neccessaryes for the husbondry Item . . . for dyverse necessaryes pertayninge unto the husbondrye . . . xxiii s ob

[*13v*] Reparacions in the brwehowse Item . . . for Mendynge of brwynge vessels . . . xvi s

Unto the Cowper Item . . . for hopes and other worke uppon the brwyng vessels . . . xv s iii d

Unto the Smythes Item . . . unto dyverse Smythes aswell for Nayles as other workes at dyverse and sondry tymes with xiii s v d for Shoyinge of horses . . . iiii li vii s ix d

14 Substituted for iiii^{xx}xvii s x d.

Carpenters Item . . . unto dyverse Carpenters for theyr worke at dyverse and sondry tymes . . . viii li vii s iiii d

[*14*ʳ] Sawyers Item . . . unto the Sawyers for Sawynge at dyverse tymes . . . xxxii s vi d

lathe makers Item . . . for clevyng of lathes . . . x s

Tylers Item . . . unto dyverse menne for Tylinge . . . lxvii s ii d

dychers Item . . . unto dyverse persons for Clensinge and Castynge of dyches . . . Cxv s iiii d ob

[*14*ᵛ] Closinge of Sprynges . . . for thenclosure of Sprynges . . . lxi s vii d ob

Cuttinge of wood for fuell . . . for woodd Cutte by the lode . . . xxi s viii d

Thatchinge and Shynglynge . . . for thachinge of howses xxiiii s ii d ob and for Shynglynge lx s iii d . . . iiii li iiii s v d

foren Charges Item . . . unto dyverse persons at dyverse and sondry tymes foren Charges . . . ix li xi s iii d ob

[*15*ʳ] Makinge of Shyppe borde and Clove borde Item . . . for makinge of Shyppeborde and Clove borde . . . lxviii s

Servants wages Item . . . for servants wages . . . xviii li ix s
Sum iiii^{xx} li xvii s x d ob
And yett Ci li ix s vi d

Wherof

[*15*ᵛ] (*blank*)
[*16*ʳ] pannyngrydge he askythe to be allowed of Money by hym layde owte and payde unto dyverse and sondrye persons aswell for the buyldinge of the new fornesse as for myne bowght, with xx s gyvyn unto the parson of Penherst and xxxi s for serchinge for Myne and xii s vi d for woodd bowght of the parson of penherst aforesayd all which dothe amownte unto[15] lxv li xvi s ix d ob
Item . . . payde within the tyme of this accompte viz unto

[15] Part of 373 (Furnace Book) is printed above [2].

dyverse woodcutters[16] ther xvii li xiiii s ob. Item unto the Colyers[17] ther Ciii s. Item unto the Myners for Mynynge[18] ther ix li iiii d all which dothe amownte unto the sume of

xxxi li xvii s iii d ob

Sum iiii^xx^xvii li xiiii s ii d

And yett he owythe xxii li xv s iiii d

Wherof

[*16v*] . . . viz unto a shyngler for Repayringe of the Channcell at Udymore xxiiii s vi d. Item to Mr browne for Reparacions of the parsonage of Udymore as apperith by his bylle xxii s. Item Mr darell for Reparacions at lamberhurst viii s viii d. all which dothe amownte lv s ii d

Item . . . for fees and annuyties, viz to Mr Sakvyle for his di yeres fee due at Michellmas last past xxvi s viii d. Item to Richard halle for his annuyte due for i quarter at Chrystmas laste past, xxv s, all which amownth to xxxi s viii d

Item . . . unto Mistress welsshe for reknynge of Gwyllms Covenante made with her xlvi s viii d, and of Money layd owte for his Charges in the tyme of his trowble xxxii s xi d, all which amownth unto lxxix s vii d

[*17r*] Item . . . payd at my Masters Comandement unto dyvers persons viz unto the thre Collins for theyr lyvereys lx s. Item in Reward to Godffrey the Carpenter x s
Item to a bocher of wynchelsey ii s viii d which amownteth unto lxxii s viii d

Item . . . of ii qrtes of Malte price xii s which was received of William Stubbes the laste yere and not payde for untyll within the tyme of this reknynge xii s

Sum xii li xi s i d

and yett he owyth x li iiii s iii d

wherof he requyreth to be allowed of xl s by hym payde unto Mr Chowte for his di yeres fee endynge at Myghellmas last past and also of lxvi s viii d due unto the sayde accomptannte for one hole yeres wages due at Crystmas last passed and yett he owythe of his owne

[16] 373 gives an excellent impression of the seasonal pattern of woodcutting; whereas 12 men were paid in April and 14 in November, the numbers for July, August and September are 4, 4 and 5 respectively.

[17] Although there are far fewer colliers than woodcutters, the seasonal pattern is again clear, with no payments from August to October (373).

[18] 373 shows searches for ore in May 1543, and purchases from Mr. Ashburnham's ground. However, mining was carried out in Hasilden wood consistently from March to December, 10 men being involved.

propre arrerages within the tyme of this his accompte iiii li xvii s vii d
Item more for his arrerages determyned uppon his accompte Anno xxxiiii° xxiii li xviii s vii d which amowntyth in the hole unto the sume of xxviii li xvi s ii d

[*17ᵛ*] *blank*
[*18ʳ*] *blank*
[*18ᵛ*] *blank*
[*19ʳ*] *blank*
[*19ᵛ*] *blank*
[*20ʳ*] *blank*

[*20ᵛ*] Thaccompte of henry westall of such Iron as he hathe bene charged with within the tyme of this accompte
Memorandum that ther dyd Remayne in the Iron howse with iii^{t} di vi ^{C} lxxvii lib solde by the sayde henry westall for which he hadde nott receyvyd Money for the laste daye of december Anno Regni Regis henrici viii xxxv° over and above iiii^{C}vi lib solde by John Collyns at Sowthampton the which is yett unpayde xlviii^{t} di vi^{C} di xxi lib
Item Made this yere viz bytwene the laste daye of december Anno Regis henrici viii xxxiiii° and the sayd laste daye of december Anno xxxv° the sum of vii^{xxt} ix^{C} iii qrt
Sum ix^{xx} ix^{t} vi^{C} qrt xxi lib wherof
solde unto John Collyns at xiii li ix s
as maye appere by the recept therof ii^{t} xii^{C}
Item unto the Castell at the Chamber at Cvi s viii d as lykewyse maye appere i^{t}
Item to philpott at Cvi s viii d . . . i^{t}
Item to the Smyth of Ewherst C

[*21ʳ*] Item more unto John Collins at Cxvi s viii d as by the sayde Receyte maye appere i^{t}
Item to Gybbons of Rye at lyke price . . . i^{t}
Item Thomas Bedle at vi li vi s . . . i^{t} C
Item to the Castell at viii li xi s iiii d i^{t} di iiii^{C} xiii lib
Item to peter lawlesse at xii li ii^{t}
Item to philpott at xi li ii s i^{t} di vii
Item to a Smyth of Battell at xxii s i d CCC iii qrt
Item to Kensham at xxx s v^{C}
Item Bradde at iiii s vi d iii qrt
Item to henry Shether at iii s di C
Item to andres and draper of London xlv^{t} xi^{C} iiiqrt x lib
Item to theym the seconde tyme lxx^{t}
Item to theym the thirde tyme xl^{t}

Item to andres Ciii qrt
Item to the prince locksmyth i^t^
Item to a Smyth of the west iiii^t^
Item to the Ironmongers and Roger Brusshe iii^C^ di Item to padyham di C vii lib Item to Mr darell[19] di C xiiii lib iiii^C^ di xxi lib

[*21^v^*] Item spent in the workes[20] with CC di ii lib for the new fornesse vii^C^ di xi lib
Item ther Remain in the Iron howse at the daye of the determynacion of this Reknynge xvii^t^ xv^C^
Sum Totalis ix^xx^ xii^t^ xv^C^ iii qrt xxiii lib
And so he is in supplus by the Receyte of the forge wayght iii^t^ ix^C^ di ii lib
Memorandum solde of Caste Iron unto the Kynges workes ii^t^ xiii^C^ at liii s iiii d the tonne as maye appere by the recepts of the sayd henry which dothe amownte unto vii li ii s iiii d

[*22^r^*] Money Owinge for Iron
delivered per J. h. First John Collyns owyth for iiii^C^ vi lib of Iron which he solde at Sowthampton at the delyvery of Mr Webbes Iron xxiii s vi d
Received per westall Item John phillpott for i tonne of iron vi li
Received per westall Item peter lawlesse for di^t^ lx s
Item delyvered for the kynges workes at the Castell of Camber di t xiii^C^ xiii lib

[*22^v^*] Sowes Remaynynge at the fornesse the last daye of december Anno xxxv^o^ iiii^xx^iii
Coles Remaining at the fornesse and the forge lx lodes
Myne Remaining yett uncaryed xlvi lodes and at the fornesse vi lodes lii lodes
Cordes of woodd Remaining vi^C^

[*23^r^*] *blank*
[*23^v^*] *blank*
[*24^r^*] *blank*
[*24^v^*] *blank*

[*25^r^*] Money payd by henry westall uppon a New Reknynge viz Robertsbrydge
to the hamerman and fyners lxxviii s ii d
to the Colyers ix s ix d
to the Myners xvi s viii d

19 2 'Formoldes' (379/1).
20 The items used in the forge and furnaces are recorded in detail in 379/1.

to the woodcutters	lxi s iiii d ob
to the dychers	viii s
Pannynge Rydge	
woodcutters	lxxv s
fyller	xx d
Colyers	xxii s
Caryers	xi s ii d
Sum	xiiii li iii s ix d ob
Item Remaining in his hands in Ready Money	xvi li xviii s
Item more by hym received for the dett of George the Colyer which is runne awaye in parte of payment of viii s iiii d which he dyd owe	v s v d
Item for lyke dett of peter frenchman	ii s iii d
Sum	xvii li v s viii d
Sum Totales	xxxi li ix s v d ob
Et he in supplus	liii s iii d ob

[4] SUMMARY ACCOUNT FOR PANNINGRIDGE FURNACE AND ROBERTSBRIDGE FORGE, 1547

377/5 *U 1475 B1/5*

[*1r*] Robertsbridge: The accompte of the Iorne mynes there the fyrst yere of the reigne of our sovereigne lorde Kyng Edwarde the vi[ti] Anno primo E vi[ti]

[*1r*] *blank*

[*2v*] Declaracon of accompte of Henry Westall Clarke of the Iorne Workes to the Right Worshipfull Sir William Sydney Knyght at his Manor of Robertsbridge in the Countye of Sussex aswell of all and singular suche somes of money by hym receyvyd: as also all suche sommes of money by the seyd henry ymployd to the use of the seyd Sir William from the feast of the Nativite of our lorde god in the yere of the reigne of our late souvereigne lorde Kynge Henry theight xxxviiii[ti] untyll the same feast of the Nativitie of our lorde god then nexte ensuyng in the yere of the reigne of our souvereigne lorde Edwarde the vi[th] by the grace of god of Inglonde Frannce and Irelonde Kyng defendor of the fayth and in the yerth of the Churche of Inglond and also of Irelonde supreme hede fyrste that ys for one hole yere

In primis he chargith hymselff with tharrages dependyng in the fote of the last accopte — Cxliii li xviii s x d ob

Item he chargeth hymself with money received at the seyd syr William Sydney lx li and of mr henry Sydney xx li as it appereth by a boke of Receypte upon this accompte showed and examined — iiii[xx] li

Item he chargith hymselff with money received of John hawes as yt appereth by the seyd boke — CCxvii li xvii s

Item for Catall sold hoc anno as it appereth by the seyd boke — xii li ii s

Item for ix ton of tymber sold hoc anno as it appereth by the boke — xxvi s iiii d

[*2v*] Item for xii[C]xxxiiii fete of borde solde at divers prices hoc anno — xxxv s vii d

Item received for plankes hoc anno solde — xx d

Item received for woodde solde at Robertsbridge — lxvi s iiii d

Item received for wodde and wodeasshes solde at pannyngridge hoc anno — xi s viii d

Item for pasturying of catall hoc anno xiis xd
Item received for xviii ton iC and xxiiii lli of Iorne solde hoc anno to divers persons ut per librum predictum Cxxv li ixs iiid
Item received for caste yorne solde hoc anno xxvis vid
Item received for Corne solde oute of the garners this yere that ys xix quarters di bushels of whete viii li xviiis iid
Item received for mill Corne solde hoc anno xiiis viiid
Item received for Clxviii kylderkens of bere sold hoc anno as it appereth by the seyde boke xiiii li iis
Item received of denysens for money layde oute for them by my master as it appereth by the seyd boke xi li xvs
Item received for mete solde to the frensshemen xiiiis iiiid
Item received for onyons solde hoc anno iiiis viiid
Item received for felles and hydes solde hoc anno xxxs vid
Item received for Talowe solde hoc anno vis xd
Sum totall of all the receptes aforeseyd with tharragiis DCxxvi li xiiis iid ob

whereof

[*3r*] layd oute at Robertsbridge
and in primis for Cuttyng of woode Rayling and Dykyng ther hoc anno as the particelles dothe appere by the seyde boke vii li xvs vid ob
Item for mowyng and makyng of hay there hoc anno as it appereth by the seyd boke xliiiis
Item payd in Rydyng expenses this yere iiii li xs
Item for sawyng of xx^M^viC xxiiii fete of bordes at divers prices as it appereth by the seyd boke xv li iiiis iiid
Item for hewyng of CCxiii tun xvi fete of tymber at divers prices hoc anno viii li xixs viid
Item for Repacions there hoc anno as well to the Kerpentters as also to the Tylers iiii li xviis viid
Item for necessaries bought hoc anno lxiis id ob
Item to the smyth for showyng and other necessaries boughte for husbondrye lxviis iiiid
Item for the makyng of the new ponde by the Chapull as it appereth by the seyd boke ix li iiis xd
Item payd to the Glasier for glasyng xiiis xid ob
Item for caryng of tymber and corne hoc Anno lis iiiid
Item payd for wages there hoc anno with vi li xx d for martens borde xx li xviiis xd
Item payd to divers persons helpyng in the Brewhowse this yere as it appereth xxs viiid

Item to the hamermen and fyners for makyng of Clxx ton viii^c di quarters of Iorne at xiii s iiii d the ton as it appereth and C Cxiii li xii s viii d

Item for hepyng of coles and sowes of Iorne and mendyng of belowes as it appereth lxv s iiii d

Item for makyn of ix^cxxxvii cordes of wood ad divers prices hoc anno xi li xiiii s iiii d ob

[*3^v*] Item for colyng viii^cxl lodes of Coles there as it appereth by the seyd boke xlvii li xiii s ix d

Item for the caryng of viii^cxl lodes of coles xi li xvi d

Item payd for repacions of the forge the dyches and the Ryver as it appereth by the seyd boke vii li xv s

Item for carying of Iorne which was solde by my master hoc Anno xi li xv s vii d ob

Item payd for xiii seme of otes of hoc Anno lxxvi s

Item for xx^ti quarter of malte boughte hoc anno vi li vi s viii d

Item payd for the neccessaries bought when my master was here at ester as it [pc] viii li xv s ix d ob

Item for di ton of wyne bought hoc anno xlvi s viii d

Item for ii Oxen bought of mr henry Sydney as it appereth by the seyd boke liii s iiii d

Item in expenses of howsholde hoc anno over and besydes xiii li ix s vii d spente of the store that ys in the price of Cx Kylderkyns [ix li ix s iiii d] of bere at xx d and in the price of x quarters of whete viz iiii li v s ii d and one pecke at viii s the quarter as it appereth by the seyd boke xxvi li xii s x d ob

Sum of all the paymentes aforeseyd at Robertsbridge CCCxli li xviii s v d ob

[*4^r*] and at pannyngridge[1]

Item for Cuttyng of iiiM Dxv cordes of wodde there hoc anno as it appereth by the seyd boke[2] xlvi li vii s

Item in expenses there at my comyng thether at divers tymes as it appereth by the seyd boke ix s ii d

Item payd to the founder and filler for (*blank*) foundes and (*blank*) dayes at xiiii s the foundy and ii s iiii d the day as it appereth by the seyd boke[3] xl li xiiii s viii d

[1] Based on 383/1.

[2] The employment pattern is particularly fragmented. 37 individuals appear; 5 are mentioned on more than 8 of the 17 pay days, 22 on less than 3. The miners did much of the cutting from January to April, but did not resume in the autumn. There is the usual lack of cutting in the harvest period, only 1 man being paid in late August.

[3] 58 foundays and 1 day; 383/1 shows 57 foundays and 2 days; indicating

Item for the colyng of Mli lodes of coles[4] lvi li xviii d ob
Item for iii waynes bought hoc anno xxxi s iii d ob
Item for the caryng of Mli lodes of coles[5] xx li xv s
Item payd to the myners for dyggyng of myne hoc anno as appereth by the seyd boke[6] xxxiii li ix s x d
Item for caryng of the same myne[7] iiii li xix s iii d q
Item for caryng of sowes to Robertsbridge hoc Anno[8] xvi li ix s viii d
Item for dyggyng of stone and sannde and caryng the same as it appereth by the seyd boke xliii s ii d ob
Item to mr Burwell for myne hoc Anno[9] xxvi s viii d
Item for rent of the ponde and tythe of the same xxv s
Item to mr Channcellor for the rente of pannyngridge hoc anno xx li
Item for Raylyng ther hoc anno xliii s vii d
Item to divers persons for libertye thowrow there grounde for caryng of sowes hoc anno xiiii s iiii d
. . . for neccessaries bought ther hoc anno xxvi s ix d ob
. . . payd to laborers for neccessaries done at the furnes there hoc anno[10] v s vii d
. . . for Repacions aboute the bay there hoc anno as it appereth by the seyd boke[11] iiii li v s v d
Sum of all the paymentes aforeseyd at pannyngridge hoc anno CClv li iiii s vi d q

[*4v*] Sum of all the paymentes aforeseyd Diiii^xx^xvii li ii s xi d ob q

---

that payments for making the hearth, dressing the bellows and repairing the furnace wall (13s in 383/1) have been included but not specified in the summary total.

[4] Employment runs from March to October, all but 73 cords being made by two men, Duggyn and Geoffrey Totayn. Two others, Adryan and Joachym worked in April and May.

[5] Within this are the purchase of 3 carts (9s each) and differing cartage rates: Panningridge: 4d/load, Elmswood 4½d, Hassilden 6d.

[6] 6 miners from May onwards, being paid 7½d each load.

[7] Only one man, Thos. Smythe is recorded, being paid 1¼ per load, with an occasional and unexplained bonus of 12d a hundred.

[8] John and William Stonestrete were well established here, supplemented on occasion by 3 other carters. The rate was 16d per load (2 sows).

[9] Stated in 383/1 as 1959 loads at 1d each: an unexplained discrepancy.

[10] Includes carrying cinder to repair the furnace wall.

[11] This appears to have been a substantial repair, 2 men worked for 42 days (paid 17s 4d, with 12s 3d for their lodging paid to Atkins' wife). Piles and rails were cut for the bay(dam) by Sawyers paid 1s 4d a day, feeding themselves. There are further payments to labourers for hauling and ramming piles and clay.

and Oweth xxix li x s ii d ob q. Of the which he askyth allowannce of xix li for suche money as depended upon Sknowe (*blank*) and drewe in the fote of the accompte of the laste yere which is payd to the handes of the seyd Sir William Sydney as it appereth by the accompte of John Bagoot hoc anno, and he asketh allowance of iii s viii d for paper and ynke by hym bought this yere, and he askythe allowance of ii s vi d for money by hym payd to a rate taken by the comanndement of mr henry Sydney, and so askethe
x li iiii s ob q

[5^{r}] *blank*

[5^{v}] Cordes of wodde at Robertsbridge The remayne of cordes of anno xxxviii^{vo} MMCCiiii^{xx} cordes
Item made ther hoc anno ix^{C}xxxvii cordes
Some of all the cordes MMMCCxvii wherof spente hoc anno MMiii^{C}iiii^{xx}xii cordes di and remayneth in the woodde hoc anno
viii^{C}xxiiii cordes and di

Coles Item the remayne of lodes Anno xxxviii^{vo} DCl
Item made and caried ther hoc anno viii^{C}xl
Some of all the lodes Miiii^{C}iiii^{xx}x lodes wherof spente hoc anno DCCCCxl lodes and remayneth Dl lodes

lodes of myne Item the remayne of lodes of myne Anno xxxviii^{vo}
C lodes
Item caried hoc anno nil
Sum of all the lodes of myne C lodes which remayneth

Sowes there Item ther is in Sowes by estymacion DClxviii

Pannyngridge
Item ther is in sowes by tale CCxxxii
Sum of all the sowes ix^{C} which remain

[6^{r}] The accompte of Iorne The remayne of Iorne anno xxxviii^{vo} xvi ton xii^{C} di
Item made ther hoc anno Clxx ton viii^{C}iii qtrs
Some of all the Iorne aforeseyd Ciii^{xx}vii ton iC qtr, wherof solde by henry westall as the particelles particularly doth appere by a boke upon this accompte showed xviii ton iC xxiiii lli, also spente this yere aboute the forge and furnes as it appereth by the seyd boke iii^{C} qtr and x lli, also delyvered to mr Webbe xl ton, and also delyvered to mr draper by my masters comanndement lx ton, also delyvered to mr draper for my master xi ton, and also delyvered to George

Covyld by masters comanndement i ton, and remayneth lvi ton xvi^{C} di qtr and xxii lli, unto the which he ys charged with iii ton vC and vi lli which is gayned in the wayte of Iorne, and so ther is remaynyng the xxi^{ti} day of december lx ton and CC

Pannyngridge
cordes of wood there Item the remayne of cordes Anno xxxviii^{vo} MMCCiiii^{xx}
Item ther is made hoc anno MMMDxv
Sum totall of all the cordes v^{M}vii^{C}iiii^{xx}xv cordes wherof spente hoc anno iii^{M}CCiiii^{xx} cordes and so remayneth MMv^{C}xiiii cordes

[*6^{v}*] Coles ther Item the remayne of Anno xxxviii^{vo} iii^{C}iiii^{xx} lodes
Item made ther hoc anno primo Regis E vi^{ti} Mli lode
Sum of the lodes Miiii^{C}xxxi lodes wherof spente hoc anno Mii^{C}lxxi lodes and remayneth Clx lodes

Myne ther Item the remayne of anno xxxviii^{vo} MMD lodes
Item ther is caried and digged hoc anno Mlxviii lodes
Sum of the lodes iii^{M}Dlxviii wherof spent hoc anno MDlxviii and remain MM

Shipborde at Robertsbridge Item the remayne of anno xxxviii^{vo} viii^{C}
Item made ther hoc Anno nil
Sum of all the shipborde viii^{C} which remain

tymber Item the remayne of Anno xxxviii^{vo} Cxlvii ton xv fete
Item hewed ther this yere CCxiii ton xvi fete
Sum of all the tones iii^{C}lx ton xxxi fete which is sold and delyverd to mr holton to the use of the kynges grace
Memorandum ther is in tymber by estimacon vi^{xx} ton ult D ton sold and delyverd to mr holton

[*7^{r}*] ynche bordes The remayne of anno xxxviii^{vo} iii^{C} di
Item sawen hoc anno xxvi^{M}Cxxiiii fete
Sum of the bordes xxvi^{M} iiii^{C} di wherof solde hoc anno xii^{C}xxxiiii fete and spente hoc anno by estymacion vii^{C} and remayneth xx^{v}M and xvi fete

Shiplankes The remayne of anno xxxviii^{vo} lxvi^{C} di and xv fete
Item made hoc anno nil
Sum lxvi^{C} di and xv fete which remain

[*7^{v}*] The remaynes of the Stoke at Robertsbridge and pannyngridge aforeseyd the xxi^{ti} day of december anno primo Regis E vi^{ti}

pannyngridge

In primis MMv^{C}xiiii cordes of wod at iiii d	xli li xviii s
and Item in lodes of coles ther Clx at iii s the lode	xxiiii li
Item myne ther MM lodes at x d	iiii^{xx}iii li vi s viii d

Robertsbridge

Item in cordes of wood viii^{C}xiiii and di at iii d	x li iii s vii d ob
Item in coles ther v^{C}l lodes at iii s	iiii^{xx}ii li x s
Item in lodes of myne ther C at x d	iiii li iii s iiii d
Item in sowes ther vi^{C}lxviii Item in sowes at pannyngridge CCxxxii } in toto ix^{C} at xx s	ix^{C} li
Item in the storehowse of Iorne lx ton and CC at vi li xiii s iiii d	iiii^{C} li xiii s iiii d
Item in Shippe bordes vii^{C} di at xxx s	xi li v s
Item in tymber by estimation vi^{xx} ton at ii s viii d	xvi li
Item in Shiplankes lxx^{C} and xv fote at v s	xvii li x s
Item in ynche borde xxv^{M} and xvi fote at ii s	xxv li
Some totall of all the remayne aforeseyd	MDCxv li iiii s xi d ob

[*8^{r}*] A declaracon of the clere gayne of the Iorne Workes aforseyd dicto anno primo Regis E vi^{ti}

In primis in price of Cxxi sowes of Iorne at Robertsbridge and pannyngridge hoc anno at xx s the sowe over and besydes the remayne of the laste yere Cxxi li

Item in the price of Clxxiii ton xiii^{C} and iii qtrs and vi lli of Iorne made there this yere at vi li xiii s iiii d the ton MClxii li xviii s iiii d

Item in sawyng of xxv^{M} of bordes at xiii d the C xiii li x s iiii d

Some of all the Incresse or gayne hoc Anno MCCiiii^{xx} xii li viii s viii d wherof to be abated DCx li xviii s viii d ob q for money payd in divers kyndes of the seyd workes this yere as the particulers doth appere in a boke Also to be abated of xxx li iii s ix d for wood and Cole spente of the store of the laste yere at Robertsbridge as appereth by the accomptes therof. And also to be abated of l li x s iiii d for wodde Cole and Myne spente of the store at pannyngridge of the laste yere as it appereth by the accomptes therof, and so remayneth clerly this yere gayned DC li xv s x d q

[*8^{v}*] *blank*

[5] SUMMARY ACCOUNT FOR PANNINGRIDGE FURNACE AND ROBERTSBRIDGE FORGE, 1548

377/6[1] *U 1475 B1/6*

[*1r*] Robertsbridge
The accompte of the Iorne mynes there the seconde yere of the reigne of our Souvereigne lorde kyng Edwarde the vi^ti^ Anno secundo R E vi^ti^

[*1v*] *blank*

[*2r*] Declaracon of accompte of henry westall Clarke of the Iorne Workes to the right Worshipfull Sir William Sydney Knyght at his mannor of Robertsbridge in the Countye of Sussex aswell of all and singuler suche somes of money by hym receyvyd. As also all suche sommes of money by the seyd henry ymploed to the use of the seyd Sir William from the feast of the Natyvytie of our lorde god in the yere of the reigne of our soveraynge lorde Edwarde vi^ti^ by the grace of god of Inglonde Frannce and Irelonde Kyng defendor of the fayth and in erthe of the Churche of Inglonde and also of Irelonde supreme hede fryste untyll the same feaste o the Nativitie of our lorde god then nexte ensuyng the seconnde that ys for one hole yere.

and In primis he chargeth himselff with arrears dependyng in the fote of the last accompte	x li iiii s ob q
and Item he chargeth hymselff with money received of mr henry within the tyme of this accompte with xxii li by thandes of John Bagot as it appereth by a boke of recepte upon this accompte showed and examined	CCCiiii^xx^ii li x s vii d ob
Item he chargeth hymselff with money received of John hawes as it appereth by the seyd boke	Clxxvi li xii s iiii d ob
Item for Catall solde hoc Anno as it appereth by the seyd boke	xviii li xiii s
Item received for tymber solde ther hoc anno	iiii s x d
. . . for xi^C^xxv fete of bordes with ii slabbes solde hoc anno ut per dictum librum	xxxii s vii d

[1] 1548 is a year for which several preliminary books survive. There is one, in 372A (B8/2), for the forge, which has a number of discrepancies from the final summary account, 377/6 (above). For the furnace, however, there are three. 372A (B10/2) and 382/1 (B10/3) take the usual form, the latter being rather more tidily laid out and closer in totals to the summary account. There is also 375(B2/1) which contains much less detail and adds nothing to the others.

[*2*^{v}] . . . iiii^{C} of shipbordes sold hoc anno Cviii s

. . . woode solde hoc anno at per librum predictum li s xi d

. . . xx^{C}viii quarters of Shipplankes and vii slabbes solde hoc anno . . . viii li xiiii s x d

. . . woodasshes solde at pannyngridge hoc anno . . . xxiiii s iii d

. . . pasturyng of Catall hoc anno xix s xi d

. . . ii ton ix^{C} di and x lli of Iorne solde hoc anno[2] . . .
xvii li xix s ii d ob

. . . xxvi quarters vi bushels di of whete solde hoc anno . . .
xi li vi s

. . . xi bushels of oten malte sold hoc anno vi s v d

. . . Clxvii K di of bere solde hoc anno . . . xiii li xix s ii d

. . . herynge and veale solde hoc Anno iii s

. . . for onyons and branne solde hoc anno iiii s i d

. . . hides and felles solde hoc anno viii s xi d

. . . Capons solde hoc anno vi s vi d

. . . hey solde hoc anno vi s

. . . the carege of a lode of cole duste viii d

. . . lviii cordes of woode burnte by dogen the Colier hoc anno . . . ix s viii d

. . . denyson money hoc anno[3] vi s viii d

. . . viii^{C} of lathe hoc anno ii s v d ob

. . . of John Bacheler for sawyng of tymber hoc anno . . . viii d

[*3*^{r}] . . . xv quarters vii bushels of barley and ii bushels of musterde sede solde hoc anno . . . Cxi s vi d

Sum totall of all the receptes aforeseyd with tharragiis
DClx li vii s iii d ob q

wherof

[*3*^{v}] layd oute at Robertsbridge

Item in primis payd for cuttyng of wood and heggyng and and dychyng hoc anno as the particulers dothe appere by the seyd boke xi li x s ob

Item for mowynge and makynge of hey hoc Anno lxviii s ii d

Item in Rydyng expenses and in foren charges hoc anno
Cix s viii d ob

Item to the sawyers for sawyng of bordes plankes and other tymber hoc anno ut per librum predictum x li xiii s iiii d

[2] This tallies exactly with 372A (B8/2), which while showing the usual pattern of small sales to smiths, also records, but does not value, larger consignments: 40 tons to Mr. Webb and 80 tons to Mr. Draper.

[3] This corresponds with an entry in the Furnace Book, 372A (B10/2), and relates to Letters Patent for John Margo.

Item payd to the Kerpenters for makyng a newe barne and mendyng of other howses hoc anno Cvii s iiii d

Item payd for neccessaries bought for the howse hoc anno . . . xxv s iiii d ob

Item to the Smythe aswell for showyng nayles and other yorne worke as for howsbondrye hoc anno ix li x s iiii d

Item payd to the Thecher, masons, and for strawe and for cariage of the same, stones, synder and Corne hoc anno . . . vii li xviii s ii d ob

Item payd for wages there hoc anno with vi li xvi d for martyns borde hoc anno xxix li xv s vii d

Item payd to laborers in neccessarie busynes in the place and the brewhowse hoc anno iiii li xii s v d ob

Item payd to hamermen and fyners for making of Cxliii ton and xviii^C of Iorne at xiii s iiii d the ton[4] . . . iiii^xx xv li xviii s viii d

Item for hepyng of coles of coles and sowes of Iorne and mendyng of belowes hoc anno[5] xlvi s ii d

Item for makyng of MMiii^C xxi cords of woodde ad divers prices hoc anno xxviii li xvii s xi d

Item for colynge of viii^C lxxv Cordes of coles liiii li viii s v d

Item for the caryng of viii^C lxxii lodes of coles ad divers prices[6] xiiii li iii s iii d

[*4*^r] Item payd to laborers and kerpentters for Repacions at the forge diches and Ryvere there, and hydes lether and gresse for the seyd forge hoc anno[7] ut per etc x li xviii s ii d ob

Item for caryng and wayng of Iorne hoc anno[8] xii li viii s ob

Item for xliiii quarters of ottes bought hoc anno vii li xvii s viii d

Item for Catall bought hoc anno ut per librum predictum xii li xiiii s viii d

Item payd in Rewardes hoc anno . . xlii s x d

[4] The details in 372A (B8/2) are incomplete; work to the value of £66.16.8 is recorded.

[5] Cutting had become concentrated among fewer men since the last surviving detailed record (1543): 17 men appear, 8 are paid on 5 or more out of 11 pay days, although 7 are only referred to once. No cutting was done in July, August or September.

[6] 4 burners are paid, the great bulk of work being done by only 2, Duggyn and Adryan.

[7] 372A (B8/1) gives particularly full details of repairs; although there was no major rebuilding there is an excellent picture of the constant repair needed by wheels, bellows, hearths and chimneys.

[8] This is an amalgamation of sections in 372A (B8/1), covering lighterage, land carriage and weighing. There is a full list of carters (normal rate 2s per day), and details of the cost of lighterage to Rye (1s 3d per ton).

Item payd to the plomer and other workemen aboute the Condyte hoc anno . . . xi li xviii s vi d

Item for palyng withoute the mote in the basecorte and in the Iner orcheyarde the Reddyng and grobbyng of the seyd orcheyardes and other places of the grownde hoc anno . . . xiiii li viii s ix d ob

Item payd to the cowper for neccessaries for the brew howse bought hoc anno xxix s vii d

Item for neccessaries bought for the ii boyes in the kychen hoc anno xxii s iiii d

Item in expenses of howsholde hoc anno over and besydes xxiiii li v s vi d spend of the store that ys in the price CCx kilderkin, xvii li x s, of bere at xx d the kilderkin and in the price of xvi quarters vii bushels di of whete vi li xv s vi d at (*blank*) the quarter as it appereth by the seyd boke lxiiii li xv s ii d ob

Sum of all the paymentes aforeseyd at Robertsbridge CCCCxxiiii li ix d ob

[*4v*] and at pannyngridge

Item for the Cuttynge of MMCxxv cordes of wood ther hoc anno ut per librum predictum xxvi li xviii s iii d

Item in expenses there at my comyng thether at duvers tymes[9] . . . xvi s xi d

Item payd to the founder and fyller for xxxiiii foundes at xiiii s the foundy[10] . . . xxiii li xvi s

Item for colynge of Dlxvii lodes of Coles hoc anno[11] xxxiii li viii s iii d

Item for caryng of Dlxvii lodes of coles hoc anno[12] xii li v s ob

Item for castyng of MCClvii lodes of myne at vii d ob the lode[13] . . . xxxix li v s vii d ob

Item for caryng of Mvi lodes of myne[14] hoc anno vi li v s ix d

[9] Includes expenses of John Jackson riding to Buxted (furnace) to speak with Charles (Pulleyn), and to Charles' man for cost of coming to Robertsbridge; also costs of measuring woodlands (Estons Wood and Kemehyd). Peter the Founder and Martin went to Birchenden (8d)—perhaps Birchenden Forge.

[10] 372A (B10/2), is not a reliable source for this. It gives a total of £24 11s 0d but items which only add up to £15 3s 0d.

[11] No coling was done in June, July or August. 338 of these loads were made by Duggyn: 5 other men did the rest; 3 of the latter were paid 1s 3d a load, as against 2s.

[12] All by one man, Hawkins. Rates: Panningridge 4d, Tottersdown 4d and 4½d, Hasilden 6d.

[13] Four miners (372A:B10/2).

[14] Entirely by Thos. Smyth (372A: B10/2).

. . . for caryng of Sowes from pannyngridge to Robertsbridge hoc anno[15] . . . xiiii li x s viii d

Item payd for myne[16] hoc anno . . . xxxi s

Item payd for the ferme of the woodd hyer of wayes thowrowe mennes growndes the rent of the ponde and the tythe of the same[17] hoc anno xxii li x s iiii d

Item payd in empcions of divers neccessaries bought for the furnysshe ther and for Repacions aboute the the same furnysshe[18] hoc anno iiii li v s x d

Item payd to Richard aneston and to Nicholas vynehall for woodde of them bought hoc anno lvii li v s

Sum of all the paymentes at pannyngridge CCxlii li xiiii s i d

[5^r] Sum of all the paymentes foreseyd DClxvi li xiiii s x d ob and so is in surplus, vi li vii s vi d ob q, unto the which he askythe allowannce of ix d in the price of iii quyre of paper by hym bought hoc anno. And sic yet supplus vi li viii s iii d ob q, whiche the seyd accomptannt hathe receyvyd by thande of mr henry Sydney upon this declaracion

(*illegible signature*)

[5^v] *blank*

[6^r] Cordes of woodde at Robertsbridge The remayne of cordes anno per pceden viii^C xxiiii and di

Item made ther hoc anno MMCCCxxi cordes

and Sum of all the cordes iii^M Cxlv and di, wherof spent hoc anno MMlvii cordes, and burned by the neclygens of the coliers lviii cordes. And so remain in the woodde hoc anno ix^C xxx cordes and di ad se li cordes gayned in the rekenyng hoc anno, and so remain there ix^C iiii^xx i cordes di

Coles Item the remayne of lodes anno . . . Dl

Item made and caried hoc anno viii^C lxxv lodes

Sum of all the lodes Miiii^C xx wherof spente hoc anno Mlxx lodes and so remayneth CCCl lodes

15 The rate of 1s 4d per load still applies. 3 carters were involved.

16 Bought from Mr. Burwell at 1¼d per load (372A: B10/2).

17 Woodland rents were paid to Mr. Chancellor; pond rent to the vicar of Penhurst, the tithe to the vicar of Ashburnham. Wayleave for sow carriage was paid to Hawkins, James Ryve of Mountfield (who was one of the carriers of sow iron) and Longley.

18 This includes 'felling, framing and setting up a new house for George Maryatt, my master's collier, 13s 4d . . . for carriage of wood for this house, 11s 3d . . . thatching and daubing it, 11s 3d'. Also making a 'bogge' for the furnace; this may be a corruption of 'bridge'.

lodes of myne Item the remayne of lodes of myne . . . C lodes
Item caried hoc anno nil
and Sum of all the lodes of myne C whiche remaynethe

Sowes there Item there ys in sowes by estimacion DCCCxx

Pannyngridge
Item there is in Sowes by tale Ciiii
Sum of all the sowes is DCCCCxxiiii which remain

[*6*^{v}] The accompte of Iorne Item the remayne of the last yere lx ton and CC
Item made ther hoc anno Cxliii ton and xviii^{C}
Sum of all the Iorne aforeseyd CCiiii ton, wherof solde by henry westall as the particelles particulerly dothe appere by a boke upon this accompte showed ii ton ix^{C} di and x lli, and also delyvered to George Covyle at my masters comanndement iiii ton, and also delyverd to mr Webbe and his servant by hys seyd comanndement xliii ton and delyverd to master by his seyd comanndement iiii^{xx} ton. And also delyverd to a smythe of farnyngham i ton. And so remayneth lxxiii ton di qtr and xviii lli, unto the whiche he is charged with iii ton vi^{C} di and iii lli, which is gayned in the wayte of Iorne hoc anno, and so ther ys remaynyng the xxi^{ti} day of december hoc anno lxxvi ton xvi^{C}iii qrts and xxi lli.

Cordes of woodde at pannyngridge Item the remayne of cordes anno per pceden ii^{M}v^{C}xiiii
Item made there hoc anno MMCxxv
Sum totall of all the cordes v^{M}vii^{C}iiii^{xx}xv cordes, wherof spente hoc anno MMiii^{C}iiii^{xx}v cordes, and so remayneth in cordes MMCCliiii cordes

[*7*^{r}] Coles there Item the remayne . . . Clx lodes
Item made there in lodes hoc anno Dlxvii
Sum of all the lodes vii^{C}xxvii lodes, wherof spente hoc anno vii^{C}xiii lodes, and remayneth xiiii lodes
lodes of myne ther Item the remayne . . . MM
Item ther ys caried and dyged hoc anno MCClvii
Sum of all the lodes of myne iii^{M}CClvii, wherof spente hoc anno Miii lodes, and remain MMCCliiii lodes
Shipborde at Robertsbridge Item the remain . . . viii^{C}
Item made hoc anno nil
Sum of all the shipborde viii^{C}, wherof solde hoc anno iiii^{C}, and so remain iiii^{C}
tymber ther Item the remain . . . Cxx ton

Item hewed ther hoc anno xx ton
Sum of all the tones of tymber Cxl, wherof spente in buldynge hoc anno per estimation xx ton, and sawen in bordes and plankes per estimation hoc anno xl ton. So remain iiii^{xx} ton

[7^{v}] ynche borde there Item the remayne . . .
xxv^{M} and xvi fete
Item sawen ther hoc anno per estimation xv^{M}ix^{C} lix fete
Sum of all the bordes xl^{M}ix^{C}lxxv fete, wherof solde hoc anno Mxxi fete, and spente eodem anno iiii^{M}D fete, and remaynethe
xxxv^{M}iiii^{C}liiii fete
Shiplankes there Item the remayne . . . lxvi^{C} di and xv fete
Item sawen ther hoc anno MCC
Sum of all the shiplankes vii^{M}viii^{C}lxv fete, wherof solde hoc anno MMvii^{C}lxxv fete to duvers persons, and spente hoc anno per estimation M fete and remain iiii^{M}iiii^{xx}x fete
Catall there Item the remain de anno . . . vi oxen at xxxiii s iiii d
x li
Item iiii oxen bought hoc anno at xxxiii s vi li xii s
Item kyne bought of mr fitzherbet at xvii s iiii d lxix s
Item ii kye bought of William Stonestrete xlv s
Item ii fate oxen Cvi s viii d
Sum of all the monny for Catall xxvii li xii s viii d
Noted ther ys one oxe dede of the moren

[8^{r}] *blank*
[8^{v}] *blank*

[9^{r}] The remaynes of the Stoke at Robertsbridge and pannyngridge aforeseyd the xxi^{ti} day of december anno ii^{de} Regis E vi^{ti}

pannyngridge
In primis MMCCliiii cordes of woodde at iiii d xxxvii li xi s iiii d
Item in lodes of coles there xiiii at iii s xlii s
Item in lodes of myne there MMCCliiii at x d iiii^{xx}xiii li xviii s iiii d

Robertsbridge
Item in cordes of woodde ther ix^{C}iiii^{xx}i at iii d xi li xvi s iii s
Item in lodes of coles CCCl at iii s the lode lii li x s
Item in lodes of myne there C at x d iiii li iii s iiii d
Item in sowes ther viii^{C}xx
Item in sowes at pannyngridge Ciiii } ix^{C}xxiiii at xx s DCCCCxxiiii l
Item in the store howse of Iorne lxxvi ton xvi^{C}iii qrts xxi lli at vii li Dxxxviili xviii s vi d ob q

Item in shipbordes iiii^{C} at xxx s the C vi li

Item in tymber per estimation iiii^{xx} ton at ii s viii d x li xiii s iiii d

Item in shiplankes x^{C}liiii^{xx}x fete at v s x li iiii s iiii d ob

Item in ynche bordes xxxv^{M}iiii^{C}liiii fete at ii s xxxv li ix s

Item in Catall there eodem die price xxvii li xii s viii d

Sum totall of all the remayne aforeseyd MDCCliii li xix s ii d q

[*9*^{v}] A declaracon of the clere gayne of the Iorne workes aforeseyd anno ii^{de} Regis E vi^{ti}

In Primis in price of xxiiii Sowes of Iorne at Robertsbridge and pannyngridge hoc anno at xx s over and besydes the remayne of the last yere xxiiii li

Item in the price of Cxliii ton and xviii^{C} of Iorne made there hoc anno at vii li the ton Mvii li vi s

Item in sawyng of x^{M} of ynche borde at xiii d the C Cviii s iiii d

Item payd for wood hoc anno and not spente lvii li v s

Item in myne at pannyngridge CCliiii lodes at x d the lode x li xi s viii d

Sum of all the Incresse or gayne hoc anno MCiiii li xi s

wherof to be abated of DClxvi li xv s vii d ob

for money payd in duvers kyndes of the seyd workes this yere as the particulers doth appere in a boke. Also to be abated of xxx li for coles spente of the store of the last yere at Robertsbridge as it appereth by the accompte therof. And also to be abated of xxvi li iiii s viii d for wood and Cole spente of store of the laste yere at pannyngridge as it appereth by the accompte therof made hoc Anno and so remayneth clerely this yere gayned CCCiiii^{xx}i li x s viii d ob

[6] SUMMARY ACCOUNT FOR PANNINGRIDGE FURNACE AND ROBERTSBRIDGE FORGE, 1549

377/7 *U 1475 B1/7*

[*1r*] Robertsbridge
The accompte of the Iorne mynes there the iii[de] yere of the reigne of Our Sovereigne lorde Kyng Edwarde the vi[ti], Anno iii[tio] regis E vi[ti]

[*1v*] *blank*

[*2r*] Declaracon of accompte of henry westall Clarke of the Iorne Workes to the right Worshipfull Sir William Sydney Knyght at his mannor of Robertsbridge in the Countye of Sussex aswell of all and singuler suche sommes of money by hym receyvyd. as also all suche sommes of money by the seyd henry Imploed to the use of the seyd Sir William from the feast of the Natyvytie of our lorde god in the yere of the reigne of our lorde Edwarde the vi[ti] by the grace of god of Inglonde frannce and Irelonde kyng defendor of the fayth and in erthe of the Churche of Inglonde and also of Irelonde supreme hede ii[de] untyll the same feaste of the Natyvytie of our lorde god then next ensuyng the iii[de] that ys for one hole yere.

In primis he Chargeth hymselff with money receyvyd of master Henry Sydney within the tyme of this accompte, with xxx li by thandes of John Bagoot, as it aperethe by a boke of receypte upon this accompte showed and examyned — CCClxvi li x s

Item he chargeth hymself with money received of John hawes as it appereth by the seyd boke — Ciiii[xx]xiiii li xii s ix d

Item he chargeth him selff with money received for Catall solde hoc Anno ut per librum predictum — xxxiii li v s x d

Item received for wood solde hoc anno — lx s v d

Item for asshes and wood solde at pannyngridge — xxi s ii d

Item of Anthony Normand for a nolde howse to hym solde by Mr henry — xiii s iiii d

[*2v*] Item for hoppys and hydes solde hoc anno . . . — xxxiii s iii d

Item for xiii[C]xxxiiii li of Iorne sold hoc anno to divers persons as it appereth by the seyd boke — vi li ix s vii d

Item of master draper for Casting of one ton of andernes at my masters comanndement — xiii s iiii d

F

Item for iii qrters and one bz of barley hoc anno solde ut . . . xxix s x d ob
Item for xxv qrters iiii bz and di of whete solde hoc anno at divers prices xv li iiii s iii d
Item for xiii bz of oten malte solde hoc anno ut . . . viii s iiii d
Item for iiii^{xx}vii kylderkens of bere sold ther hoc anno to the workemen ad divers prices ut . . . vii li viii s vi d
Sum totall of all the receptes aforeseyd DCxxxii li x s vii d ob

wherof

[*3^r*] layd oute at Robertsbridge[1]
In primis for the Cuttynge of Mvii^{C}xxx cordes and di of wood ad diverse prices as the particulars dothe appere by the seyd boke[2] xxi li xiii s ii d
Item payd for mowyng and making of hay hoc anno ut . . . lxviii s ix d
Item payd in Rydyng expenses and foren charges hoc anno ut . . . ix li xi s[3]
Item payd for sawyng of tymber for Repacions of howses hoc anno xxiii s i d ob
Item payd to kerpentters and Sawyers for Repacions of the forge hoc anno xii li xvi s xi d ob
Item payd to laborers about the forge hoc anno iiii li iiii s v d
Item payd to kerpentters hoc anno lxxiii s vii d
Item payd to the Smythe aswell for showyng nayles and other Iorne worke as for howsbondry hoc anno xi li xix s i d ob
Item payd to the Thecher glasyer mason and plomer and Strawe bought hoc anno[4] lxix s vii d ob
Item payd for Servantes wage hoc anno with gere bought for the boy of the kychen xxii li xi s i d ob
Item payd to laborers in necessarie busynes in the place and the brewhouse hoc anno lxviii s x d ob
Item payd to the hammerman and fyners for makyng of C ton vi^{C}iii qrts of Iorne at xiii s iiii d the ton ut . . . lxvi li xvii s i d

[1] This summary is based on 372A: B8/2, B8/3, between which there is little material difference.

[2] The pattern differs little from previous years; out of 6 pay days 1 wood-cutter appears at all, 3 at 5, 2 at 4, 5 at 3, 6 at 2, and 2 at 1. There is the usual summer interval.

[3] This includes expenses of riding to London after the forge was pulled down by rioters in June 1549. For local feeling against ironworks see *H.M.C., Salisbury*, xiii, p. 19.

[4] The glazier from Battle provided 22 feet of new glass. Including fitting and metalwork this cost 4¼d per foot. (372A: B8/2).

Item payd for hepyng of Coles Sowes and mendyng of belowes xxxii s x d ob

Item for the Colyng of vi^c^vi lodes of Cole ad diverse prices ut . . . xxxvii li vi s ii d

[*3^v^*] Item payd for the Carying of the seyd vi^c^ and vi lodes of Coles ad diverse prices xi li xv s vii d

Item payd for caryng of Iorne and wayng of the same which was solde to diverse persons ix li xix s iii d ob

Item payd for Catall bought hoc anno xxxi li xvii s i d

Item for hydes and felles for the forge hoc anno xliii s x d

Item for the makyng of bryckes and tyles hoc anno ut[5] . . . xiiii li xix s i d

Item for palyng heggyng and Cuttyng of woode for the howse hoc anno vi li iii s x d

Item for caryng of woodde for the howshold x s iiii d

Item in expenses of howsholde hoc anno over and besydes xxxiiii li xiiii s viii d spente of the store that is in the price, CCiiii^xx^vi K of bere at xx d and in the price of xx qrts iii bz and di of whete at x s viii d ut . . . iiii^xx^xviii li ii s vi d ob

Item payd for hennes and Capons bought to sende to London to my master xxxvii s i d ob

Sum of all the paymentes aforeseyd at Robertsbridge CCCiiii^xx^i li iiii s vii d

[*4^r^*] and at pannyngridge[6]

Item for the Cuttynge of iiii^M^iii^C^xviii Cordes and di of woodde ad diverse prices hoc anno[7] lxiiii li xiii s v d

Item for myne expenses Blakenalles and others in goying thether ad diverse Temporily xiii s

[5] There are 3 pages giving details of William Ovenden's making of brick and tiles in 372A (B8/2).

[6] 382/2 (B10/3) is a complete and informative furnace book; it is duplicated by another version, 383/2 (B11/2), which omits totals. 383/4 (B11/3) perhaps relates to 1549, for although most totals are different, those for mining and ore carriage fit *377/7*.

[7] The expansion of the area of wood supply becomes clear in 1549. In the spring large quantities came from Eston's Wood (see 1548). Hasilden was still in use, but in December Couper's Wood was largely used, with a new group of woodcutters, including a man named Couper. Small quantities came from Hornden Wood, The High Wood and Keentrethe. Panningridge Wood still appears throughout. No cutting was paid for between June 23rd and November 28th; the number of cutters mentioned is 54; the pattern of employment, between regular and occasional workers was comparable with earlier years.

Item payd to the founder and filler for xxviii foundes and di at xiiii s the foundy[8] xx li iiii d

Item for the Colyng of Mlxxii lodes of Cole at xv d the lode hoc anno[9] lxvii li

Item for the Caryng of MClv lodes of Coles ad diverse prices[10] xxviii li xii s ix d

Item for Castyng of iii^C^xv lodes of myne[11] x li vi s x d ob

Item for Caryng of ii^C^lxiiii lodes of myne[12] lxi s xi d ob

Item for caryng of Sowes and hyer of grounde for the Cartes hoc anno iiii li xv s viii d

Item payd for the woodde pounde and tythe of the fornes with martens wages and other ther hoc anno ut . . . xli li iii s x d

Item payd to laborers for the reparyng of the fornys wall and the fornysshe and for neccessaries bought for the same hoc anno[13] xiiii li xix s viii d

Item payd to Kerpentters for hewyng of tymber and makyng of lathes hoc anno ix li ii s vi d

Sum of all the paymentes at pannyngridge CClxiiii li x s

[*4^v^*] Sum of all the paymentes aforeseyd DCxlv li xiiii s vii d, and so is in surplus xiii li iii s xi d ob, of the whiche he is allowed of iiii li xvi s iiii d for money by hym layde oute in preste the laste yere and hath it allowed agayne thys yere and so yet surplus viii li vii s vii d ob

[*5^r^*] Cordes of woodde at Robertsbridge anno per pceden — The remayne of Cordes ix^C^iiii^xx^i cordes and di

Item made there hoc anno M vii^C^xxx cordes and di

Sum of all the cordes ii^M^vii^C^xii wherof spente hoc anno Miiii^C^xlii cordes and di So remain in the woodde hoc anno MCClxix cordes and di

Coles there Item the remayne of lodes . . . iii^C^l

Item made there hoc anno vi^C^vi

[8] Peter the Founder, for all smelting except 2 Foundays, ending June 11th, worked by Nicholas. Nicholas cast 1 ton of brandirons.

[9] Two men only are mentioned.

[10] Costs: Panningridge: 4d and 5½d; Hornden 6d; Hasilden 6d and 7d; Neston 9d per load. The last is the highest yet paid.

[11] Cresse's land was increasingly in use, although ore still came from Panningridge. Two miners were employed. There is an entry in the furnace book for three men searching for ore.

[12] Carriage: Panningridge 1½d, John Cresse's Wood 3d, Hasilden 4d.

[13] The repair entries at the furnace are well detailed in 382/2. Charles, probably the Buxted founder, repaired the furnace wall, bellows and hearth; John Alye made the furnace wheel, a new penstock, and 'pieced' the floodgate; the furnace wall was repaired (23 man-days) in October, using clay and cinder.

Sum of all the lodes ix^{C}lvi lodes wherof spente hoc anno vii^{C}lxxvi lodes
and so remayneth Ciiii^{xx}

lodes of myne Item the remayne of lodes . . . C lodes
Item caried hoc anno nil
Sum of all the lodes C which remain

Sowes there Item ther is in Sowes per estimat vi^{C}xi
pannyngridge Item in sowes there by tale ii^{C}iiii^{xx}xii
Sum of all the Sowes ys per estimat ix^{C}iii

[*5^v^*] Iorne there Item the remain . . . lxxvi ton xvi^{C}iii qrts and xxi li
Item made ther hoc anno C ton vi^{C}iii qrters
Sum of all the Iorne aforeseyd Clxxvi ton ix C iii qrts and xxi li
wherof solde hoc anno xiii^{C}xxxiiii li by henry westall as the particulars doth appere by a boke upon this accompte showed and examyned and delyverd to mr draper by my masters comandement in mense Junii C ton. And delyvered to mr White in eodem mense 1 ton, and delyverd to Colvyld in eodm mense i ton and delyvered to the seyd Colvylde xxiiii^{to} die october i ton and delyverd to the seyd Colvyld in mense december i ton and delyverd to the workemen for repacions of the workes hoc anno iiii^{xx}iii li. So sic remain lxxii ton iii qrters of an C and xvi li. so remain in the storehowse lxxiiii ton ix^{C} and so gayned in wayte hoc anno ii ton viii^{C} and i qtr

[*6^r^*] Cordes of wood at pannyngridge Item the remain of cordes . . . MMCCliiii
Item made there hoc anno iiii^{M}iii^{C}xxviii and di
Sum totall of all the cordes vi^{M}v^{C}iiii^{xx}ii cordes and di
wherof spent hoc anno iii^{M}Diiii^{xx}xvi and di So remain MMix^{C}iiii^{xx}vi cordes

Coles there Item the remain of lodes there . . . xiiii lodes
Item made there hoc anno Mlxxii
Sum of all the lodes Miiii^{xx}vi lodes wherof spente hoc anno vii^{C}xlvi lodes So remain iii^{C}xl

lodes of myne[14] Item the remain . . . MMCCliiii
Item ther is caried hoc anno CCCxv lodes
Sum of all the lodes MMDlxix wherof spent hoc anno v^{C}lxix lodes
So remain MM lodes

Shipbordes at Robertsbridge Item the remain . . . iiii^{C}

[14] The Panningridge ore carriage entry shows 264 loads (382/2).

Item ther hoc anno nil
Sum of all the Shipborde iiii^C^ which remain

[*6^v^*] tonnes of tymber Item the remain . . . iiii^xx^ ton
Item hewed hoc anno nil
Sum of all the tonnes of tymber iiii^xx^ which remain

ynch bordes ther Item the remain . . . xxxv^M^ iiii^C^ liiii fete
Item sawen hoc anno nil
Sum of all the bordes xxxv^M^iiii^C^liiii fete wherof solde hoc anno di C lent to lawrence derby one C and spent hoc anno viii^C^ and remain xxvi^M^iiii fete

Shiplankes Item the remain . . . iiii^M^iiii^xx^x fete
Item made and Sawen hoc anno nil
Sum of all the shiplankes iiii^M^iiii^xx^x fete which remain

Catall there Item the remain . . . in oxen xii
Item in oxen bought hoc anno v
Item in kye the remain . . . vi
Item in kye bought hoc anno ix
Sum of the oxen and kye xxxii wherof solde hoc anno in oxen vii
solde in kye hoc anno x
So remain xv

unde

[*7^r^*] oxen ix at xlvi s x d
kye v at xxiii s i d

lathes made at pannyngridge Item in lathes made there hoc anno xxxi lodes
Sum of the lathes xxxi lodes wherof solde hoc anno ii lodes So remain xxix lodes at vii s iiii d the lode

[*7^v^*] *blank*

[*8^r^*] The remayne of the Stoke at Robertsbridge and pannyngridge aforeseyd the xxi^th^ day of december anno iii^tio^ Regis predicto

pannyngridge
In primis MMix^C^iiii^xx^vi cordes of wood there at v d the corde lxii li iiii s ii d
Item in lodes of Coles ther iii^C^xl at iii s 4 d lvi li xiii s iiii d
Item in lodes of myne there MM at x d iiii^xx^iii li vi s viii d
Item in lodes of lathes there xxxi at vii s iiii d xi li vii s iiii d

Robertsbridge

Item in cordes of wood there Mii^{C}lxix and di at iiii d xxi li iii s ii d

Item in lodes of coles there Ciiii^{xx} at iii s 4 d xxx li

Item in lodes of myne there C at x d iiii li iii s iiii d

Item in Sowes there vi^{C}xi
Item in Sowes at pannyngridge ii^{C}iiii^{xx}xii } ix^{C}iii at xxiii s 4 d
Mliii li x s

Item in the storehowse of Iorne lxxiiii ton and ix^{C} at viii li x s the ton DCxxxii li

Item in shippe bordes there iiii^{C} at xxx s vi li

Item in tymber per estimation iiii^{xx} ton at ii s x d x li xiii s iiii d

Item in shiplankes x^{C}liiii^{xx} and x fete at v s x li iiii s iiii d ob

Item in ynchebordes xxvi^{M} and iiii fete at ii s the C xxvi li

Item in Catall ther eodem die xxvi li xvi s x d

Sum totall of all the remayne aforeseyd MMxxxiiii li ii s iiii d ob

[*8*^{r}] A declaracon of the clere gayne of the Iorne workes aforeseyd dco anno iii^{tio} Regis predicti

In primis in the price of C ton vi^{C}iii qrts of Iorne made there hoc anno at viii li x s the ton DCCClii li xvii s

Item gayned in cordes of wood hoc anno over and besydes the remayne of the last yere at Robertsbridge CCiiii^{xx}viii at iiii d iiii li xvi s

Item in cordes of wood at pannyngridge vii^{C}xxxii over and besydes the remain of the last yere at v d the corde xv li v s

Item in lodes of Coles there hoc anno over and besydes the remayne of the last yere CCCxxvi at iii s xlviii li xviii s

Sum of all the Incresse or gayne hoc anno iii^{tio} DCCCCxxi li xvi s wherof to be abated of DCxlv li xiiii s vii d for money payd in divers kyndes of the seyd workes hoc anno as the particulars doth appere in a boke therof made and so remayneth clerely this yere gayned CClxxvi li xvii d

[7] PANNINGRIDGE FURNACE BOOK, 1550

383/3 *U 1475 B11/2*

[*1r*] The Boke of paymentes at Robrt pannyngrig made the first day of January Anno Edwardi Regis tertio ut Sequitur[1]

[*1v–2v*] *blank*

[*3r*] xxviii[th] January
hassilden

paid to harry olyver for xx[ti] cordes	vi s
. . . Stephen affild for xxv cordes	vii s vi d
. . . laurens Erle for xl cordes	xii s
. . . John baker for xxx cordes	ix s vi d
. . . Bogge for xxxii cordes	ix s vii d

panyngrig

. . . John Smithe for xxii cordes	vi s vii d
. . . philpot for iii[xx]vi cordes	xix s ix d ob
. . . william Affild for xx[ti] cordes	vi s

Cops woode

. . . markes for xx[ti] cordes	vi s
. . . henry maurice for xxx cordes	ix s
. . . William smalffild for xiii cordes	iii s x d
. . . Robert heward for v cordes	xviii d
. . . William Ovenden for xxvi cordes	vii s ix d ob
. . . willis for iiii cordes	xiiii d
. . . Edmonde coper for xx[ti] cordes	vi s
. . . John welche for x cordes	iii s
. . . Wat hoopson for xiii cordes	iii s x d ob
. . . John Atkyn for xxx cordes	ix s

[*3v*] ultimo february
hassilden

. . . henry olyver for xx[ti] cordes	vi s
. . . Richard Slayt for xl cordes	xii s
. . . stephen Affild for xl cordes	xii s
. . . John Smyth for xxv cordes	vii s vi d

[1] There seems little doubt that this account relates to 1550. The entries, when totalled, do not correspond with the summary for 1549. This book must have been *started* on 1st January 1550.

. . . Robert barnet for xx^ti^ cordes vi s
. . . laurens Erle for x cordes iii s

panyngrig
. . . William Affild for xx^ti^ cordes vi s
. . . george morrall for xxx^ti^ cordes ix s
. . . Philpyng for ix cordes ii s viii d ob

Cops wood
. . . William coper for xlii cordes di xii s viii d ob
. . . Edmonde coper for xx^ti^ cordes vi s
. . . Henry maurice for xxx^ti^ cordes ix s
. . . Wm Ovenden for xx^ti^ cordes vi s
. . . Robert heward for xviii cordes v s v d ob
. . . Wat hoppson for x cordes iii s
. . . markes for xx^ti^ cordes vi s
. . . Edmonde Welche for xii cordes iii s vii d
. . . thomas batty and John Elis for iii^xx^ cordes xviii s

[*4^r^*] xxi^th^ martii
panningridge wood
. . . William Affild for xx^ti^ cordes vi s
. . . lawrens Erle for xli cordes xii s v d
di more unto hym for xi cordes di in hassilden iii s vi d
. . . stephen Affild for xl cordes xii s
. . . George morrall for xix cordes v s viii d
. . . barnet for x cordes in high wood iii s
. . . philpot for vi cordes xxi d

Cops woode
. . . wat hopson for xv cordes iiii s vi d
. . . maurice for xx^ti^ cordes vi s
more unto hym in Recompence for brussyng of homes in the same woode iiii d
. . . markes for xx^ti^ cordes vi s
. . . William smallffild for xl cordes xii s
. . . atkyn for l cordes xv s
. . . Ovenden for xxx^ti^ cordes ix s
. . . Edmonde Welche for xv cordes iiii s vi d
. . . Thomas batty for xx^ti^ cordes vi s

iii^th^ Aprilis

panningridge woode
. . . William Affild for xx^ti^ cordes vi s

. . . laurens Erle for xxx^{ti} cordes ix s
. . . henry olyver for x cordes iii s
. . . John Smith for xx^{ti} cordes vi s
. . . William glaiser for xvii cordes vi s i d
more unto hym for v cordes in panningridge xviii d
. . . Robert barnet for xx^{ti} cordes in high vi s
. . . Stephen Affild for xv cordes iiii s vi d

Coops woode
. . . henry mauryce for xx^{ti}ii cordes vi s vii d
. . . wat hoppson for xxx^{ti} cordes ix s
. . . markes for xvi cordes di iiii s xi d

[*4*^{v}] John Atkyn for xi cordes iii s iii d ob
. . . Thomas batty for xxx cordes ix s
. . . John whelche for v cordes xviii d
. . . William Smalffild for xxx^{ti} cordes ix s
. . . William Ovenden for x cordes iii s

ultimo Aprilis
panningridge
. . . William Affilde for xv cordes iiii s vi d
. . . William Olyver for xxv cordes vii s vi d
. . . laurens Erle for xxxii cordes ix s vii d
. . . Richard Slayter and his brother for xxx cordes ix s
. . . Stepson Affild for xxv cordes vii s vi d
. . . John Smithe for xx cordes vi s
. . . henry Olyver for xx^{ti}ii cordes vi s vii d

highewood
. . . Robert burnet for x corddes iii s

cops woodd
. . . henry maurice for xxx^{ti} cordes ix s
. . . William Smalffild for xi cordes xii s
. . . John Atkyn for xx^{ti} cordes vi s
. . . William Ovenden for x cordes iii s

xxiiith may
panningridge
. . . William affilde for xxx^{ti} cordes ix s
. . . hary olyver and T Olyver for xxxv corddes x s vi d

hassilden
... Laurens erle for for xl cordes xii s
... John martyn and Richard olyver for xl corddes xiis
... William olyver and his man for xxii cordes vi s vii d
... William glaiser for xx^{ti} cordes vi s
... Robert barnet for x corddes iii s
... stephen Affild for x cordes iii s

Coops woode
... John atkyn for xvi cordes iiii s ix d ob
... William smalfild for xx^{ti} corddes vi s
... spray for xlvi cordes xiii s ix d ob
... hary mauryce for xx^{ti} cordes vi s
... John den for xx^{ti} cordes vi s
... wat hopson for for xxxi cordes ix s iii d ob

[5^{r}] xxiiith Junii
panningridge
... William Affild for xxx^{ti} corddes ix s
... hary olyver thomas olyver and John olyver for iii^{xx}xv cordes xxii s vii d
... laurens erle for xxxii^{ti} corddes ix s vii d

hassilden
... hary olyver John olyver for xxx^{ti}ii corddes ix s vii d
... John martyn Richard olyver and John olyver for lv corddes xvi s vi d
... William glaiser for xli corddes xii s iii d ob
... laurens erle for x corddes iii s
... stephen affild for xx^{ti}v corddes vii s vi d
... William olyver for xxv corddes vii s vi d
... Robert barnet for xxiiii corddes vii s ii d

cops woode
... hary olyver Thomas olyver Richard olyver and John martyn for l corddes xv s
... John Smithe for xxvii corddes di viii s ii d ob
more to hym and dew for iii cordes di xii d
... John den for xxviii corddes viii s v d ob
... laurens erle for xxiiii corddes vii s ii d
... Sprey for iii^{xx}iiii corddes xix s ii d
... John Atkyn for xviii corddes v s iiii d ob
... Sprey for brussyng and maykng oken [ ] in his worke xii d

xiiiith July
cops wood

. . . Sprey for xliiii cordes	xiii s ii d
. . . markes for xxi corde di	vi s v d
. . . William coper for xx^{ti} corddes	vi s
. . . maurice for xxv corddes	vii s vi d
. . . barnet for x cordes	iii s
. . . Richard Slayter for xiii cordes in hassilden	iii s x d ob[2]

[5^{v}]
v^{to} Augustii

. . . pray to xl corddes	xiii s ix d

x^{to} Augustii

. . . markes for x cordes	iii s

xx^{ti} Augustii

. . . sprey for xl corddes	xii s

primo septebris

. . . markes for xxii corrdes	vi s vii d
. . . henry maurice for xxx corddes	ix s

vi^{to} octobris
cops wood

. . . Sprey for iii^{xx}iiii cordes	xix s ii d
. . . William Coper for iii^{xx}vii cordes	xx s i d
. . . Mighell bellet for xx^{ti} cordes	vi s
. . . John Atkyn for xl cordes	xii s

xxi^{mo} octobris
cops wood

. . . myghell bellet for xxiiii^{ti} cordes	vii s ii d
. . . Sprey for xxx^{ti} cordes	ix s
. . . daniell for xiii cordes di	iiii s
. . . William coper for xx cordes	vi s

hassilden

. . . harry mauryce for xx cordes	vi s[3]
. . . William glayser for xl cordes	xii s
. . . stephen affild for xx^{ti} cordes	vi s

panningridge

. . . William affild for xv cordes	iiii s vi d
. . Richard olyver and hary olyver for iii^{xx}xv corde di	xxii s vii d ob
. . hym more for the Cuttyng of a gret loge	viii d[3]

[2] Crossed out in *ms.*

[3] Later insertions in a different hand.

[*6r*] ix° novembris[4]
panningridge
. . . William affeld for xii cordes di iii s ix d
. . . laurens erle for iiii^{xx} cordes xxiiii s
more unto hym for iii cordes at iiii d the corde xii d

hasselden
. . . William glaiser for xx^{ti} cordes vi s
. . . Stewen affild for xv cordes iiii s vi d
more unto hym for x cordes at iiii d the cord iii s iiii d
. . . Richard Slayter for xv di cordes iiii s vii d ob
more unto hym for vii cordes at iiii d the corde iii s iiii d

cops wood
. . . Sprey for xl cordes xii s
. . . myghell bellet for xl cordes xii s
. . . John den for xxx^{ti} cordes ix s
. . . William den for xxx^{ti} cordes ix s
. . . henry maurice for xx^{ti} cordes vi s
more to hym for cuttyng of a gret log and brussing of homes in his woorke iiii d
. . . Atkyn for xx^{ti} cordes vi s
. . . William smalffield iiii cordes xiiii d
last of novembris
Cops wood
. . . myghell bellet for xxxi cordes di ix s v d
. . . symond sprey for xlviii cordes xiiii s iiii d
. . . Roger Willes for xxx^{ti} cordes ix s
. . . William smalffeld for xl cordes xii s
. . . hoke and dyne for xxii cordes vi s viii d ob
. . . William coper for xii cordes iii s vii d[5]
. . . barnet for xx^{ti} cordes vi s
. . . margo for iiii^{xx} cordes in hordens at iiii d the corde xxvi s viii d
. . . philpot for l cordes in the same wood xvi s viii d

[*6v*] xxii° decebris
hasselden
. . . laurens erle for xxx^{ti} cordes of woodd ix s
more unto hym for xxx cordes of old motes x s
. . . stephen affild for xii cordes iii s viii d ob

[4] Originally entered xviii°.
[5] This is a later addition, for although in the same hand, it is inserted between lines and a different, fading, ink has been used.

more unto hym for xxi corddes di of old mottes vii s ii d
. . . William glaser for iii^xx^i corddes di xviii s v d

hordens wood
. . . philpot for xxxii corddes at iiii d the corde x s viii d
. . . John margo for l cordes at iiii d the cord xvi s viii d
. . . george morrall for lii corddes xvii s iiii d

Cops wood
. . . sprey for l corddes in cops woodd xv s
. . . myghell bellet for xl corddes xii s
. . . Roger Wylles for xxx^ti^ corddes ix s
. . . William den for xl corddes xii s
. . . William smalffeld for l corddes xv s
. . . hary mauryce for xl corddes xii s
. . . John atkyns for xx^ti^ corddes vi s
. . . Slaytter for vi corddes of old mottes ii s

[7^r^–8^v^] *blank*

[9^r^] Colyars
xxiii^th^ aprilis
. . . peter uncle for the collyng of v^xx^xi loodes of cole owt of panyng-rigg at xv d the loodde vi li vi s iii d
ultimo aprilis
. . . George morrall in full contentacion and payment for the collyng of vii^xx^xi loodes of coles owt of pannyngrig at xv d the loode viii li xvi s iii d
more unto hym for the collyng of xiiii loodes of colles owt of highe wood xvii s vi d
xxiii^th^ may
. . . lewes Bannson for the collyng of of xlii loodes of colles owt of highewood at xv d the loode lii s vi d
. . . peter for the collyng of xliiii loodes of coles out of neston wood at xv d the loode lv s
xii^th^ July
. . . peter uncle in full payment for the collyng of iii^xx^vii loodes of coles at xv d the loode (owt of neston wood)[6] iiii li iii s ix d
xiiii^th^ July
. . . Sampson in full payment for the collyng of xxviii loods of coles owt of neston at xv d the loode xxxv s

[6] Crossed out.

[9^{v}] . . . George morrall in full payment for the collyng of vii^{xx}xv lodes of coles owt of cops wood at xv d the lood ix li xiii s ix d
. . . Sampson for the collyng of xxxvii loodes of coles owt of neston wood at xv d the loode xlvi s iii d
primo Septembris
. . . Sampson for the collyng of xxiiii^{ti} loodes of coles owt of neston woode at xv d the loode xxx s
vii^{to} Septembris
. . . Stephen for the collyng of xx^{ti} looddes of colles owt of neston wood at xv d the loode xxv s
xiii^{o} septembris
. . . peter uncle for the collyng of v^{xx} loodes of colles owt of cops woode at xv d the loode vi li v s
. . . George morrall for the collyng of vii^{xx} loodes of colles owt of cops wood at xv d the loode viii li xv s
. . . Sampson for the colling of xxxvii looddes of colles out of neston wood at xv d the lood xxxviii s ix d[7]

[*10*^{r}] vi^{to} Octobris
. . . Sampson for the collyng of xxx^{ti}vii loodes of cooles owt of neston wood at xv d the loode xlvi s iii d[8]
xx^{mo} octobris
. . . peter unckyll for the collyng of lv looddes of colles owt of copswood at xv d the loode iii li viii s ix d
xvii novembris
. . . George morrall for the collyng of iiii^{xx}vii loodes of coles owt of hasselden at xv d the loode v li viii s ix d
xxix^{mo} novembris
noted viz
. . . the parson of penherst for ix loodes of coles bought of [ ] at his owne charge at the pyt at iiii s the loode xxxvi s[9]
xxii decebris
. . . George morrall for the collyng of xxxvi looddes of colle owt of hasselden at xv d the loode xlv s
. . . peter uncle for the collyng of xlvi loodes of the Cole owt of hasselden at xv d the loode lvii s vi d

[*10*^{v}–*11*^{v}] *blank*

[*12*^{r}] Carege of Colles
iiith Aprilis

[7] Crossed out in *ms*; the corrected entry is at the head of fo. 10^{r}.
[8] The incorrect xxxviii s ix d is again entered, but crossed out and replaced by xlvi s iii d.
[9] Originally entered xvi s.

. . . Thomas Smithe for the caryeng of iiii^{xx}i loodes of Coles owt of panyngrig at iiii d the Lood xxvii s
. . . James affild for the caryeng of iiii^{xx}iiii loodes owt of the same woode at iiii d the Loode xxviii s
ultimo Aprilis
. . . Thomas Smithe for the caryeng of xxxviiith loodes of coles owt of panynrigg at iiii d ob the Loode xiiii s iii d
. . . James affyld the same tyme for the caryeng of xxxviiith loodes of coles at iiii d ob the loode xiiii s iii d
paid more unto thomas smithe for the carege of xi loodes of coles owt of hassilden at viii d the loode vii s iiii d
paid also to James affild for the carege of xv loodes of coles owt of hassilden x s
xxiiith may
. . . James affyld for the caredge of xix loodes of colles owt of the same wood at vi d the loode ix s vi d
. . . Thomas Smithe for the carege of xi loodes of colles owt of highe woodde at vi d the lood v s vi d

[*12v*] xxii Junii
. . . John Slaytter for the careg of iii^{xx}viii looddes of cole owt of cops woodde at xiiii d the loode iii li xix s iiii d
xiiii July
. . . T hankyns in full payment for the carege of v^{xx}xi loodes of coles owt of neston wood at ix d the loode iiii li iii s iii d
xix July
. . . John Slayter in Full payment for the carege of v^{xx}i loode of coles owt of Cops wood at xiiii d the loode v li xvii s x d
xxi Augustii
. . . John Slayter for the carege of iii^{xx}xvii loodes of coles owt of cops woodd at xiiii d the loode iiii li ix s x d
. . hym more for the carege of xlviii loodde of colles owt of cops wood at xiiii d the Loode lvi s
xiii^{o} septembris
. . . John Slayter for the carege of v^{xx}ii looddes of coles owt of cops wood at xiiii d the loode v li xix s
. . . John Slaytter for the carege of lvi looddes of coles owt of cops wood at xiiii d the loode iii li v s iiii d

[*13r*] xxix^{mo} novembris
. . . Thomas Smithe for the caryeng of iiii^{xx}vi loodes owt of hassilden at vi d the lood xliii s
note paid to the slayter for carege of ix loodes of cole bought of the parson of peneherst at iiii d the loode iii s

xxii^{o} decembris
. . . Thomas Smythe for the caregg of iiii^{xx} and ii looddes of colle owt of hasselden at vi d the loodde xli s
. . . Thomas hankyns for the carege of vii^{xx}vi looddes of colles at ix d the loode owt of neston woodd v li ix s vi d

[*13*^{v}] *blank*

[*14*^{r}] dygging of myne
xiiith Junii
. . . philpot in Full payment for the dyggyng of xiiii^{xx} loodes of myne owt of Cresseys wood at viii d the loode ix li x s
xiiiith July
. . . John margo in Full payment for the dyggyng of iii^{C}iiii^{xx}xi looddes of myne owt of Cressis woode at viii d the Loode xiii li viii d

xx Augustii
. . . Cressye sones for the dyggyng of a C xii loodes of myne owt of his owne land at viii d the lood iii li xv s
v^{to} Septembris
. . . Cresses sones for the dyggyng of iiii^{xx} loodes of myne owt of his owne woodd at viii d the loode liii s iiii d
xiii^{o} septembris
. . . John margo for the dyggyng of CCv loodes of myne owt of hassilden at x d the loode viii li x s x d
note that thes iii payments folowing is diggyd and destarged and not caryed to the phurnes
. . . John margo for the diggyng of viii^{xx} and x loodes of myne in hassilden at x d the loode vii li xx d
. . . philpot for the diggying of CClix loodes of myne at x d the lood in hassilden x li xv s x d
paid more unto hym for the diggyng of xxx loodes of myne in Cressis wood at viii d the lood xx s

[*14*^{v}–*16*^{v}] *blank*

[*17*^{r}] Carege of myne
xxiiith may
. . . thomas Smythe for in full payment for the carege of xi^{xx}viii loodes of myne owt of cresseis woode at iii d the loode lvii s
xiiiith July
. . . T Smythe For the carege of iii^{C}xii looddes of myne owt of cresseis woode at iii d the lode iii li xviii s

xiii° Septembris
. . . T Smithe for the carege of viii^{xx}iiii loodes of myne owt of hassilden at v d the loode iii li viii s iiii d
more paid to hym for the careg of vii^{xx}xix loodes of myne at owt of cressis wood at iii d the loode xxxix s ix d

[*17^{v}*] Myne bought
. . . John Cressey of moundeffeld for vii^{xx} and x loodes of myne dygged within his pastoure grounde beying gret loodes at i d ob the lood xviii s ix d
paid more unto hym for v^{C}xxxvii loodes beying gret loodes dyggyd within his wood land at i d q^{w} and ii s in every C iii li v s iiii d ob

[*18^{r}–18^{v}*] *blank*

[*19^{r}*] fownder and filler
xxiiiith January
. . . peter the fownder for iiii foundeis and v dais endyd the xxiiith of January xxxii s
. . . to the filler for like fowndeis xxiiii s
iiiith of february
. . . peter fownder for ii fowndeis endyd the same day xvi s
. . . to the filler for like fowndeis xii s
ultimo february
. . . the founder for iiii foundeis endyd the same day xxxii s
. . . the filler for the same xxiiii s
xxiiiith marcii
. . . the fownder for iiii foundeis endyd the xxiiii of march xxxii s
. . . to the filler for like foundeis xxiiii s
iiith Aprilis
. . . the founder for ii foundeis endyd the vth day of Aprell xvi s
. . . to the filler for like foundeis xii s

[*19^{v}*] ultimo Aprilis
. . . peter founder for v foundeis endyd the vth day of aprell[10] xl s
. . . the filler for like foundeis xxx s
xx^{ti} Augustii
. . . peter founder for iiii foundeis endyd the xxvth Augustii xxxii s
. . . the filler for like foundeis xxiiii s
xii Septembris
. . . peter founder for iii foundeis endyd the xii of September xxiiii s
. . . the filler for like foundeis xviii s

10 This should perhaps read xxxth.

vi^to^ octobris
. . . peter the founder for iiii foundeis endyd the same day xxxii s
. . . the filler for like foundeis xxiiii s
xxi^o^ octobris
. . . peter the founder for ii foundeis [di] endyd the same day xx s
. . . the filler like foundeis xv s
. . . peter the founder for iii foundeis di endyd the xii of novembre xxviii s
. . . the filler for like foundes xxi s

[*20^r^*] xxix^mo^ Novembris
. . . peter the founder for iii foundeis endyd the same day xxiiii s
. . . the filler for like foundeis xviii s
xxii^o^ decembris
. . . peter the founder for v foundeis endyd the xxix of decebre xl s
. . . the filler for like foundeis xxx s

[*20^v^–22^v^*] *blank*

[*23^r^*] Careg thorow mens land for coles and Sowes
iii^th^ Aprilis
. . . William mereman for the carege thorowe his land for one hole yere with our coles owt of cops lande x s
. . . Richard Standen the lybertye thorowe his lande for carege of coles iii s iiii d
. . . Roger hale for the lybertie thorowe his lande for carege of coles iii s iiii d
. . . William Saunders for the lyberty of his grounde vi s viii d
. . . John longley for the lyberty thorow his lande for our carge of coles vii s vi d
. . . William coper for the libertie thorowe his land ii s viii d
. . . hankyns for the libertie thorow his lande for our carege of Sowes ix s iiii d
. . . James Reve for carege thorow his lande v s
. . . John [Awwk] for the libertie thorow his land xiii s iiii d

[*23^v^*] *blank*

[*24^r^*] for farmes tythes and wages owr Lady day
iii^th^ Aprilis
. . . master channceler for his half yeris farme of pannyngrigg ended at our Lady day x li
. . . the parson of penherste for his di yeris farme of the phurnis pounde due ut supra x s
. . . the vicar of Assheburneham for the tythe of the phurnis due . . . ii s vi d

. . . peter unckell for his quarters wages due . . . vi s viii d
. . . George morrall for his quarters wages due vi s viii d
. . . Richard martyn for his quarters wages due . . . xvi s viii d
more unto hym for his borde wages viz for xiii[th] wekes xxx s iiii d
mydsomer quarter
. . . peter uncle for his quarters wages due at mydsomer vi s viii d
. . . George morrall for his qwarters wages due at the same tyme vi s viii d
. . . Richard martyn for his quarters wages due at the same tyme xvi s viii d
more unto hym for his bord wages due then viz for xiii weekes xxx s iiii d
[*25v*] myghtlmas quarter
. . . mr chanceler for his half yeris farme of panyngrig x li
. . . peter uncle for his quarters wages vi s viii d
. . . georg morrall for his quarter wages vi s viii d
. . . peter for his lyvery viii s
. . . georg for his lyvery viii s
. . . more to peter for colyng of [certen] wood lyeng abrod in high wood by my masters commandment x s
. . . george for worke like don within the same wood by my masters commandment x s
. . . the parson of penherst for the farme of the pownd of pannyngrig x s
. . . the vicar of assheburnham for the thyth of the phurnis ii s vi d
. . . Richard martyn for his quarters wages xvi s viii d
. . . hym for his bord wages for xiiii wekes at ii s iiii d xxxii s viii d
Cristmas quarter
. . . George morrall for his quarters wages vi s viii d
. . . peter uncle for his quarter wages vi s viii d
. . . Richard martyn for his quarters wages xvi s viii d
. . . hym for his bord wages for xiii wekes at ii s iiii d the weke xxx s iiii d
[*26r*] necessary charges and Empcions for the Phurnis
paid for one yeren sthole viii d
paid for ii galons and a pottill of greyse for the phurnis at xvi d the gallon iii s iiii d
Sand ut februarii
. . . page and John alyn for dyggyng of Sande ii days a pece ether of them at vii d the day ii s iiii d
. . . thomas Smith for the carage of the same sande xii d
more to hym for caryeng of a pole for the phurnis bellos vi d
. . . more to hym for caryeng of a colyar dust at our ned ii s

. . . William Saunders for his paynes in showyng my master mens landes for our carege of coles viii d

sand

paid more to page for iiii dais diggyng of sand at vii d the day xxi d[11]

. . . thomas Smith for the carege of the same sand iiii d

laithe

. . . Roger hale for the makyng iii loodes of laithe x s

. . . hym more for the byndyng of xvi loodes of laithe at viii d the lood x s viii d

ultimo Aprilis

paid for a new iron sthole for the phurnis ix d

. . . John margo for ii cole baskettes xvi d

. . . Atkyns wiff for a pottill of gresse for the phurnis viii d

paid for martin dyne and nicholas wynall at hastyng when I whent to hym for to speke for another yeris utterance of his wood xii d

paid for martyn dyne at warbleton to spek with one petyd for the sale of his wood iiii d

. . . T Smith for carieg of synder to mend the waies for carege of myne vii d

[*26v*] Slaytter

. . . Slaytter for iii pere of new whelles for his carege xvii s

more unto hym for iii newe cole waynes xxx s

xiiii June

more unto hym for makyng of yren worke for his waynes (viz for iii^{xx}xli[12]) vii s vii d

. . . hym for settyng of new whelles xii d[12]

. . . page and John alyn for helpe to mend the ways by the space of vi dais apece ether of them at viii d the daye viii s

paid more to slayter for the fetchyng of iii pere of whelles from cobbeche xii d

paid for a newe payle for the phurnis bought on mydsomer day iii d

. . . synderforth for mendyng of the waynes the same tyme iiii d

. . . Atkynses wife for a pottell of gresse viii d

. . . Slaytter for fetchyng of iii pere of newe whelles from cobech xii d

paid more to hym for makyng of a hedge in mr burwelles land for our careg of colles iiii s

more unto hym for makyng of vi gattes goyng thorowe mens lande for our colles iiii s

[11] ii s iiii d was entered originally, and crossed out.

[12] Crossed out in the manuscript.

xiii^th^ Junii

. . . peter founder and John nevyll for mendyng of a brig and the ways for careg of our sowes from panyngridge xvi d

. . . thomas smythe for the carege of sande

[*27^r^*] Stone xxi June

. . . page and John Alyn for dyggyn of stone for the phurnis harthe ether of them by the space of iiii dais apece v s iiii d

more to them for dygging of sande and loodyng of the same stone for the phurnis harth iiii s viii d

xxix Novembris

. . . J Alyn and page and the parson(s) man of brightlyng for ii dais work ether of them in dyggyng of stone for the fornis at viii d p diem iiii s

paid more unto them for dyggyng of sand iiii days ether of them at viii d the day v s iiii d

. . . peter the founder for the dyggyng of iiii loodes of sand x d

xi July

. . . hankyns for iii newe gates for the carege of sowes owt of his lande and new postes for the same gates and Settyng up of them vii s

paid more unto hym for iii pere of hokes and iii pere of thymbles for the said gates waying xx li att ii d ob the li iiii s ii d

. . . ii workmen for settyng on a new gogyn for the phurnis whele iiii d

. . . Charles for makyng of the phurnis harth v s

more unto hym for the new dressyng of the phurnis bellows lethers and corying of the same lethers and sowyng vi s viii d

paid more to hym for ii plates one for the twerne and the other for the shamyons xxi d

xxiiii martii

for the phurnis walles in westalls tyme

paid more unto hym for the new makyn of the phurnis walles xx s

. . . margo for ii cole baskettes xvi d

[*27^v^*] . . . burges for iiii gret ox hiddes for the phurnis bellowes xl s

paid for the dressyng and corying of the same ii s

. . . georg morrall for ii galles of gresse iii s

paid for [as] for sprey xiii d

. . . german for a pick for the phurnis viii d

paid for the settyng on of the goodgyn of the phornis whele iiii d

iii Aprilis

. . . T Smith for the careg of v loodes of sand x d

paid more to hym for careg of a cole dust ii s

. . . peter for dyggyng of ii loodes of sand iiii d
. . . T Smith for the careg of x loodes of sande xx d
. . . page and his felowe for the dyggyn of sande iiii dais apece at viii d the day v s iiii d
. . . thomas smyth for caryng the same sand xvi d
. . . T Smyth for the careg of viii loodes of sand xvi d
. . . Slaytter for makyng of iiii hokes to hang the gate in mr burrell land iiii d
paid more to hym for nailles i d
. . . hym for a stole ii d

[*28*ʳ] . . . Stewen the filler berying of coles this laste Sommer when the phurnis staid still by the space of a qwarter of yere viii s
. . . John margo for makyng A newe [bog][13] for the phurnis iiii d
. . . the Carpenter for settyng on of a newe brass[14] and a gogyn on the Round beam x d
paid for ii newe Rak heddes and a whele barowe viii d
. . . mr Burrell for vi yeres past for sand of hym had for the phurnis est iii s iiii d for every yere xx s
. . . charles for the new makyng of the phurnis harth the ii day of August the begyning to blow v s
paid more unto hym for the new dressyng of the bellows in the same tym with new lethers x s
paid more unto hym for makyng of the kames[15] vi d
more unto hym for makyng of ii new storoppes[16] viii d
paid more to hym for his labor ix dais workyng in the amending of the phurnis wheele xii s
. . . charles man for helpe to serve hym in work iiii s

[*29ᵛ–32ᵛ*] *blank*

[13] 'Bridge' is a possible meaning.
[14] This could refer to a bearing for the main shaft driving the bellows.
[15] cams (set in the wheel shaft to operate the bellows).
[16] stirrups in the bellows mechanism.

[8] SUMMARY ACCOUNT FOR PANNINGRIDGE FURNACE AND ROBERTSBRIDGE FORGE, 1551

378/1 *U 1475 B3/1*

[*1r*] Robertsbridge The accompte of the Iorne mynes there the vth yere of the reigne of Our sovereigne Lorde Kyng Edwarde the vi[th] Anno v[to] Regis E vi[ti]

[*1v*] *blank*

[*2r*] A declaracon of accompte of William Blackenall Clarke of the Iorne workes to the right worshipfull Sir William Sydney Knyght at his mannor of Robertsbridge in the Countye of Sussex aswell of all and singuler suche sommes of money by hym receyvyd as also alsuche sommes of money by the seyd William Imploed to the use of the seyd Sir William from the feast of the Nativity of our lorde god in the yere of the reigne of our sovereigne lorde Edwarde the vi[ti] by the grace of god of Inglonde frannce and Irelande Kyng defendor of the faythe and in erth of the Churche of Inglond and also of Irelonde supreme hede the iiii[th] untyll the same feast of the Nativity of our lorde god then nexte ensuyng the vth that ys for one hole yere

In primis he chargeth hym selff with tharrarages of his last accompte as it appereth in the fote of the same xiiii li vi s ii d q

Item he chargeth hym selff with money receyvyd of Sir henry Sidney Knyght within the tyme of this accompte as it appereth by a boke of Recepte uppon this accompte showed and examined Cxx li

. . . of John Baggot as it appereth by the seyd boke CCCxvii li

. . . of John hawes as . . . CCCix li xviii s ix d

. . . for Catall solde hoc anno ut per librum predictum ix li vi s viii d

Item received for wood and olde tymber on hewen olde motes and asshes solde hoc anno ut . . .[1] ix li xvi s iii d

. . . for hydes and felles solde there hoc anno ut . . . ii s viii d

[*2v*] . . . for xii ton xv[C] qrt and viii lli of Iorne solde hoc anno ut . . .[2] Cxvii li xiiii s v d

[1] There is a preponderance of old or fallen timber amongst these sales.

[2] 380/1 records the buyers of this iron, largely local smiths, although Draper the ironmonger took delivery of small lots during the summer.

. . . for xxxiii qrt v bz and di of whete solde at divers prices hoc anno xxxvii li xii s iiii d

. . . for vii qrt and v bz of Barley solde hoc anno at divers prices vi li xx d

. . . for xiii qrts of ottes solde hoc anno lxi s i d ob

. . . for ii bz of beanes solde hoc anno ii s i d

. . . for iiii qrt ii bz di of malte solde there hoc anno ut . . . xliii s viii d

. . . for xii Kilderkins of bere solde to the workemen hoc anno ad divers prices xxiii s

. . . for CC di of qrt borde sold hoc anno vi s viii d

. . . for x lodes of lathe solde hoc anno with v lodes at pannyngridge lxxiiii s ix d

. . . for CC qrt of olde Iorne solde hoc anno . . . xix s

. . . for appulles sold hoc anno vii li x s

Sum Totall of all the receptes aforeseyd DCCCClx ll xix s ii d ob q[3]

wherof

[*3r*] layde out at Robertsbridge

In primis for the Cuttynge of iiii^{M}vii^{C}iiii^{xx}ii cordes and di of woodde hoc anno at divers prices as it dothe appere by the seyd boke[4] lxvii li xiiii s x d ob

Item for the mowyng and makynge of hay hoc anno ut per librum predictum xlviii s

Item payd in Rydynge expenses in foren charges and showyng of horses hoc anno[5] xxvii li ix s ob

. . . to kerpentters for the mendyng of Serten howses and for hewynge of tymber[6] lxxvii s viii d ob

. . . to Tylers Thechers and other labores in necessary busynes hoc anno[7] viii li vi s v d

. . . to the Smyth for nayles . . . lx s iii d

3 An incomplete set of receipts appears in the Forge Book, 380/1: the tota there is £768 14s 11¼d.

4 The detailed record in 380/1 is less well laid out than in earlier books; the rates paid per load also vary more, with many lump payments for batches, working out between 3d and 3½d per cord. Many of the entries are undated, but of those that are, none were made between June 29th and September 28th.

5 380/1 contains a list of expenses incurred by Blacknall riding to Harting (Norfolk) and to London.

6 Much of this involved fencing off woodlands; in addition, a new hammer block was cut and shaped in Park Wood, it took 5 days work to cut and square, and 5 to install, agreeing well with the large size of block excavated at Chingley (see introduction, n. 17).

7 The tilers and thatchers did not do work connected with the forge: tilers were paid 5d per day with food in addition, thatchers 6d with food.

. . . for Servantes wages . . . xviii li xii s iii d
. . . to a laborer which dede helpe huggens to brewe . . . viii s xi d
. . . for the lande cariage of sowes from pannyngridge to Robertsbridge . . .[8] xxiiii li xviii s iiii d
. . . to the hamer men and fyners for the makyng of Cli ton iii qrt of a C of Iorne . . .[9] Cii li xxii d
. . . payd for hepyng of Coles and sowes xxxii s i d ob
. . . for Colyng of ix^{C}viii lodes of Coles ad divers prices . . .[10] lvii li viii s iiii d
. . . for the cariyng of ix^{C}xxxv lodes of Coles ad divers prices . . .[11] xxvi li xii s iiii d
. . . for the cariyng of Iorne aswell by land as by water . . . xix s
. . . for Catall bought . . . xv li xvii s iiii d

. . . for the dressyng of the belowes there . . .[12] xv s v d

[*3*^{v}] . . . for vi oxe hides bought for the forge belowes . . . xxxix s
. . . for the lande cariage of rent Corne . . . viii s viii d
. . . in expenses of howsholde hoc anno, over and above l li iii s xi d spent of the store, viz xxi li ii s vii d in price CCxxx and di Kylderkyns of bere at xxii d le Kylderkyn, xxi li xiii s in price xviii quarters iii bushels of whete at xxiiii s le quarter, vi li xiii s iiii d de price vi bolockes and xv s in price fyve calves as it appereth by the seyd boke xli li viii s v d
Sum of all the payments foreseyd at Robertsbridge CCCCv li xviii s vii d

[*4*^{r}] and at pannyngridge
. . . for the Cuttyng of iii^{M}iiii^{C}xv Cordes of wood at divers prices ut per librum predictum liii li ix s ii d
. . . for my expenses and other when we wente to pannyngridge at divers tymes hoc anno[13] xi s v d

[8] This includes the carriage of sows bought in. 380/1 contains an important confirmation of sows' weights; the 100 tons bought in comprised 193 sows, close to the 10 cwt used as a basis for reckoning in the 1560s.

[9] There is a change of hammerman this year: 380/1 records Gwyllam up to March 28th, and John Collins thereafter.

[10] 380/1 records two colliers working in four woods, Welhead, Bishops Wood, Morgays Wood and Badland Wood. Both work through the year, including July and August.

[11] Cressy is the only carrier (probably Cressy of Mountfield, owner of land where ore was mined for Panningridge in this period). The rates vary between Welhead, the nearest, at 3d/load and Andrews land, 10d.

[12] 380/1 makes it clear that there were two pairs of finery bellows.

[13] Includes payment to Hogens in Panningridge, Cowpers and Glede Wood to see 'how long it would serve my masters furnace'.

. . . to the founder and filler for xliii foundes and one day at divers prices with the mendyng and makyng of the hathes[14] hoc anno ut per librum predictum xxxiii li vi s iiii d

. . . for the Colynge of MClxxiiii lodes of Cole at xv d the lode hoc anno lxxiii li xix s ii d

. . . for the Caryng of MClxxiiii lodes of Cole ad divers prices hoc anno[15] xlvi li xiii s vii d

. . . for the Castyng of Miiii^{C}lxii lodes of myne at divers prices hoc anno lix li xvii s v d ob

. . . for the Caryng of MCiiii^{xx} lode of myne at divers prices ut per librum predictum xxiiii li viii s i d

. . . for the rente of the woode Tythe of the furnesse martens wages and libertie thorowe mennes grownde xxxvi li x s x d

. . . to laborers for the reparyng of the furnesse caryng of sande and stone and neccessaries bought for the same hoc anno[16] iiii li xix d

. . . for the makyng of x lodes of lathes and to ii Kerpentters for worke x li s

. . . to frannces prior for wood of hym bought hoc anno ut per librum predictum[17] xxx li

. . . to William Spyser of dallyngton for dette to hym oughte for woodde hoc anno xxv li

[*4v*] . . . to mr draper henry westall and Charles (blank) in full contentacon and paymet of| CClxi li xiii s iiii d in the price of one hunderde ton of sowes of them bought at lii s iiii d the ton ult. Cxl li payd by my master Sir henry Sydney

14 The furnace book hints that some attempt was being made to improve performance. In addition to Peter the Founder's pay of 6s per founday (6 days), up to the end of April Charles was paid 2s per founday; he relined the hearth and supervised repairs. He also took charge (at 8s per founday) during May. It seems from this account that early in the year he was being paid a retainer to be available. Despite this, no campaigns were lengthy (21 Feb.–10 April; 23 April–25 July; 26 Sept.–30 Nov.; 7 Dec.–?) and pig had to be bought in for the forge. Peter the founder was being paid the new high rate of 8s a founday after October. It is not clear if he or Charles was working in the summer. Peter gathered 2 tons of iron from among the cinders in June, suggesting that the break-out of molten iron was not uncommon.

15 The cost reaches a new maximum, of 1s 2d per load from Cowper's land; however charcoal was still coming from Panningridge Wood at 4d per load.

16 There were no major repairs; 382/3 (B10/5) makes clear that such stone as was required came from a nearby quarry, at Penhurst. 380/1(B8/4) refers to a tymp being sent to the furnace; this was of iron, not stone as may have been the practice at some early sites.

17 Francis Prior is described in 382/3 as a yeoman of Dagenham, Essex. A parcel of wood was bought, of unspecified acreage, 'near' Panningridge.

Knyght hoc anno ut per librum predictum[18] Cxxi li xiii s iiii d
Sum of all the paymentes at pannyngridge Dxi li xi s xi d ob
Sum totall of all thallowances and payments foresed
DCCCCxvii li x s vi d ob

and so owethe xliiii li viii s viii d q wherof to be allowed of xx li iiii s vii d for the losse which is in the some of iiii^{xx} li xviii s v d in money remayning in thandes of the seyd accomptante at the tyme of the firste fall of money after the rate of v s in the pounde And to be allowed to hym of xv li iii s ii d ob for the losse whiche is in the some of xlv li ix s v d in money remayning in the handes of the seyd accomptannte at the tyme of the Seconde fayll of money after the

[*5*^{r}] rate of vi s viii d in every pounde as it ys testified upon this accompte and so owethe clerly[19] viii li x d ob q

[*5*^{v}] *blank*

[*6*^{r}] Cordes of woodde at Robertsbridge In primis the remayne anno per pceden v^{C}xxix cordes

Item made there hoc anno iiii^{M}vii^{C}iiii^{xx}ii cordes di
Sum of all the cordes v^{M}iiii^{C}xi cordes di

[18] This unexpected item indicates a temporary inadequacy of the supply of pig from Panningridge. 380/1 (the Forge Book) shows that the 100 tons were brought from Westall's and Charles' furnace. The carriage rate, 20d. per ton, is no more than that from Panningridge to Robertsbridge; thus the source must be sought within a 6–8 mile radius of the latter. Charles, thought of as the founder at Buxted (some 15 miles distant) may thus have worked another furnace. Henry Westall, the former clerk at Robertsbridge, although still an estate official, must by 1551 have entered into a partnership with Charles. The references to Mr Draper, ironmonger, suggest a source of capital for this otherwise unknown combination.

[19] 380/1 (The Forge Book) includes the following entries, (i) on a loose sheet, (ii) in the sewn book;

(i) Md that ther dyd Remayne in my hands the xith day of July in Anno v^{to} E vi^{ti} of my masters money after the ratt of xii d to the shyllyng and iiii d the grott whych hath ben seen and tolde be ffore Wylliam Walter Clerk and John hawes ymmedyatly apon the first heryng of the proclamacyon for the alteryng of the sayd mony iiii^{xx} li xviii s v d
per me William blackinhall William walter clark John hawes

(ii) Md that ther dyd Remayne in my hands the xviith day of August in A*nno* v^{to} E vi^{ti} of my masters money after the ratt of ix d to the shyllyng and iii d to the grott whych hath been seen and told beffore
William walter John hawes
noted that xl li thereof was Received at my Masters handes the xvth of August

For the background to the calling down of the currency see R. de Roover, *Gresham on Foreign Exchange* (Cambridge, Mass., 1949) pp. 56–59; A. Feaveryear, *The Pound Sterling* (2nd edn., Oxford, 1963), pp. 64–71.

wherof spente hoc anno iii^M^Cxlviii cordes and remain in the woodde hoc anno MMCCxliii cordes and di

Coles there Item the remain . . . in lodes iii^C^
Item made there hoc anno ix^C^xviii lodes
Sum of all the lodes xii^C^viii lodes
wherof spente hoc anno ix^C^viii lodes so remain iii^C^ lodes

Myne there Item the remain . . . C lodes
caryed hoc anno nil
Sum of all the lodes C which remain

Sowes there Item is ther in sowes per estimacion ix^C^

Sowes at Pannyngridge Item in sowes there by tale CCxl
Sum of all the sowes MCxl

[*6^v^*] The accompte of Iorne Item the remayne . . .
xxiii ton iiii^xx^vii lli
Item made there hoc anno Cli ton iiii^xx^iiii lli of Iorne
Sum of all the Iorne Clxxiiii ton one hunderde lix lli, wherof solde hoc anno by the seyd William Blackenall as it appereth by his boke of receptes xii ton xv^C^ qrt and viii lli. And delyverd to mr draper to performe his bargayne of laste yere viz iiii^to^ die Junii v ton xii^C^xxxix lli also delyverd to hym the same day for mr lovell i ton also delyverd to hym eodem die for mr [wend] v^C^ Also delyverd to hym eodem die for mr Lombarde CC, and also delyverd to hym eodem die i ton ii^C^ iii qrt and xi lli also delyverd to George Covyll which is unpayde the xv^th^ day of october i ton, and also delyverd to the furnesse and for makyng of Iorne worke for the Cole waynes hoc anno as the particelles dothe appere in the seyd boke C iii qrts and xxv lli and so remayneth there in the store howse on Cristemas Eve Clii ton CC and iiii lli of Iorne
Note That the Iorne is not wayed at this tyme whiche gayne in the wayte is to be remembered the nexte yere
Note Also that George Covyle owethe for one ton of Iorne upon this accompte which is delyvered and accompted for.

[*7^r^*] tonnes of tymber Item the remain anno per pceden
l tonnes
Item hewed hoc anno nil
Sum of all the tonnes of tymber l which remain
Ynche bordes Item the remain . . . xxxi^M^lxxvii fete
Item Sawen hoc anno nil
Sum of all the bordes xxxi^M^lxxvii fete wherof solde hoc anno as it appereth in the seyd boke in the title of receptes CC di and spent at

Robertsbridge aboute the garners loftes and kychen per estimacion iii^{M} and so remain xxvii^{M}viii^{C}xxvii fete of bordes

latthes Item the remain . . . iii lodes
Item made hoc anno x lodes
Sum of all the latthes xiii lodes wherof solde hoc anno ut per librum predictum x lodes
and spent aboute the barnes and other howses hoc anno per estimacion ii lodes and remayneth i lode

[*7^{v}*] Catall there Item the remain . . . in oxen ix
Item the remain eodem anno in kyen v
Item in oxen bought hoc anno ii
item in kyen bought hoc anno viii
Item in steres bought hoc anno ii
Item there ys for heryotte hoc anno in Oxen iiii
Sum of all the oxen and Kyen xxx, wherof solde hoc anno iii and spente in the howse hoc anno vi kyen, and dyed hoc anno i cowe and remain xx
unde in oxen xii
in kyen viii

[*8^{r}*] pannyngridge
Cordes of wood ther Item the remain anno per pceden iii^{M}v^{C}xxxii cordes
Item made ther hoc anno iii^{M}iiii^{C}xv cordes
Sum of all the cordes vi^{M}ix^{C}xlvii cordes
wherof spent hoc anno iii^{M}ix^{C}xxxii cordes and remain iii^{M}xv cordes

Coles Item the remain of lodes of coles anno pceden iii^{C}xxx lodes
Item made there hoc anno MClxxiiii lodes
Sum of all the lodes Mv^{C}iiii wherof spente hoc anno MClxiiii lodes of Coles and remain CCCxl lodes
lodes of myne Item the remain anno per pceden MCCC lodes
Item caried hoc anno MCiiii^{xx}i lodes
Sum of all the lodes of myne MMiiii^{C}iiii^{xx}i lode
wherof spente hoc anno MCCiiii^{xx}i lode
Et remain MCC lodes

[*8^{v}*] *blank*

[*9^{r}*] The remayne of the Stoke at Robertsbridge and pannyngridge aforeseyd the xxi^{ti} of december anno v^{to} regis E vi^{ti}

Pannyngridge

In primis iii^{M}xv cordes of wood there at vi d the corde lxxv li vii s vi d

Item in lodes of Cole iii^{C}xl at iiii s the lode lxviii li

Item in lodes of myne here MCCC at xii d the lode lx li

Robertsbridge

Item in cordes of woode MMCCxliii and di at vi d the corde lvi li xxi d

Item in lodes of coles CCC at iiii s the lode lx li

Item in lodes of myne C at x d the lode iiii li iii s iiii d

Item in sowes there ix^{C} }
Item in sowes at pannyngridge CCxl } MCxl at xxvi s viii d MDxx li

Item in the Storehowse of Iorne Clii ton CC and iiii li at viii li x s le ton MCCiiii^{xx}xii li viii s

Item in tonnes of tymber per estimation l at ii s viii d vi li xiii s iiii d

Item in ynche bordes xxvii^{M}viii^{C} and xxvii^{ti} fete at xx s the M xxvii li xvi s

Item in lathes one lode price viii s

Item in Catall there eodem die viz xii oxen and viii kyen price xxxiii li vi s viii d

Sum totall of all the remayne aforeseyd MMMCCiiii li iiii s vii d

[*9*^{v}] A declaracion of the clere gayne of the Iorne workes aforeseyd dco anno v^{to} Regni Regis predicti

In primis in the price of Cli ton iiii^{xx}iiii lli of Iorne made there hoc anno at viii li x s les ton MCCiiii^{xx}iii li xv s

Sum of all the Incresse or gayne dicto anno v^{to} MCCiiii^{xx}iii li xv s

wherof to be abated of DCCCCxvii li x s vi d ob for money payd in divers kyndes of the seyd workes hoc anno as the particulers dothe appere in a boke therof made and examined and so remain clere this yere gayned CCClxvi li iiii s v d ob

[9] SUMMARY ACCOUNT FOR PANNINGRIDGE FURNACE AND ROBERTSBRIDGE FORGE, 1553

378/4 *U 1475 B3/4*

[*1r*] Robertsbridge
The accompte of the Iorne mynes ther the fyrst yere of the reigne of our Sovereigne lady Quyne mary the firste
anno regni Rege marie prime primo

[*1v*] *blank*

[*2r*] A declaracon of accompte of William Blackenall Clarke of the Iorne Workes to the right Worshipfull Sir Henry Sydney Knyght at his mannor of Robertsbridge in the Countye of Sussex aswell of all and singuler suche sommes of money by hym receyvyd as also suche sommes of money by the seyd William Imploed to the use of the seyd Sir Henry from the feaste of the Nativity of our lorde god in the yere of the reigne of our late sovereigne lorde Edwarde the vi^ti^ untyll the same feaste of the Nativity of our lorde god nexte ensuying in the fryste yere of the reigne of our sovereigne lady mary the fryste by the grace of god of Inglonde frannce and Irelonde quene defendor of the fayth and in Erthe of the Churche of Ingelonde and also of Irelonde supreme hede that ys for one hole yere.

fryste he chargeth hymselff with tharragiis of his last accompte as it appereth in the foote of the same — xl li iiii s ix d q

Item he chargeth hym selffe with money remaynyng in his handes which he askede allowannce of in hys accompte in Anno v^to^ nuper Regis E vi^ti^ as for money payd to william spyser and not payd wherin ys loste xii li x s by the fayll of monny in the seyd yere — xii li x s

Item he chargeth hym selff for money received of George Coke for Corne solde oute of the parsonage barne of Salehurste hoc anno as it appereth by a boke of Recepte upon this accompte showed and examined — xlv li xiii s iiii d

ad xii li of the Issues of this yere

[*2v*] Item received of the vyker of monvyle for Corne by hym solde with lx s for vi qtrs of Rente Barley as it appereth by the seyd boke — vi li

. . . of John hawes of the Issue of his officio hoc anno ut per dictum librum CCliii li xiiii s viii d
. . . for one ton di iiii^C and xv lli of Iorne solde hoc anno . . . xiii li xv s vi d
. . . for xi^C of olde Iorne solde . . . lxxiii s iiii d
. . . for xxxii oxen solde hoc anno at l s le oxe with one oxe geven in . . . lxxvii li x s
. . . for x qtrs vii bz and iii peckes of whete solde hoc anno at divers prises . . . viii li xvii s iiii d
. . . for one quarter of barley solde . . . viii s
. . . for iiii qtrs and one bz of oten malte solde hoc anno . . . xxxiii s
. . . for x bz of otes solde hoc anno vi s
. . . for ii bz of Bay salte ii s
. . . for ii bz of Barlye malte ii s viii d
. . . for hydes hoc anno . . . xvi s iiii d
. . . for wood solde ther this yere . . . xxxii s ix d

[3^r] Sum totall of all the Receptes which appear aforeseyd CCCClxvi li xix s vii d q

wherof

[3^v] layde oute at Robertsbridge
In primis for the Cuttynge of iii^M lxviii cordes and di of wood at divers prises as it appereth by a boke therof upon the declaracon showed and examyned[1] l li xvii s ix d
Item payd to the hamer men and fyners for the makyng and fynyng of Cxxv ton one hunderd di of Iorne at xiii s iiii d le ton[2] ut per dictum librum iiii^xx iii li vii s viii d
. . . for Colyng of Mxlii lodes of Coles at xv d le lode[3] . . . lxv li ii s vi d
. . . for the caryng of Mxliii lodes of Coles at divers prices[4] . . . xxi li vii s x d
. . . for the dressyng of belowes there hoc anno . . . xiiii s vi d
. . . for servantes wages and borde wages ther hoc anno . . . xxvi li xix s ii d

[1] The expansion in wood sources continues; the Forge Book (380/2:B8/5) shows work at 11 woods, compared with 8 in 1551. 46 men were employed, irregularity of employment being particularly marked.
[2] John Collins was hammerman for the entire year.
[3] Three colliers worked throughout the year.
[4] Ranging from 3d (Welhed Wood) to 10d (Hollowall Wood).

. . . for the cariage of xvi lodes of sowes from pannyngridge to Robertsbridge[5] . . . xxvi s viii d

. . . for the hepyng of Coles there hoc anno . . . xlvii s vii d

. . . payd for neccessaries bought for the forge with vi li for herynges sente to pensehurste . . . vii li viii s vii d

. . . to laborers in neccessarie busynes hoc anno . . . vii li xvi s v d ob

. . . to Kerpentters in mendyng of divers decaies aboute the forge as other places . . . xiiii s xi d

[*4*^r] . . . in foren charges hoc anno[6] . . . vi li xvii d ob

. . . for the londe carage of Iorne from the storehowse to the water syde hoc anno . . . vi li iii s v d

. . . for the water cariage of Iorne hoc anno ix li iiii s iiii d

. . . for the cariage of certen stuff from Robertsbridge to pensehurst hoc anno . . . xx s

. . . for nayles bought as well for pensehurst as for Robertsbridge . . . lii s

. . . for waterworke ther hoc anno . . . lxxviii s vii d

. . . for the cariage of hay there hoc anno . . . xviii s viii d

. . . for the cariagine as well of Rente Corne as also of synder and other neccessaries . . . lxi s iii d

Sum of all the paymentes foreseyd at Robertsbridge CCCi li iii s iiii d

[*4*^v] and at pannyngridge

Item payd for the Cuttyng of MDliii cordes and di of woode at divers prises[7] hoc anno ut per dictum librum xxiii li xix s vi d

. . . for the Colynge of DCCxix lodes of Cole at xvi d the lode[8] . . . xlvii li xviii s vi d [ ]

. . . for the caryng of DCCxiiii lodes of Coles at divers prises[9] . . . xvii li ii s iii d

. . . for the Caryng of Clv lodes of myne . . . xxxviii s ix d

[5] The standard price was 1s 8d per ton (load).

[6] This includes the cost of delivering 80 tons of iron to Xpofer Draper. It is not stated where, but as inclusion of transport charges in the heading is unusual, it must be presumed that delivery was made to a point other than Rye.

[7] The first sheets of 382/4(B10/6), are damaged; nevertheless it appears that 16 cutters worked in three woods (perhaps four, for Panningridge may be included in the damaged section). No payments are recorded between July 14th and September 19th. There is rather less contrast between regular and occasional workers than in the late 1540s: out of 11 pay days only 2 men appear in as many as 6 and one in 5.

[8] By two colliers working throughout the year.

[9] Costs range between 4d and 7d per load.

. . . to divers persons for liberties thorowe there grounde[10] . . . viii s iiii d

. . . to the founder and filler for xxviii foundes and ii dayes with xiii s ii d for the makyng the fyrnysshe hathe and mendyng the Belowes hoc anno . . .[11] xx li x s x d

. . . for the rente of the wood thythe of the furnes wages and borde wages of marten and other . . .[12] xxxiii li xi s vi d

. . . for divers neccessaries bought for the furnes hoc anno . . . iiii li i d

. . . to laborers in repayng of the furnes caryng and dyggyng of stone . . .[13] lxiiii s iii d

. . . for my expenses and other in goyng to pannyngridge at divers tymes . . . vi s i d

Sum of all the paymentes at pannyngridge foreseyd Cliii li iii d

[5^r] Sum totall of all thalowannces and paymentes foreseyd CCCCliiii li iii s vii d

and so oweth xii li xvi s q

[5^v] *blank*

[6^r] Robertsbridge

Cordes of wood there In primis the remayne anno per pceden MMMxli

Item made ther hoc anno iii^M lxviii cordes di

Sum of all the cordes vi^M Cix cordes di wherof spente hoc anno iii^M vi^C lxv cordes di and so remain in the wood MMiiii^C xliiii cordes

Coles there Item the remain . . . iiii^C lx lodes

Item made there hoc anno in lodes Mxlii

Sum of all the lodes MDii wherof spente hoc anno ix^C ii lodes and remain in the storehowse DC lodes

Myne there Item the remain . . . C lodes

Item caried hoc anno nil

Sum of the lodes of myne C which remain

10 Wayleave payments for pig iron include one to Thomas Hawkins, the major carrier of charcoal and ore; he would thus appear to be a farmer in the Netherfield or Mountfield area.

11 The founder's name is Warnett, but Charles still repaired the hearth.

12 The Panningridge rent was paid to Sir John Baker.

13 382/4 makes it clear that the smith at Dallington (3 miles west of the furnace) was carrying out repairs to metalwork 'pipes and thin iron stuff'. The furnace seems to have required a good deal of work, including digging 3 loads of stone 'to make the fore part of the furnace which was fallen down'.

Sowes there pannyngridge Item ther ys in sowes by tale Cxxxii
Item in sowes ther per estimation ix^{C}
Sum of all the sowes Mxxxii

[*6*^{v}] The accompte of Iorne Item the remayne . . . Cxlvii ton xv^{C} di and i lli
Item made there hoc anno Cxxv ton C and di
Sum of all the tonnes CClxxii ton xvii^{C} i lli wherof solde hoc anno by the seyd William Blakenall as it appereth by his boke of receptes upon this accompte showed and examined one ton di iiii^{C} and xv lli, and delyverd to the forge and furnes as it appereth by the seyd boke CCC qrt and iiii lli, and delyverd to John harrysson the xi day of July Ciiii^{xx}iiii lli. And delyverd to Thomas hyckeby by me masters comandement the xith day of may iiii^{xx} ton and delyverd to xpofer draper by the seyd comandement the xvii^{ti} day of may lx ton, and delyverd to the seyd xpofer draper by hys seyd comandement to the use of mr FitzWilliams the xxiii day of June iiii^{xx} ton C xxvii lli, and so remayneth l ton di vi^{C}lxvii lli tunc remain in the store howse primo die Januari anno primo regni Regine marie primo lvii ton C lx lli
noted ther ys gayned in the waye in iii yeres paste vi ton iiii^{C} qrt and xxi lli

[*7*^{r}] lathes Item the remain . . . i lode
Item made there hoc anno nil
Sum of all the lathes one lode which remain

Totall accompte for the oxen and Kyen there for the laste yere[14]

pannyngridge
Cordes of wodd there Item the remain . . . MCx
. . . made there hoc anno MDliii cordes and di
Sum of all the cordes MMDClxiii cordes and di wherof spente hoc anno MMlxviii cordes di and so remain vi^{C}iiii^{xx}xv cordes

lodes of Coles Item the remain . . . iiii^{C}xl
Item mad there hoc anno DCCxix
Sum of all the lodes of Coles MClix wherof spente hoc anno DCCxxix lodes and so remain iiii^{C}xxx lodes

[*7*^{v}] myne Item the remayne . . . MCC lodes
Item caried there hoc anno Clv lodes

14 There is no account to correspond with this heading.

Sum of all the lodes of myne Miii^{C}lv lodes wherof spente hoc anno vii^{C}lv lodes and so remain vi^{C} lodes

[8^{r}] *blank*

[8^{v}] The remayne of the Stoke at Robertsbridge and pannyng ridge foreseyd the xxi^{ti} day of december anno primo regni Regine marie prime

pannyngridge

In primis vi^{C}iiii^{xx}xv cordes of wood there at vi d the corde	xvii li vii s vi d
Item in lodes of Coles iiii^{C}xxx at iiii s the lode	iiii^{xx}vi li
Item lodes of myne vi^{C} at xii d	xxx li

Robertsbridge

Item cordes of woode MMiiii^{C}xliiii at vi d the corde	lxi li ii s
Item lodes of Coles there DC at iiii s the lode	Cxx li
Item lodes of myne ther C at x d	iiii li iii s iiii d
Item Sowes there Cxxxii Item sowes at pannyngridge ix^{C} } Mxxxii at xxvi s viii d	MCCClxxvi li
Item in the Storehowse of Iorne lvii ton one hundred lx lli at vi li x s the ton	CCClxx li xix s vi d
Item lathes one lode price	viii s
Sum totall of all the remayne foreseyd	MMlxvi li iiii d

[9^{r}] A declaracon of the clere gayne of the Iorne workes aforeseyd dicto anno primo regni Regine marie prime

In primis in the price of Cxxv ton C di of Iorne made there hoc anno at vi li x s the ton	DCCCxii li xix s vi d
and Item incressed in the stoke of wood Coles Sowes and myne ther hoc anno	nil

Sum of all the incresse or gayne dicto anno primo viii^{C}xii li xix s vi d, wher of to be abated CCCCliiii li iii s vii d for money payd in divers kyndes of the seyd worke hoc anno as the particelles dothe appere in a boke therof made and examyned. And also to be abated of l li xii s viii d whiche ys spent oute of the stoke there hoc anno as it appereth by accompte of the same, and so remayneth clere gayned hoc anno CCCviii li iii s iii d

[10] SUMMARY ACCOUNT FOR PANNINGRIDGE FURNACE AND ROBERTSBRIDGE FORGE, 1554

378/6 *U 1475 B3/6*

[*1r*] The declaracon of the Iorne mynes there the fryste and seconnde yere of the regnes of Kyng phelyppe and Quyne mary Anno primo and ii^do^ phi and marie
Robertsbridege

[*1v*] *blank*

[*2r*] A declaracon of accompte of William Blackenall Clarke of the Iorne Workes to the Right Worshipfull Sir Henry Sydney Knyght at his mannor of Robertsbridge in the Countye of Sussex aswell of all and synguler suche sommes of money by hym receyvyd as also all suche sommes of money by the seyd William Imploed to the use of the seyd Sir Henry from the feast of the Nativity of our lorde god in the yere fryste of the reigne of our sovereigne lady mary by the grace of god of Inglonde frannce and Irelonde quene defendor of the fayth untyll the same feaste of the Nativity of our lorde god then next ensuyng in the fryst and seconde yere of the Rayne of phelipp and mary by the grace of god kyng and quene of Inglond frannce and Irelonde Naples and Jerusalem defendor of the fayth prynce of Spayne and Cusell archeduke of austryche dewke of Mylleyn Burgundy and Brabband Counte of haustburge flannders and Tyroll that is for one hole yere ut inferius per

fryste he is charged[1] with tharraragiis of his last accompte as it appereth in the foote of the same xii li xvi s q
Item he is charged with suche monny as he hath receyvyd of John hawes Receyvor of the Issues of his offyce hoc anno as it appereth by a boke of recepte upon this declaracon showed and examyned CCCxxiii li vii s i d

[*2v*] Item he is charged with monny receyvyd of John Thomas as the particulars doth appere by the seyd boke Cx li
Item he hath receyvyd of George Coke of the Issues of the parsonage of Salehurste with lxvii s i d for the arrears of his laste accompte ut per dictum librum x li vii s i d

[1] The Forge Book for 1554 is 382/9(B8/6), wrongly labelled in pencil as a Furnace Book, perhaps during the preparation of the H.M.C. Calendar.

. . . of olde kechery Colier for Serten wood by hym burned in a wood called the Glene ut per dictum librum vs

. . . for xiiii ton xii C and ix lli of Iorne solde hoc anno as the particelles doth appere by a boke therof upon this declaracon showed and examyned Ciii li xs iii d

. . . for woodde solde hoc anno as it appereth by the seyde boke[2] lvis ii d

Sum totall of all the Receptes foreseyd with arrears Dlxiii li xixd q

wherof

[*3*^r] layd oute at Robertsbridge

In primis for the Cuttynge of MMCv cordes of woodde ad divers prices as it appereth by a boke therof showed upon this declaracon examyned xxix li xis id

Item payd for the Colyng of vii^C xxxvii lodes of Coles as it appereth by the seyd boke[3] xlvi li xvd

. . . for the caryng of the seyd vii^C xxxvii lodes of coles at dyvers prices . . .[4] xix li xs iiii d

. . . for hepyng of Coles hoc anno xxviiis xd ob

. . . to the hamermen and fyners for the makynge of Cxxvii ton and xiiii^C qrt of Iorne at xiiis iiii d le ton . . .[5] iiii^xx v li iiis

. . . for the dressyng of the Belowes hoc anno ut per dictum librum xvis

. . . for Servantes wages and borde wages ther . . . xiii li xiiiis

. . . for the londe cariage of iii^C lxiii lodes of sowes from pannyngridge to Robertsbridge at xxd the lode as it appereth by the seyd book[6] xxix li xviiis iiii d

. . . for the londe cariage of Iorne hoc anno . . . vi li viis xd

. . . for the Water cariage of Iorne hoc anno . . . viii li xiis vid

[*3*^v] . . . to the Kerpentters aswell for the mendyng of the forge as also for hewyng of Ci ton of tymber . . . vi li xis iii d

. . . for the hepyng of sowes hoc anno . . . xxviis ii d

[2] A number of trees were sold, illustrating the complementary nature of cutting for charcoal, which ideally used small wood, and for large timber. John Pellyng of Horstmonses (*sic*), carpenter, was one purchaser; in this case there is a note: 'and the said oak would not serve for his purpose and there remaineth (in Timberwood) which should have been for the spindle of a windmill'.

[3] Two colliers, working through the year, with a single appearance of a third in July.

[4] Cressy is again the carrier; costs range from 3d to 9d.

[5] John Collins: hammerman.

[6] A notable variety of carriers: nine men in all.

.. to the sawyers for sawyng of plankes and jestes hoc anno ... xs

... to laborers in neccessary besynes hoc anno ... iiii li xviii s ix d ob

... in empcions of neccessaries for the forge hoc anno ...[7] Cv s x d ob

... in foren charges hoc anno with C s for a geldyng of hym bought vi li xii s

... for Thechyng of the priorie howse there and other ... xviii d

Item for the londe cariage of Serten neccessaries as well to pensehurste as at Robertsbridge hoc anno ... Cvii s v d

Item for nayles bought ther hoc anno as it appereth by the seyd boke xix s xi d ob

Sum of all the paymentes foreseyd at Robertsbridge CClxxii li xvii s ii d

[*4*r] and at pannyngridge[8]

Item payd for the Cuttyng of MMviii^C xlvi cordes and di of wood ad divers prices as it appereth bi a boke therof upon this declaracon showed and examined[9] xl li vii s i d ob

... to the founder and fyller for xxix foundes and one day with v s for the mendyng of the hathe ut per dictum librum[10] xx li xiii s iiii d

... for neccessaries bought for the furnes hoc anno ...[11] xxvi s viii d ob

... to John Egleston for wood bought of hym hoc anno ...[12] xix li vi s viii d

7 Including new hursts for the hammer; one was brought from Hodesdale Forge and three from Mr. Weekes of Battle at Darvel Furnace.

8 There are two draft Furnace Books, 382/5 (B10/7) and 383/5 (B11/4).

9 Thirty-three woodcutters are mentioned: a great increase over the previous year; eight of these were paid only on June 22nd, suggesting a sudden shortage of wood stocks for the colliers. No payments were made between July 12th and October 26th. Panningridge Wood was definitely out of use, although Hasilden remained among the four referred to.

10 The furnace was less used in 1554; after a long campaign which appears to have run from October 23rd, 1553 until February 12th, there was only a short blow (from about February 12th until March 31st) before a break until October 6th. Warnett was then replaced as founder by Peter, whose campaign ran until March 3rd. The very rapid re-start in February 1554 is of interest: Charles certainly did the relining, but the Furnace Book suggests this was done in a day or so.

11 This includes payment for fetching the weight from Mr. Ashburnham's furnace to weigh a sow. This is the first reference to this site, downstream from Panningridge.

12 Neston's Wood, 9½ acres.

. . . for MCxxiii lodes of myne bought of the seyd John Egleston hoc anno . . .[13] vi li vii s x d

. . . to laborers for repayng the furnes and other necessaries ther hoc anno as it appereth by the seyd boke[14] vi li iii s vii d

. . . for the rent of the woodde tythe of the furnes wages and borde wages of marten and libtie thowrowe mennes grownde hoc anno . . . xxxii li xiiii s iiii d

. . . for the Castyng of MCxxiii lodes of myne at ix d the lode . . .[15] xlii li ii s iii d

. . . for the caryng of ix^C xl lodes and di of myne at divers prises as it appereth by the seyd boke xx li xi s ix d

[*4^v^*] . . . for the Coling of vii^C lx lodes of Coles at xv d the lode as it appereth by the seyd boke[16] xlvii li x s

. . . for the caryng of Diiii^xx xviii lodes of Coles at divers prises . . .[17] xxii li iiii s viii d

. . . in expenses in goyng to pannyngridge at divers tymes as it appereth by the seyd boke . . . iii s xi d

noted that master assheborham oweth for Clxi lode of Coles[18]

Sum of all the paymentes at pannyngridge foreseyd CClix li xii s ii d

[*5^r^*] Sum totall of all thalowannces and paymentes foreseyd Dxxxii li ix s iiii d

and so oweth xxx li xii s iii d q

[*5^v^*] The remaynes aswell at Robertsbridge as at pannyngridge anno predicto viz at Robertsbridge

Cordes of woodde there In primis the remayne anno per pceden MMiiii^C xliiii

Item made ther hoc anno MMCv

Sum of all the cordes iiii^M Dxlix cordes wherof spente hoc anno MMMClxxv cordes and di and so remain in the woodde MCCClxxiii cordes and di

Coles ther Item the remain . . . DC lodes

13 Three hundred loads at 1d; 823 at 1½d.

14 This includes a reference to the building of a new furnace wheel (21s) by Roger Baker in contrast to the usual patching.

15 The dispersal of ore mining led to a larger labour force; six miners are named.

16 The Forge Book shows two colliers.

17 These range from 6d (Hasilden) to 12d (Glyde Wood).

18 Addition in left hand margin.

Item made ther hoc anno in lodes vii^{C}xxxvii
Sum of all the lodes Miii^{C}xxxvii wherof spente hoc anno DCCCxxxvii lodes and so remain in lodes in the storehowse D lodes

myne Item the remain . . . C lodes
Item caried hoc anno nil
Sum of all the lodes of myne C which remain

Sowes there and at pannyngridge Item is in sowes by tale Dxl
Item in sowes ther by estymacion iiii^{C}xxxiii
Sum of all the sowes DCCCClxxiii

[*6r*] The accompte of Iorne Item the remayne anno per pceden lvii ton Clx lli
Item made ther hoc anno Cxxvii ton xiiii^{C} and one qtr

Sum of all the tonnes Ciiii^{xx}iiii ton xv^{C}iii qtrs and iiii lli, wherof solde hoc anno by the seyd William Blackenall as it doth appere by his boke of Receptes upon the accompte showed and examined xiiii ton xii^{C} ix lli. And delyverd to the forge and furnes hoc anno as it appereth by the seyd boke CC xx lli, and delyverd to divers persons within the tyme of this accompte at divers tymes viz xxi^{mo} die february to mr Bacon xl tonnes, ii^{da} vice xvi^{o} die april to edwarde mynnes taker for the quenes maiestie ii ton, alia vice xx^{o} die april to mr Golston and to mr Bacon
xl ton, alia vice ultimo die may to mr Bacon and to mr Golston xxxii ton, alia vice eodem die to mr hyggeby v^{C} of Iorne, alia vice vii^{o} die november to Edmond Roberts xx ton, alia vice xii^{o} die december to the seyd Edmond Roberts xx ton, in toto [pnt] per librum dcm William super hunc [comp osten] et examinat Cliiii ton v^{C} and so remayneth xv ton xvi^{C} di and iii lli wherof delyverd to George Covylde xxix^{mo} die of aprell as it appereth by his seyd boke one ton and so remayneth[19] xiiii ton xvi^{C} die iii lli, tunc remain in the Store howse primo die January anno primo and ii^{de} R phillip and marie xviii ton v^{C} lxvi lli

noted ther ys gayned in the wayte hoc anno iii ton ix^{C} and vii lli

[*6v*] lathes Item the remain anno per pceden one lode
Item made ther hoc anno nil
Sum of all the lathes one lode, wherof spente hoc anno (*blank*) and so remain

pannyngridge
Cordes of wood there Item the remain . . . vi^{C}iiii^{xx}xv
Item made ther hoc anno MMviii^{C}xlvi and di corde

[19] In margin: 'note that George Covyld did pay for this iron in anno sequente.'

Sum of all the cordes iii^{M}v^{C}xli corde and di wherof spent hoc anno MMix^{C}lxv cordes and di and so remain Dlxxvi cordes

[7^{r}] lodes of Coles Item the remayne . . . iiii^{C}xxx lodes
Item made ther hoc anno vii^{C}lx lodes
Sum of all the lodes MCiii^{xx}x wherof spente hoc anno vii^{C}lxx lodes and so remain iiii^{C}xx lodes

Lodes of myne Item the remain . . . vi^{C}
Item cast and cared hoc anno MCxxiii
Sum of all the lodes of myne MDCCxxiii lodes wherof spente hoc anno viii^{C}lxxiii lodes and so remain viii^{C}l lodes

[7^{v}–8^{r}] *blank*

[*8^{v}*] The remayne of the Stoke at Robertsbridge and pannyngridge the xxi^{ti} day of december anno predicto

pannyngridge
In primis v^{C}lxxvi cordes of wood there at vi d the corde xiiii li viii s
Item in lodes of Coles iiii^{C}xx at iiii^{s} the lode iiii^{xx}iiii li
Item in lodes of myne viii^{C}l at xii d xlii li x s

Robertsbridge
Item in cordes of woodde there Miii^{C}lxxiii and di at vi d the corde xxxiiii li vi s ix d
Item in lodes of Coles ther D at iiii s the lode C li
Item in lodes of myne ther C at x d iiii li iii s iiii d
Item in sowes ther Cxl } ix^{C}lxxiii at
Item in sowes at pannyngridge iiii^{C}xxxiii } xxvi s viii d
MCCiiii^{xx}xvii li vi s viii d
Item in the store howse of Iorne xviii ton v^{C}lxvi lli at xii li the ton Cxxvii li xvi s
Item one lode of lathes viii s
Sum totall of all the remayne foreseyd MDCCiiii li xviii s ix d

[*9^{r}*] A declaracon of the clere gayne of the Iorne workes aforeseyd dicto anno primo and ii^{do} regno philip and marie

In primis in the price of Cxxvii ton xiiii^{C} and one qtr of Iorne made there hoc anno at vi li x s le ton DCCCxxx li ii s vii d ob
Item incressed in the stoke of woodde coles sowes and myne hoc anno nil
Sum of all the incresse or gayne anno predicto DCCCxxx li ii s vii d ob wherof to be abated of Dxxxii li ix s iiii d for monny

payd in divers kyndes of the seyd worke hoc anno as the particelles dothe appere in a boke therof made and examined and also to be abated of Cxvii li xviii s i d whiche is spente oute of the stoke there hoc anno as it appereth by accompte of the same and so remayneth clere gayned hoc anno

Clxxix li xv s ii d ob

[11] ROBERTSBRIDGE FORGE BOOK, 1555

381/1 *U 1475 B8/7*

[*1r*] The forge booke
[*1v*] *blank*

[*2r*] Anno ii marie regine
My debet ys xxx li xii s iii d q at myne acount
Recetts of money
iiii^to^ february
Recevyd of George coke for hys debets at hys laste accounte iii li iiii s
viii^mo^ februarii
. . . Hawes the viiith day of februarii for hys debetts viii li viii d ob
. . . Audryan dogen for the denysons of francys longley and davy longley the whych he was suerty for to my master and the sayd davy longley departyd within the halfe yeer folowyng as it aperith bi bill iii li
xxiii february
. . . hawes the xxiii^ti^ day of february vi li x s
Sum li li vi s xi d ob q

[*2v*] Recetts of money
xix^no^ marcii
. . . John Thomas at pensorst the xix daye of march xx li
xxvi^to^ marcii
. . . Hawes the xxvi^to^ die marcii to pay workemen at Robartts-bridge ix li i d
xiii^o^ aprilis
. . . Hawes the xiii day of aprell xiiii li
xviii^vo^ aprilis
. . . mystres Hawes the viii^th^ day of aprell xvi li
xii^mo^ maii
. . . Hawes the xii day Maii iii^xx^ix li
xxii^mo^ august
. . . Hawes the xxi^ti^ day of august xi li xvi s iii d[1]
Sum Cxxviii li i d

[*3r*] x^o^ July
. . . Hawes the xth day of July xxi li xi s vi d

[1] Crossed out in the original.

xxix^{no} July	
. . . Hawes the xxix^{ti} day of July	xxi li viii d ob
xxi^{mo} August	
. . . Hawes the xxi^{ti} day of August	xi li xvi s iii d
xiiii^{to} September	
. . . George Colfyld for on ton of yeren to hym delyvered in Anno predicto marie regine And paid now in the presence of Rychard marten the xiiii day of September in anno 1555	vi li vi s viii d
Sum	iii^{xx} li xv s i d ob
[*3*^{v}] iiii^{to} october	
. . . Hawes the iiiith day of october	xxxix li xiii s iiii d
xxi^{mo} october	
. . . Hawes the xxi^{ti} day october	xlv li xv s i d
ultimo october	
. . . Hawes the last day of october	xxx li vii s
xiiii^{to} november	
. . . Hawes the xiiii day of november for Mr rylandes rent	xli s viii d
more of hym the same tyme	x li
Item the more recevyd of hym the same day	xiiii li ii s x d
xxiiii^{to} november	
. . . hawes the xxiiii^{ti} day of november for the halfe yeres rent of the parsonage of Sallehorst	vi li x s
Sum	Cxlviii li ix s xi d
[*4*^{r}] Receipts of money	
xxix november	
. . . Hawes the xxix day of november	xxviii li
. . . Hawes the xxiii day of Januarii	xiii li vi s viii d
Sum	xxviii li[2]
. . . Hawes the xxviii day of Januari	viii li ii s ii d q
Sum pagine	xlix li viii s x d q
Sum totalis rec pdm	iiii^{C}xxxviii li xi d ob[3]
	unde
Arrears	xxx li xii s iii d q
Johne Thomas	xx li
John hawes	CCClxxiiii li xviii s q[4]
Adriano dogen beyng suertye for frannces langley and davy langley	lx s

[2] Crossed out in the original.

[3] iiii^{c} xvi li xii s (or xv s) i d ob q crossed out.

[4] CCClvi li xiii s ii d crossed out.

Georgie Colfelde for one ton of Iorne sold to hym in Anno primo regni Regine marie prime — vi li vi s viii d
Georgio Coke de predic Rectorie de Salehurste — lxiiii s

[*4*ᵛ, *5*ʳ, *5*ᵛ] *blank*

[*6*ʳ] Yeren Sold
Receved of fylpott for CC of yeren — xiiii s viii d
xxii Januarii
. . . fylpott for C of yeren — vii s iiii d
xxvi[to] January
. . . fylpott for CC of yeren lackyng ii lli — xiiii s vi d ob
xxvi[to] Januarii
. . . Edmond Robartts of hawkhorst for iii tonnes of yeren at viii li the tonne in ende ix[xx]xvi ende — xxiiii li
xxxi[o] Januarii
. . . peter Lawles of Redynge Smyth for halfe a ton of yeren price fore pounde to be payd the xxi day of Aprell (as it aperyth by a byll)[5] — iiii li
. . . the Smyth of norbrydge for di C yeren and iiii li — iii s xi d
Sum — xxx li v d ob

[*6*ᵛ] yeren sold
. . . Richard harpar for on smale barre of yeren wayeng ix lli at ob q the pound — vi d ob
ix[no] februarii
delyvred unto the hamerman iii blomes and a halfe to be leed under the andvyld wayeng — on hondred of yeren

ix[no] februarii
. . . fylpott for CC yeren lackyng on pound at vii s vi d the hoderd — xiiii s xi d ob
xxii[do] februarii
. . . Edmond Robartts of hawkhurst for one ton of yeren in ende iii[xx]vi price — viii li
xxii[do] februarii
. . . John Upton for CC yeren and on pound at viii s the honderd — xvi s i d
. . . the Smyth of norbrydge for di C and iiii lli of yeren — iiii s iiii d
Sum — ix li xv s xi d

[*7*ʳ] xxii[do] februarii
. . . fylpott for halfe a ton of yeren at vii s vi d the C — iii li xv s

[5] Crossed out.

. . . the Smyth of nordyam for C yeren price viii s
xi^mo martii
. . . Shether of stapelcros for di C of yeren price iiii s
xxvii^mo martii
. . . John Trencham of Apeldore for halfe a ton of yeren price iiii li
. . . nycolas vynall for C yeren viii s
v^to aprilis
. . . nycolas vynall for C yeren lackyng ii pounds vii s x d ob
Sum ix li ii s x d ob

[*7^v*] yeren sold
vii^mo aprilis
delyvered unto master Robartts off hawkhorst be my masters comandement the vii^ti day of Aprell and carried it to the Oke xxi^ti tonnes of yeren
Received for a crow of yeren wayeng xiiii lli xii d
xxvi^ti Aprilis
. . . the smyth of geslyng for C yeren price viii s iiii d
xxix^no Aprilis
. . . nycolas vynall for C yeren viii s iiii d
v^to maii
. . . fylpott for CC yeren xvi s viii d
. . . nycolas vynall for C yeren viii s iiii d
v^to maii
Delyvered unto Master Robartts off hawkhorst be my masters comandement on v^th day of mai xxi^ti tonnes of yeren
Sum xlii s viii d

[*8^r*] yeren sold
xi^mo maii
. . . fylpott for halfe a ton of yeren at viii s iiii d the C iiii li iii s iiii d
. . . nycolas vynall for a C yeren lackyng v lli vii s viii d ob
xiiii^to maii
Delyvered ii barres of yeren to John collyan for to macke ii hopes for the hamer beme at the forge wayeng di C iiii lli
xvi^to maii
. . . peter lawles of redyng smyth for on ton of yeren to hym sold the xvi daye of maii at viii li vi s viii d the ton to be payd at bartellmew next comyng as it apereth by a bill viii li vi s viii d
Delyvered to Richard cresy of barrs of yeren wayeng xxviii lli to mack bolltts for the colle wayens xxviii lli[6]
Sum xii li xvii s viii d ob

[6] The complete entry crossed out.

[*8v*] xx^{mo} maii
Delyvered unto master Robartts of hawkhorst be my masters comandment the xx^{ti} day off mai xxi^{ti} tonnes of yeren delyvered to peter lawles
. . . John whytwood of halden for ii barres of yeren to macke ii spyttes wayeng xliiii lli price iii s viii d
xxii^{do} maii
Delyvered unto Cresy one barre of yeren to macke boltts for the collwaynes waying xxix lli
xxiii^{o} maii
. . . nycolas vynall for C yeren lackyng iiii lli at viii s iiii d the hondred viii s i d
. . . the Smyth of rye for CC yeren xvi s viii d
. . . the Smyth of norbrydge for halfe a honderd of yren iiii s ii d
xiiii^{to} maii
Delivered to mr hadlow iii boltts of yeren for the bemes in the mylhouse wayeng xiii lli
Sum xxxii s vii d

[*9r*] yeren Sold
xxvii^{mo} maii
. . . the Smyth of nordyam for C di of yeren lackyng vi lli at viii s the honderd xii s ob
xxviii^{mo} maii
Delyvered to the fornes ii ryngars waying halfe a honderd and twynty poundes
. . . the Smyth of nordyam for C yeren viii s iiii d
. . . vynall for a C yeren viii s iiii d
xiiii^{to} June
. . . the Smyth of nordyam for C di of yeren lackyng iiii lli at viii s iiii d the hondred xii s iii d
. . . nycolas vynall for C yeren viii s iiii d
. . . marten of Stapell crose for di C of yeren iiii s ii d
xvii^{o} June
. . . Rychard Shether of Stapell crose for C yeren viii s iiii d
Sum iii li xxi d ob
[*9v*] yeren sold
xx^{mo} June
. . . John harryson for CC xiiii lli of yeren at viii s iiii d the hondred xvi s viii d
xxii^{do} June
. . . nycolas vynall for C yeren viii s iiii d
Delyvered to mr hadlow ii barres of yeren for the mendyng

of the roffe over the garners wayeng halfe a honderd and xiiii pounds

. . . marten of Stapell crose for di C of yeren iiii s ii d

viii^vo^ July

. . . a Smyth of rye for xii C of yeren v li

xxvi^to^ July

. . . fylpott for CC vii lli of yeren xvii s iii d

xxix^mo^ July

delyvered to Cresy ii barres of yeren to make barres for wyndowes wayeng halfe a honderd

Sum vii li vi s v d

[*10^r^*] yeren sold

iii^o^ august

. . . the Smyth of nordyam for C yeren viii s iiii d

iii^o^ august

. . . fylpott for CCC di of yeren at viii s iiii d the honderd (xiii barres) xxix s ii d

Delyvered unto Cresy on barre of yeren to make hokes rydes and henges for hys new [dore] wayeng thirty on pounde

xvii^o^ august

. . . nycolas vynall for C yeren viii s iiii d

xx^mo^ August

delyvered unto Mr Robartts the xxi^ti^ day of August be my masters commandment as it aperyth by hys byll xiii tonnes of yeren

. . . the Smyth of hestyng for C yeren viii s iiii d

. . . the Smyth of brede for C yeren viii s iiii d

Sum iii li ii s vi d

[*10^v^*] yeren sold

xxx^mo^ August

. . . the Smyth of hastyng for C yeren viii s iiii d

ultimo August

. . . peter lawles of Smalled for halfe a ton of yeren to be payd at allhalowtyd iiii li iii s iiii d

. . . the lokear of hastyng for C yeren viii s iiii d

ultimo August

. . . Gray of nordyam for C yeren viii s iiii d

debet ii lli . . . nycolas vynall for C yeren viii s iiii d

ultimo August

. . . fylpott for iiii C di of yeren at viii s iiii d the honderd xxxvii s vi d

iii^o September
. . . the Smyth of hastyng for CC yeren xvi s viii d
x^mo September
Delyvered unto Sir John baker be my masters commandement the x day of september on ton of yeren
ende iii^xx v
Sum viii li x s x d

[*II*^r] yeren Sold
ix^mo Septebris
. . . Shether of stapell crose for di C of yeren iiii s ii d
. . . John Upton for CC yeren xvi s viii d
xiii^o septebris
Delyvered unto master Robartts of hawkhorst be my masters comandement the xiii^th daye of September sold by my master at viii li v the ton Syxten tonnes of yeren[7]
xiiii^to september
. . . nycolas vynall for C yeren viii s iiii d
. . . the Smyth of hastyng for C yeren viii s iiii d
. . . the Smyth of bred for C yeren viii s iiii d
xxiii^o September
. . . Shether of Stapell crose for on barre of yeren wayeng xxv[i] lli to make a pype for hys bellowes ii s
xxviii^o September
. . . the Smyth of beckley for halfe a honderd of yeren iiii s ii d
Sum lii s

[*II*^v] yeren Sold
Delyvered unto Mr Robartts of hawkhorst be my masters comandement the laste day of September Twenty on ton of yeren
primo october
. . . Cresy of hastyng Smyth for CC yeren xvi s viii d
xv^to october
. . . the Smyth of norbrydge for di C of yeren iiii s ii d
xvi^to october
delyvered unto Mr Robartts of hawkhorst be my masters comandement the xvi day of october
Twelfe tonnes xii^C iii qr and iiii lli of yeren
delyvered more unto Mr Robartts the viii^ih day of october
Syx tonnes CC iii qr and v lli of yeren
xxiiii october

[7] Note in left hand margin: 'This is parcell of the iii^xx tonnes of yeren sole be my master at viii li the ton'.

. . . John basenden for C qr iiii lli of yeren at viii s iiii d the honderd — ix s ix d

ii^do^ november

delyvered on blome of yeren to be leed under the andvyld weying — Thirty pound

Sum — xxx s vii d

[*12^r^*] yeren Sold

. . . Trentham of Apeldore for half a ton of yeren to hym sold and to be payd for yt at saynt nycolas day — iiii li iii s iiii d

iiii^to^ november

. . . wyllem gybbens of becley smyth for half a ton of yeren and delyvered to hym the iiii^th^ day of november — iiii li iii s iiii d

v^to^ november

. . . John levyd of geslyng for half a ton of yeren[8]

. . . John gebens of rye Smyth for on C xi lli of yeren — ix s iii d

. . . the Smyth of hastyng for C yeren — viii s iiii d

xvi^to^ november

delyvered unto the fornes ii shamowes wayeng — Therty on pounds

. . . John basenden for xxii pounds of yren — xxii d

Sum — ix li vi s i d

[*12^v^*] yeren Sold

xxv^to^ november

. . . Shether of Stapell crose for di C pound of yeren — iiii s ii d

ende xxii

. . . nycolas vynall of Smallhed for halfe a tone of yeren price — iiii li iii s iiii d

viii^vo^ december ende xxix

. . . gebens of Rye for halfe a ton of yeren pryc — iiii li iii s iiii d

ix^no^ december ende MviiCxxxiii

Delyvered unto master Robartts of hawkhorst the ix day of december be my masters comandement as yt aperyth be hys letter — Twenty fore tonnes of yeren

Delyvered hym more in full contentacion of iii^xx^ tonnes — iiii ton iiii^C^ xlvii lli

xiiii^to^ december

. . . Fylpott for CCC iiii li of yeren — xxv s iiii d

ultimo december

Delyvered to John collyan iii half blomes to be leed under the andvyld wayeng — half a hondred

Sum — ix li xvi s ii d

[8] Crossed out in the original.

[*13r*] Sum huius titli Cx li xviii s vii d
Cx li xviii s vii d
xiii ton xii c lv lli

[*13v*] *blank*

[*14r*] Wood Sold and Tymber
. . . Thomas hayes for ii loode of olde bechen wood in parke wood vi d
. . . Rychard Shether of youhorst for iii[xx] tonnes of tymber to hym sold by Wylliam hadlow and Wylliam blacknoll at iii s viii d the tonne as it aperyth by a byll more playnly xi li
. . . the yener of nordyam for v yardes of a beche motte in parke wood at iiii d the yard xx d
. . . charles marshall for vi yarddes of a beche motte in parkwod at iiii d the yarde ii s
Sum xi li iiii s ii d

[*14v*] Wood and Tymber sold
. . . Rychard Smyth for ii tonnes of Roufe tymber at xii d the ton ii s
xx[mo] July
. . . hym more for iiii lode of stone on the laste yere reconyng ii s
. . . Mr Stonstrett for iii loode of Stone to hym sold price xviii d
in yerneste vi d . . . the tornar of youhorst for yarde of a beche in parke wod[9]
Sum v s vi d
Sum huius Titli xi li ix s viii d[10]

[*15r*] Sum totalis Dlx li ix s ii d ob
[*15v*] *blank*

[*16r*] Wood Cottars
primo february
fannars wood
Payd to Edward Cresy for the cottyng of xxv cordes of wood in fannars wod at v s iiii d the skore vi s viii d
. . . Wr follyng for xxviii cordes vii s v d
. . . Stevyn davy for xxiii corde vi s i d
. . . Symond Kempe for xxxv corde ix s iiii d
. . . Wr davy for liii cordes xiiii s i d
. . . John Whytt for xl cordes x s viii d
. . . Marten copyn for xv cordes iiii s

[9] Crossed out in the original.
[10] In a different hand.

xxii^do^ february
... Thomas hogens Thomas mascall and to Audryan dogen for the cottyng of Cxviii cordes di of wood in fannars wod at vs iiii d the skore xxxis vii d ob
Sum iiii li ixs xd ob
Cordes iii^C^ xxxvii di

[*16^v^*] Wood Cottars
primo february
wyndars wod
... old Cathery for the cottyng of liiii cordes of wood in Wyndars wood xiiii s iiii d

fannars wood
... Whyt for the cottyng of xii cordes di of wood in fannars wod at vs iiii d the skore iii s iiii d
... Symond Kempe for the cottyng of xi cordes in fannars wod ii s xi d ob
... Wr Follyng for xxiii cords ut supra vi s ii d ob
... Edward Cresy for xxxviii cords x s ii d
... Rychard Smyth for the cottyng of iii^xx^iii Cords of wood in fannars wod xvi s x d ob
... Thomas farman for the cottyng of xlii Cords of wood in fannars wod xi s ii d ob
... Stevyn davy for the cottyng of xlviii cords ut supra xii s ix d
... John Whyt for the toppyng of on oke in fannars wood i d
Sum iii li xvii s xi d
Cordes CCiiii^xx^xi ob

[*17^r^*] wood cottars
xxiii^o^ february
wyndars wood
... Symond Kempe for the cottyng of xxxi cordes di in wyndars wood at vs iiii d the skore viii s v d
... John Whyt for the cottyng of xxxv corddes ix s iiii d
... John crefford for the cottyng of xlvi cordes xii s iii d ob
... Wr davy for the cottyng of iii^xx^vi cordes di xvii s viii d ob
... Stordygat for the cottyng of xlvi cordes of wood ut supra xii s iii d
... the old frenchman for the cottyng of lvii cordes di in wyndars wood xv s iiii d ob
... Wr follyng for the cottyng of xx cordes in wyndars wood v s iiii d

Sum iiii li viii d ob
Cordes iii^{C} ii di

[*17^{v}*] Wod Cottars
xi^{mo} Aprilis
Wyndars wood
. . . Symond Kempe for the cottyng of xxxiii cordes viii s ix d
. . . William follyng for x corddes ii s viii d
. . . John whyt for iii^{xx} corddes xvi s
. . . Stevyn davy for xli cordes x s xi d
. . . John pottar for ix cordes ii s iiii d
. . . Edward cresy for the cottyng of xl cordes x s viii d

fannars wood
. . . Symond Kempe for the cottyng of xl cordes of wood in fannars wood of oken toppes and for the toppyng of the okes ther at vi s x d the skore xiii s viii d
fannars wood
. . . Rychard Smyth for the cottyng of half a cord of wod in fannars wod i d ob

wyndars wod
. . . Rychard Smyth for the cottyng of xxv cordes di in wyndars wood vi s ix d ob
Sum iii li xi s xi d
Cordes CClix

[*18^{r}*] Wood Cottars
park wood
. . . hogens for the cuttyng off vi cordes di of great wood in the parke wood at v d the cord ii s viii d ob
. . . hym more for v cordes of topwod at v s iiii d the skore xvi d
Thomas mascall for the cottyng of xxxvi cordes of under wood at iiii d the cord xii s
Payd more to mascall and hogens for the cottyng of xxiii cordes di of great wood at v d the cord ix s ix d ob
. . . more to them for xiiii cordes of topwod at v s iiii d the skore iii s x d ob
. . . Rychard upthomas for the cottyng of iiii corddes of underwood xvi d
. . . Rychard Smyth yonger for the cuttyng of x cordes di of great wod at v d the cord iiii s iiii d ob
Sum xxxv s v d
Cordes iiii^{xx} xix di

[*18v*] Wood Cottars

Park wood

. . . Rychard Smyth the yonger for the cottyng of vi cordes of topwood xix d ob

. . . Richard Smyth the older for the cottyng of iii cordes of great wod xv d

. . . more to hym for ii cordes of topwod vii d

Park wod

. . . Rychard Smyth younger for vi cordes of great wod at v d the cord ii s vi d

. . . hym more for vii cord of topewod xxii d

Parke wood

. . . Stordygatt for the cotting of v cordes of great wood at v d the cord ii s i d

. . . hym more for on cord of toppewood iii d

wyndars wood

. . . whytt for the cottyng of v cords of wood in wyndars wood xvi d

Parke wood iii° maii

. . . Rychard uprobartts for the cottyng of iii cordes di of smale wood in parke wood at iiii d the cord xiiii d

Sum xii s vii d ob

Cordes xxxviii^{ti} cordes di

[*19r*] Wood Cottars

. . . wr follyng for the cottyng of viii cordes of oken toppes in wyndars wood ii s i d

fannars wod

. . . Symond Kempe for the cottyng of xlii cordes of wood of oken toppes in fannars wod at vi s x d the skore with the toppyng of the okes ther xiiii s iii d

park wod

. . . Stordygat for the cottyng of xiii cordes of great wod at v d the cord v s v d

. . . hym more for the cottyng of xiii cordes di of smale wod iii s vii d

. . . Rychard Smyth for the cottyng of ii cordes of smale wood in parke wod vi d ob
Sum xxv s x d ob
Cordes iii^{xx}xviii di

[*19*^{v}] Wood Cottars
Parke wood
primo June
. . . Stordygat for the cottyng of ix cordes of great wood in parke wood at v d the corde iii s ix d
. . . hym more for the cottyng of vi cordes of smalle wood xix d

parke wood
. . . Thomas hogens and to Thomas mascall for the cottyng of xxv cordes di of great wod x s vii d ob
. . . them more for the cottyng of xx cordes of smale wod at v s iiii d the skore v s iiii d

parke wood
. . . Symond Kempe for the cottyng of ii cordes of great wood x d
. . . hym more for the cottyng of ii cordes di of smalle wood viii d
Sum xxii s ix d ob
Cords iii^{xx}v cordes

[*20*^{r}] Wood Cottars
Parke wood
. . . Rychard Smyth for the cottyng of xv Cordes di of great wood in park wood at v d the cord vi s v d ob
. . . hym more for the cottyng of x cordes ther of smale wood at v s iiii d the skore ii s viii d
. . . Edward Cresy for the cottyng of vii cordes of great wod in park wod at v d the cord ii s xi d
. . . hym more for the cottyng of x cordes of smale wod in park wod at v s iiii d the skore ii s viii d
. . . Edward Cresy for the cottynge of vi cordes di of great motts at vi d the cord iii s iii d
viii^{vo} november
. . . hym more for the cottyng of iiii cords of Smale wood in parke wod xii d ob
Sum xix s[11]
Cords liii

[11] xviii s iiii d crossed out.

[*20v*] Wood Cottars

Parke wood

xxvi^{to} october

. . . Thomas hogens and to thomas mascall for the cottyng of xxvii cordes of great beche motts in park wood at vi d the cord	xiii s vi d
. . . them more for the cottyng of xii cordes di of smale wod at v s iiii d the skore	iii s iiii d

Parke wod

. . . Stordygat and to byne for the cottyng of xvii cordes of great motts in parke wood at vi d the cord	viii s vi d

Parke wood

xxiii november

. . . Thomas hogens for the cottyng of v cordes of great wood at vi d the cord	ii s vi d
. . . hym more for i cord di of smale wood in park wood	iiii d ob
. . . John byne for the cottyng of ix cordes di of great wood	iiii s ix d
. . . hym more for the cottyng of ii cordes of smale wood	vi d
Sum	xxxiii s v d ob
Cords	iii^{xx} xiiii di

[*21r*] Wood Cottars

v^{to} december

m[or]ge wod

. . . william davy for the cottyng of xxx cordes of wod in great morgey wood at v s iiii d the skore	viii s
. . . John Whytt for xxx Cordes ut supra	viii s
. . . Sharvold for xlviii cordes ut supra	xii s ix d
. . . Storydgat for xx Cordes	v s iiii d
. . . Wr Shusmyth for xxviii cordes di	vii s vii d
. . . John Shether for xxxv Cordes	ix s iiii d
. . . Wr Shether for xl cordes di	x s ix d ob
. . . John torms for xxx cordes	viii s
. . . Wr pottar for xxxvii cordes di	x s
. . . Wr crefford for lii cordes	xiii s x d
. . . Stevyn davy for xxxii cordes	viii s vi d
. . . george gerves for xxxiiii cordes di	ix s ii d
. . . george browne for xxxii cordes di	viii s viii d
. . . wr Fowllyng for xxii cordes di	vi s
. . . Thomas Levesy for xvi cordes di	iiii s iiii d ob
. . . Edward pypar for xvii cordes	iiii s vi d

Sum	vi li xiiii s x d
Cordes	vC v cordes di

[*21v*] Wood Cottars
viii[vo] december
parke wood

. . . Edward Cresy for the cottyng of xii Cordes of great wood in parke wood at vi d the cord	vi s
. . . hym more for the cottyng of viii cordes of smale wood ther	ii s i d

morgay wood

. . . Stordygat for the cottyng of xx cordes of wod in morgay wod	v s iiii d
. . . wr Shether elder for the cottyng of x cordes ther[12]	ii s viii d
. . . pottar for xvii cordes di	iiii s viii d
. . . william follyng for xiii cordes di	iii s vii d
Sum	xxiiii s iiii d
Cordes	iiii[xx]i

[*22r*] Wood Cottars
xxiii[o] december
morgay wood

. . . William davy for the cottyng of xxxv cordes of wod in great morgay wod at v s viiii d the skore	ix s iiii d
. . . John Whytt for xxxv ut supra	ix s iiii d
. . . Sharvold for xxxv cordes ut supra	ix s iiii d
. . . Shusmyth for xxvii cordes	vii s ii d
. . . Edward cresy for l cordes	xiii s iiii d
. . . John Syvear for xxx cordes	viii s
. . . John shether for xxv cordes di	vi s ix d ob
. . . Wr shether for xii cordes ut supra	iii s ii d
. . . John torms for xv cordes	iiii s
. . . Wr pottar for xi cordes di	iii s ob
. . . Robart torms for xxii cordes di	vi s
. . . William candy for xx cordes	v s iiii d
. . . William crefford for xxv cordes	vi s viii d
. . . Stevyn davy for l cordes	xiii s iiii d
. . . george gerves for xxx cordes	viii s
Sum	v li xii s x d
Cordes	iiiiC xxiii di

[12] xiii di crossed out in the original.

[*22v*] Wod Cottars
xxiii december
morgey wood
. . . george browne for the cottyng of xx cordes of wood in great morgay — v s iiii d
. . . wr Follyng for vii cordes di — ii s
. . . thomas lewsy for xvi cordes — iiii s iii d
. . . Edward pyper for xii cordes di — iii s iiii d
. . . thomas blake for xiiii cordes — iii s viii d
. . . Thomas hogens and to John byne for the cottyng of xix cordes di of great wood in parke wod at vi d the cord — ix s ix d
. . . them more for the cottyng of xi cordes di of smale wood — iii s ob
Sum — xxxi s iiii d ob
Cordes — Ci

[*23r*] Wod Cottars
ultimo december
morgay wood
. . . baker of bodyam for the cottyng of xiiii cords of wood in Great morgay — iii s viii d ob
Sum pagine — iii s viii d ob
Sum huius titli — xxxviii li xvi s viii d

[*23v*] *blank*

[*24r*] yeren Remayneng in the howse at crystonmas and wayed — xviii ton v^{C} iii^{xx}vi lli
xii^{mo} Januarii
. . . John Collyan for the homeryng of vi ton xvii C qr of yeren — xlv s ix d
. . . the fynars for the fynyng of the same — xlv s ix d
xxvi^{to} Januarii
. . . John collyan for the homeryng of vii ton viii C of yeren — xlix s iiii d
. . . the fynars for the fynyng of the same — xlix s iiii d
ix^{no} febrarii
. . . John Collyan for the homeryng of viii ton xii C di of yeren — lvii s vi d[13]
. . . the fynars for the fyning of the same — lxvii s vi d[13]
Sum — xv li v s ii d

[13] Originally iii li xvii s vi d in each case.

[*24v*]
xxiii° februarii
. . . John Collyan for the homeryng of vi ton iiiiC di of yeren
xli s vi d
. . . the fynars for the fynyng of the same xli s vi d
ixno marcii[14]
. . . John Collyan for the homeryng of vii ton viC yeren
xlviii s viii d
. . . the fynars for the fyning of the same xlviii s viii d
xxiii° marcii
. . . John Collyan for the homeryng of vii tonnes and a halfe
honderd l s ii d
. . . the fynars for the fyning of the same l s ii d
Sum xiiii li viii d

[*25r*]
vito aprilis
. . . John Collyan for the homeryng of viii ton C and a qr of
yeren liii s ix d
. . . the fynars for the fynyng of the same liii s ix d
xiii° aprilis
. . . John Collyan for the homeryng of iiii ton iii C of yeren
xxvii s viii d
ester even
. . . the fynars for the fynyng of the same xxvii s viii d
xxviimo Aprilis
. . . John Collyan for the homeryng of iiii tonnes iii C of
yeren xxvii s viii d
. . . the fynars for the fynyng of the same xxvii s viii d
Sum x li xviii s ii d

[*25v*]
ximo maii
. . . John Collyan for the homeryng of vi ton iiii C di of yeren
xli s vi d
. . . the fynars for the fynyng of the same xli s vi d
xxviti maii
. . . John Collyan for the homeryng of iiii ton xvii C yeren
xxxii s iiii d
. . . the fynars for the fynyng of the same xxxii s iiii d
viiivo June

[14] delyvered iii great blomes to be leed under the anvyld wayeng—on honderd (crossed out in the original).

. . . John Collyan for the homeryng of iiii tonnes viii C iii qr of yeren xxixs viid
. . . the fynars for the fynyng of the same xxixs viid
Sum xli vis xd

[*26*r]
xxii^do June
. . . John Collyan for the homeryng of vii ton xi C of yeren ls iiiid
. . . the fynars for the fynyng of the same ls iiiid
vi^to July
. . . John Collyan for the homeryng of v ton viii C qr of yeren xxxvis id
. . . the fynars for the fynyng of the same xxxvis id
. . . John Collyan for the homeryng of iiii tonnes on C of yeren xxviis
xx^mo July
. . . the fynars for the fynyng of ii tonn vi C di of olde hamers at viiid the C xxxis
. . . them more for the fynyng of on ton xiiii C di of new yeren at iiiid the hondred xis vid
Sum xiili iis iiiid

[*26*v] iii^o August
. . . John Collyan for the homeryng of ii ton xiiii C yeren xviiis
. . . the fynars for the fynyng of the same xviiis
xvii August
. . . John Collyan for the homeryng of iiii ton xiiii C xxxis iiiid
. . . the fynars for the fynyng of the same xxxis iiiid
ultimo August
. . . John Collyan for the homeryng of iii ton xix C di of yeren xxvis vid
. . . the fynars for the fynyng of the same xxvis vid
Sum viili xis viiid

[*27*r] xiiii^to September
. . . John Collyan for the homeryng of vi ton xi C yeren xliiis viiid
. . . to the fynars for the fynyng of the same xliiis viiid
xxviii^vo September
. . . to John Collyan for the homeryng of v tonnes of yeren xxxiiis iiiid
. . . to the fynars for the fynyng of the same xxxiiis iiiid
xvii^mo october
. . . to John Collyan for the homeryng of vi tonnes C di of yeren xls vid

. . . to the fynars for the fynyng of the same xl s vi d
Sum xi li xv s[15]

[27v] ii^do novembris
. . . John Collyan for the homeryng of ix ton xiii C di of yeren iii li iiii s vi d
. . . the fynars for the fynyng of the same iii li iiii s vi d
xvi^to november
. . . John Collyan for the homeryng off xi ton xiiii C qr of yeren iii li xviii s i d
. . . the fynars for the fynyng of the same iii li xviii s i d
xxix^no november
. . . John Collyan for the homeryng of vi ton C di xl s vi d
. . . the fynars for the fynyng of the same xl s vi d
Sum xviii li vi s ii d

[28r] xiiii^to december
. . . John Collyan for the homeryng of xi ton vii C qr of yeren iii li xv s ix d
. . . the fynars for the fynyng of the same iii li xv s ix d
ultimo december
. . . John Collyan for the homeryng of v ton xix C yeren xxxix s viii d
. . . the fynars for the fynyng of the same xxxix s viii d
Sum xi li x s x d
Sum totalis huius titli Cxi li xvi s x d
Clxvi ton xii C

[28v] *blank*

[29r] Collyars
ii^do June
Parke wood
. . . Audryan dogen for the collyng of xxiii loodes of colles in park wood at xv d the lod xxviii s ix d

xxii^do June
Stocke wood
. . . Thomas dogen for the collyng of vi^xx loodes of colles in Stockewood at xv d the lood vii li x s

vi^to July
fannars wood
. . . Audryan dogen for the collyng of iii^xxiii loodes of colles in fannars wood at xv d the lod iii li xviii s ix d

15 Originally xi li xv s viii d.

parke wood
. . . Audryan dogen for the collyng of li lodes of colles in parke wood at xv d the lod iii li iii s ix d

parke wood
. . . Audryan dogen for the collyng of xiii loode of colles in parke wood at xv d the lod xvi s iii d
Sum xvi li xvii s xi d

[*29v*] Collyars
xx^mo July
Stock wood
. . . Thomas dogen for the collyng of iiii^xx xv lodes of colles owt of Stocke wood at xv d the lod collyng v li xviii s ix d

fannars wood
. . . Audryan dogen for the collyng of xlix lodes of colles owt of fannars wod at xv d the lod iii li xv d

Stock wod
. . . Thomas dogen for the collyng of viii^xx lodes of colles owt of Stockewod at xv d the lood x li

xxviii^vo September
fannars wood
. . . Audryan dogen for the collyng of viii^xx xvii lood of coles wherof ys iiii^xx x lode in fannars wood and iiii^xx vii in wyndars wood at xv d the lod xi li xv d
Sum xxx li xv d

[*30r*] Collyars
ii^do november
wyndars wood
. . . Audryan dogen for the collyng of iii^xx ii loodes of colles owt of wyndars wood at xv d the lood iii li xvii s vi d

wyndars wood
. . . Audryan dogen for the collyng of xix lodes of colles in wyndars wod at xv d the lod xxiii s ix d

xxvi^mo november
parke wood
. . . Audryan dogen for the collyng of xv loode of colles in parke wood at xv d the lod xviii s ix d

Stock wood
. . . Thomas dogen for the collyng of xii loodes of colles owt
of Stockwood at xv d the lod xv s
Sum vi li xv s

[30^{v}] Collyars
xxvii november
park wood
. . . Thomas dogen for the collyng of iii^{xx}ii loodes of colles
owt of park wood at xv d the lod iii li xvii s vi d
Sum pagine lxxvii s vi d
Sum huius titli lvii li xi s iii d

[31^{r}–31^{v}] *blank*

[32^{r}] Lond Carriage of Colles
ii^{do} June
parke wood
. . . Cresy for the lond carriage of xxiii^{ti} Loodes of colles owt
of parke wood to the forge at iiii d the lood vi s vi[ii] d

xxii^{do} June
Stoke wood
. . . Cresy for the land carriage of vi^{xx} loodes of colles owt of
Stockwood to the forge at xii d the lod carr vi li

vi^{to} July
fannars wod
. . . Cresy for the Carriage of iii^{xx}iii lodes of Colles owt of
fannars wood at vii d the lod xxxvi s ix d

xx^{mo} July
Stockwod
. . . Cresy for the lond carriage of iiii^{xx}xv loodes of colles owt
of Stockwood at xii d the lood carriage iiii li xv s
Sum xii li xix s v d

[32^{v}] Lond Carriage of Colles
vi^{to} July
Parke wood
. . . John Smyth for the carriage of li loodes of colles owt of
park wood to the forge at iiii d the lod xvii s
xx July
. . . Cresy for the carriage of xiii lodes of colles owt of park
wood at iiii d the lod iiii s iiii d

fannars wood
. . . Cresy for the carriage of xlix lodes of colles owt of fannars wod at vii d the lod xxviii s vii d

Stock wood
. . . Cresy for the carryeng of viii^{xx} loode of colles owt of stockwood at xii d the lod viii li[16]

fannars wood
. . . cresy for the carryeng of iiii^{xx}x loodes of colles owt of fannars wood at vii d the lod lii s vi d

Stock wood
. . . cresy for the carr of xii lode of colles owt of Stokwood at xii d the lod xii s

Sum xiii li xiiii s v d

[*33*^{r}] Lond carriage of colles
Wyndars wood
. . . Cresy for the carriage of iiii^{xx}vii loodes of colles owt of wyndars wood at vi d the lod xliii s vi d
. . . Cresy for the carriage of iii^{xx}iii loodes of colles owt of wyndars wood at vi d the lod xxxi s
. . . Cresy for the carriage of xix loodes of colles owt of wyndars wod at vi d the lod ix s vi d
. . . Cresy for the carriage of iii^{xx}ii loodes of colles owt of parke wod at iiii d the lod xx s viii d
xxviii^{vo} november
. . . Cresy for the carriage of xv loodes of colles owt of parke wood at iiii d the lod v s
Sum v li ix s viii d

[*33*^{v}]
Sum huius titli xxxii li iii s vi d

[*34*^{r}–*36*^{v}] *blank*

[*37*^{r}] hepyng of colles
xxvi^{to} maii
. . . John Collyan for the beryng of xxiiii^{ti} lodes of colles into the colle howse at ob the lod xii d
primo June
. . . John Collyan for the beryng of xlviii lodes of colles ii s

16 Originally viii li iii s for vii^{xx} iii lodes.

viii^{vo} June
. . . John Collyan for the hepyng of xxvi loodes of colles at ob the lood xiii d
xxii^{do} June
. . . John Collyan for the hepyng of iii^{xx} lodes of colles at ob the lod ii s vi d
vi^{to} July
John Collyan for the hepyng of xliiii loodes of colls in the coll howse at ob the lood xxii d
Sum viii s v d

[*37*^{v}] hepyng of colles
xx^{mo} July
. . . John Collyan for the hepyng of iiii^{xx}viii loodes of colls at ob the lod iii s viii d
. . . John Collyan for the hepyng of xxii lod of colles at ob the lod xi d
iii^{o} August
. . . him more for the hepyng of xxiiii^{ti} lode of colles at i d the lod ii s
xvii August
. . . John Collyan for the hepyng of iii^{xx}i loodes of colles at i d the lod v s i d
ultimo August
. . . John collyan for the hepyng of xxviii^{ti} loode of colles at i d the lod ii s iiii d
xiii^{o} September
. . . John Collyan for the hepyng of xvii loode of colles at i d the lod xvii d
Sum xv s v d

[*38*^{r}] hepyng of Colles
xxviii^{vo} September
. . . John Collyan for the hepyng of xl loodes of colles in the colle howse at i d the lood iii s iiii d
ii^{do} november
. . . Robart tyrke for the hepyng of xvi lode of colles at i d the lod xvi d
xvi^{do} november
. . . Robart tyrke for the hepyng of xviii lode of colles at i d the lod xviii d
Sum vi s ii d
Sum huius titli xxx s

[38^v–40^v] *blank*

[41^r] dressyng of the bellowes
xxii^{do} february
. . . John Collyan for the corryeng of ii hyddes and dressyng on peer of the fynery bellowes ii s iiii d
xxiii marcii
. . . John Collyan for the dressyng of on peer of the chafery bellowes xx d
xxvi^{to} maii
. . . Peter gelly for the corryeng of iii hyddes xii d
viii^{vo} June
. . . peter gelly for the dressyng of on peer of the fynery bellowes xx d
vi^{to} July
. . . John collyan for the dressyng of on peer of the fynery bellowes xx d
Sum viii s iiii d

[41^v] xxviii^{vo} September
. . . peter gelly for the dressyng of on peer of the fynery bellowes xx d
xvii^{mo} October
. . . John Collyan for the dressyng of the chafery bellowes xx d
vii^{o} december
. . . peter gelly for the dressyng of on peer of the fynery bellowes xx d
Sum v s
Sum huius titli xiii s iiii d

[42^r–^{v}] *blank*

[43^r] Wages and bord wages payd for our lady day quarter
. . . William blacnoll for hys quarters wages dew at our lady day xvi s viii d
. . . more unto hym for hys bordwages videliz from the fyrst day of Januarii unto the xxv^{ti} day of march beying xii wekes at ii s the week xxiiii s
. . . peter gelly for hys quarters wages dew at our lady day v s
. . . Hew marchant for hys quarters wages dew at our lady day v s
Sum l s viii d

[43^v] Wages and Bord Wages payd
iii^{o} June
. . . blacknoll for hys bord wages from the xxv^{ti} day of march

unto the iii^th^ day of June by the space of x weekes at ii s the weke xx s

. . . John Collyan be my masters comandment for that he had no lyvery cott the last yeer vi s viii d

ultimo August

. . . peter gelly be the same comandement ut supra vi s viii d

. . . Audryan dogen ut supra vi s viii d

. . . Hugh marchant be the same comandement ut supra vi s viii d

paid on [ho]lyrod day

. . . Cathers dafter be my masters comandemett for yt hyr hosband shold have ben a denyson and he dyed within the tyme of the sho[ ] of the patentts xxvi s viii d

Sum total iii li xiii s iiii d

[*44^r^*] Wages payd for mydsomer quarter

. . . peter gelly for hys quartars wages dew ut supra v s

. . . hugh marchant for hys quartars wages dew ut supra v s

. . . William Blacknoll for hys quartars wages dew at mydsomer xvi s viii d

Sum xxvi s viii d

[*44^v^*] Wages payd for myghtulmas quartar

. . . peter gelly for hys quartars wages dew at myghtulmas v s

. . . hugh marchant for hys quartars wages dew ut supra v s

. . . william blackinhall for hys quartars wages dew at myghtulmas xvi s viii d

. . . hym more for hys bord wages from the iii^th^ day of June unto the fyrste day of october by the space of xvii weeke at ii s the weke[17] xxxiiii s

Sum iii li viii d

[*45^r^*] Wages payd for Crystonmas quarter

. . . william blacknoll for hys quarters wages dew at crystonmas xvi s viii d

. . . hym more for hys bord wages from the fyrst day of october unto the laste day of december beying xiii wekes and on day at ii s the weke xxvi s iiii d

. . . peter gelly for hys quarters wages dew ut supra v s

ultimo december

. . . hugh marchant for hys quarters wage dew ut supra v s

Sum liii s

Sum huius titli xiii li iiii s iiii d

[*45^v^–47^v^*] *blank*

[17] Originally xxix . . . September.

[*48r*] Lond carriage of yeren

xiimo Januarii

. . . Hawes for the lond carriage of the yeren from the forge to the yeren howse on the pay day[18] xii d

xxvito Januarii

. . . hawes . . . xii d

ixno februarii

. . . hawes . . . xii d

xxiii februarii

. . . hawes . . . xii d

ixno marcii

. . . hawes . . . xii d

Sum v s

[*48v*] Lond carriage

xxiii marcii

. . . hawes . . . xii d

viti Aprilis

. . . hawes . . . xii d

xiii aprilis

. . . hawes . . . xii d

xxvi Aprilis

. . . hawes . . . xii d

ximo maii

. . . hawes . . . xii d

Sum v s

[*49r*] Lond carriage of yeren

xxvito maii

. . . Sharvold . . . xii d

viiivo Junii

. . . Sharvold for the carr of on loode of plankes from the Sawstage to wr follyng ther to make a brydge to carry colles owt of fannars wood iiii d

. . . more to hym for the carr of vi homer helves owt of fannars wood to the forge iiii d

viiivo Junii

. . . Sharvold for the carr of the yeren from the forge to the yeren howse on the pay day xii d

Sum ii s viii d

[*49v*] Lond carriage of yeren

xxiido Junii

[18] The succeeding entries are identical in wording.

. . . Sharvold . . xii d
vi^{to} Julii
. . . Sharvold . . . xii d
xx^{mo} Julii
. . . Sharvold . . . xii d
iii August
. . . Sharvold . . . xii d
xvii^{mo} August
. . . Sharvold . . . xii d
Sum v s

[*50*^{r}] Lond carriage of yeren
ultimo August
. . . John Sharvold . . . xii d
x^{mo} Septembris
. . . for the carryage of on ton of yeren from the forge unto Sir John Bakers beyng viii mylles ii s viii d
xiii september
. . . John Sharvold . . . xii d
xviii^{vo} september
. . . John Sharvold . . . xii d
Sum v s viii d

[*50*^{v}] Lond carriage of yeren
xvii^{o} october
. . . John Sharvold . . . xii d
ii^{do} november
. . . John Sharvold . . . xii d
xvi^{to} . . .
. . . John Sharvold . . . xii d
xxix^{no} . . .
. . . John Sharvold . . . xii d
xiiii^{to} december
. . . John Sharvold . . . xii d
ultimo december
. . . John Sharvold . . . xii d
Sum vi s

[*51*^{r}] Sum huius titli xxix s iiii d

[*51*^{v}–*60*^{v}] *blank*

[*61*^{r}] Laborars in necessary work
xxvi^{to} Januarii

Payd to the forgemen for the new makyng of a horste[19] for to hold the homer helve in the forge — v s

vii^{mo} Aprilis

. . . Hogens for on days labor in helping to way yeren for Mr robartts — viii d

. . . Thomas mascall for on days labor ther ut supra — viii d

. . . Symond Kempe for the cottyng of xx loodes of fyerwood for the workemen in Welhed wod at iiii d the lood cottyng — vi s viii d

xi^{mo} Aprilis

. . . Symond Kempe and to William follyng for the hegyng of xl roddes of hege in fannars wod — iii s iiii d

. . . more unto them for the makyng of on peer of barres in the sayd wood — iiii d

Sum — xvi s viii d

[*61*^{v}] Laborers in necessary works

xi^{mo} Aprilis

. . . Edward Cresy for the toppyng of ix oks and beches on the Synder banke in dodman fyld — vi d

. . . marten Copen for on days labor in mendyng of the carryeng way in folbroke for the carriage of yeren — viii d

. . . wr byne for on days labor in mendyng of the wayes ut supra — viii d

xxii^{do} aprilis

. . . Thomas mascall for on days labor in carryeng owt of yeren owt of the yeren howse and helpyng to lad the wayens — viii d

. . . Stordygat for on days labor in carryeng owt of yeren ut supra — viii d

Sum — iii s ii d

[*62*^{r}] Laborars in necessary work

iii^{o} maii for mr robarts

. . . Thomas Hogens for halfe a days labor in wayeng of yeren for master Robartts — iiii d

. . . Thomas mascall for halfe a days work ut supra — iiii d

. . . Wr follyng for halfe a days worke ut supra — iiii d

. . . Robart tyrke for halfe a days work . . .

. . . godard the fynar for halfe a days work in wayeng of yeren — iiii d

v^{to} maii

. . . Thomas mascall for on days labour in carryeng out of yeren and helpyng to way xx^{ti} tonnes of yeren — viii d

. . . John Whytt for on days labour ut supra — viii d

[19] hurst

. . . Hught marchant for halfe a days labour in wayeng of yeren iiii d
. . . Robart tyrke for halfe a days labor in wayeng of yeren iiii d
Sum iii s viii d

[*62v*] Laborars in necessary worke
. . . Edward cresy for ii days labour in mendyng of the wayes in folbroke wod and in cranam wod for the carryeng of yeren and also mendyng of the wayes in welland for the carriage of colles xvi d
. . . marten copern for ii days labor in the same worke xvi d
ix^no^ maii
. . . wr follyng for ii days labor in the same work ut supra xvi d
. . . nycolas butlar for ii days ut supra xvi d
. . . Thomas mascall for i days worke . . . viii d
. . . John Whyt for ii days worke in brosshyng of the carryeng ways ut supra xvi d
. . . Sharvold for halfe a days labour iiii d
. . . John Shether for ii days labour in makyng of a brydge over the ryver at Stockewood gat and mendyng of the ways in the spryng ther xvi d
. . . Nycolas bottlar for on days labor ther ut supra viii d
Sum ix s viii d

[*63r*] x^o^ maii
. . . Symond Kempe and to Wylliam follyng for the hegyng of iii^xx^x roddes of hege in fannars wood a longes by the lane ther at xii d the skore hegynge iii s vi d
. . . Thomas hogens for hys labour in goynge into Stockwod ther beying on day in the avewyng of the wayes for the carriage of colles vi d
xvi^to^ maii
. . . Thomas fysher for the dyeng of ii elles di of canvas in black coller vi d
. . . Richard Smyth for on days labour in makyng of iii gatts for the carriage of colles owt of Stockwood viii d
xvi^to^ maii
. . . nycolas buttlar for on days work ther ut supra viii d
Sum v s x d

[*63v*] Laborars in necessary worke
xxii^do^ maii
. . . John Shether for the brusshyng of the carryeng way within Stockwood gatte and doyng downe of the banke ther by a bargen mad to hym iii s iiii d

. . . Thomas hogens for on days labour in carryng owt of yeren and helpyng to lade the waynes ther viii d

xxiii° maii

. . . Thomas mascall for on days labour ther ut supra viii d

. . . Thomas Hogens for halfe a days labor in helpyng John collyan to pot on ii yeren hopes of the homer beme iiii d

xxvi^to maii

. . . John Collyan for hys labor in makyng of ii great hopes of yeren for the homer beme and settyng on of them ther xviii d

. . . nycolas butlar for on days labour in makyng of a gatte betwene welhed wod and longeley for the carriage of colles viii d

Sum vii s ii d

[*64r*] Laborars in necessary worke

ii^do June

. . . Rychard Smyth for ii days labor in castyng of a dych in the lane at hodes barren at ix d the day xviii d

. . . nycolas butlar for on days labor ther ut supra viii d

. . . hogens for on days labour in cottyng of dregys of bosshes and thornes to be leed in the sayd lane viii d

. . . nycolas butlar for on days labour ther ut supra viii d

ii^do Julii

. . . Charles marshall for the settyng in of the heddes of ii hogehedde of salte and for iii new hoppes of the sayd salte to be carryed to pensorst iiii d

Sum iii s x d

[*64v*] Laborars in necessary work

ultimo Julii

. . . John Comber for iiii days labor in cottyng of busshes and a mendyng of the carryeng way in the lane at hodes barren for the carryeng of Sowes at viii d the day ii s viii d

viii August

ther beyng my lord [fewaters]

. . . hogens for ii dayes labour in fyshyng of the homer pound be my mr comandment and carryed the fyshe to pensorst xvi d

. . . John Collyan for on days labour ther ut supra vi d

. . . peter gelly for on days labour in makyng of dammes for the stoppyng of the water ther ut supra vi d

. . . Robart tyrk for on days labour ther ut supra vi d

Sum v s vi d

[*65r*] . . . Hugh marchant for hys labour in wayeng of yeren for mr robartts vi d

. . . Robart tyrk for hys labor in wayeng of the sayd yeren vi d

. . . peter gelly for the wayeng of yeren vi d

xxi^{o} August

. . . Hues servannt for hys labour in waying of yeren vi d

. . . Thomas Hogens for the settyng owt of the sayd yeren to the sayd waynes vi d

. . . Thomas mascall for hys labour in beryng owt of the sayd yeren to the waynes vi d

. . . John Collyan for on days labour ther ut supra vi d

Sum iii s vi d

[*65*^{v}] Laborars in necessary worke

xxvi^{to} August

. . . John Collyan for iiii days labor in latheyng dawbyng and makyng of the harth of the chafery chemney iiii s

. . . Robart tyrke for iiii days labor ther in the same worke ut supra iiii s

iii^{o} September

. . . Wylliam follyng for ii days di in making of a gat for fannars wood and mendyng of the hege by the lane syd ther whych was broken by the Collyars xx d

xiii^{o} September

. . . Thomas Hogens for ii days labor in wayeng of yeren and carryeng of yt owt of the howse and ladyng of the wayens xvi d

Thomas mascall for ii days labor ther ut supra xvi d

Sum xii s iiii d

[*66*^{r}] xxvi^{ti} September

. . . Thomas mascall for on days labor in byndying up of latthes that weer broken in the myllhouse viii d

. . . Thomas Hogens for two days labor in helpyng to way xxi^{ti} tones of yeren and carriage owt of the same to the waynes xvi d

xxvii September

. . . Thomas mascall for ii day labour ut supra xvi d

. . . harry Baley for on days labor in wayeng of yeren viii d

ii^{do} October

. . . Thomas Hogens and to T Mascall for on days labor ether of them in mendyng of the carryeng ways in folbrook xvi d

. . . Wr Crefford for v days worke in the amendyng of the way in molton lane and makyng of a brydge at stockwood gat for to carry colles iii s iiii d

. . . John Shether for ii days labor in the amendyng of the for sayd ways to carry colles at viii d the day xvi d

. . . John tooms for ii days labour ut supra xvi d
Sum xi s iiii d

[*66v*] Laborars in necessary work
xvi[ti] october
. . . Thomas mascall for on days labor in carrying owt of xii tonns of yeren to be carryed to the water syd viii d
xvii[o] october
. . . hugh marchant for the repayring of his chemney in the forge with stone and mortar vi d
. . . Stordygat for on days labour in mendyng of the carreng way in follbrocke to carry yeren viii d
. . . Thomas mascall for on days labour in helpyng to lade pavyng tylles at the water syd and delyvered at the place viiii d
xix[no] october
. . . T mascall for on days labor in wayeng of yeren and caryeng of yt owt to the wayens viii d
. . . Thomas mascall for hys labour in helpyng to way vi tonnes of yeren ii d
Sum iii s iiii d

[*67r*] Laborars in necessary work
xvi[to] november
. . . smalfyld for the fellyng and clevyng owt of a C postes for to set a raylle by the ryver syd after the rate of xxv postes to have for hys labor xii d iiii s[20]
xxii[do] november
. . . John Relfe of monfyld for the makyng of a new gatte in monfyld wood for the carriage off Sowes that way viii d
Sum iiii s viii d

[*67v*] Laborars in necessary worke
. . . Thomas Hogens for ii days work videlyz on day in wayeng of yeren and on day in makyng of the wayes in hyled and in downeland for the carryeng of the sayd yeren xvi d
. . . John hynshaw for ii days labor in the forsayd worke ut supra xvi d
. . . John Smyth for on days labour in wayeng of yeren viii d
. . . Thomas mascall for ii days labor in carryeng owt of yeren to the wayens xvi d
. . . nycolas buttlar for on days labour in mendyng of the carryeng ways for the carriage of the sayd yeren viii d
Sum v s iiii d

[20] Originally at xvi d: total v s iiii d.

[*68ʳ*] Laborars in necessary worke

. . . Robart candy for ii days labor in theching of the pryery howse at viii d the day fyndyng hymself xvi d

. . . John Smyth for on days labor in servyng of the sayd thecher viii d

. . . Rychard Smyth for viii days labor in fellyng and clevyng of raylles and settyng of the sayd postes and raylles from Radland brydge to the great bay at the place at viii d the day fyndyng hym selfe v s iiii d

. . . John Smalfyld for viii days labor in the sayd worke v s iiii d

. . . thomas Hogens for iii days di labour on the sayd worke ii s iiii d

. . . Edward byne for iii days labor in the forsayd worke ii s

Sum xvii s

[*68ᵛ*] Laborars in necessary worke

. . . John a thesher for the cottyng of xx lodes of fyerwod in the park wod for the workemen at iiii d the lod cottyng vi s viii d

Item iii lodes carried

ultimo december

. . . Candy for ii days work in thechyng on peter gellys howse xx d

. . . wyllm fellyng for ii days labor in servyng of the sayd thecher xvi d

Sum ix s viii d

Sum huius titli vi li ii s viii d

[*69ʳ–70ᵛ*] *blank*

[*71ʳ*] Empcions

primo februarii

Payd for v quers of paper bought at battell be rychard marten for to make my book at robarttsbrydge xvii d ob

xxii^{do} februarii

. . . John upton for ii platts of yeren to be nayled on the yeren howse dore in the forge wayeng v pound x d

. . . more unto hym for a dobell hoke for the fynery bellowes price v d

xxii^{do} februarii

. . . audryan dogen for iii new colle baskettes at viii d the piece ii s

xii^{mo} marcii

. . . godard fynar for ii new colle baskettes price xvi d

xxix^{mo} marcii

. . . banks of lamberhorst for ii new Ropes for to take down

the roffe of creses howse wayeng xxviii poundde at ii d the lli[21] iiii s viii d
Sum x s viii d ob[22]

[*71*^v^] Empcyons
. . . John Bennett of norbrydge for vi peer of gloves to way yeren for master robartts price xx d
xxvii^mo^ Aprilis
. . . for ii elles di of canvas at ix d the elle xxii d ob
. . . for vi peer of gloves bought at borryshe feer to way yeren xvi d
xxvi^to^ maii
. . . Hugh marchant for a baskett viii d
. . . for a new payle for the colle howse ii d ob
. . . goderd fynar for iiii new colle basketts price ii s viii d
vi^to^ July
. . . John collyan for ii quartts of flower to drest the bellowes at ii sondery tymmes iiii d
. . . for a quart of flower to dresse the bellowes ii d
Sum viii s xi d

[*72*^r^] Empcions
viii^vo^ Julii
. . . John Cok of Pensorst for ii barrels and a halfe of tallowe and grese for the forge at robartts brydge wayeng xxxvi stone at xv d the stone xlv s
. . . Rychard Shether of Stapull crose for on peer of hokes and thymble for a new gatt made besyddes stock wood vi d
. . . peter gelly for on new baskett ix d
. . . for ii hogesheddes to put in bay Salte and was carried to pensort price ii s iiii d
xxviii^o^ September
. . . for a quarte of flowers for to drese the bellowes ii d
Sum xlviii s ix d

[*72*^v^]
xiii^o^ September
. . . hughe marchant for iiii newe colle basketts at ix d the pece iii s
. . . for whyt thred to mend the fysheng netts vi d
xxvi^to^ September
. . . John benett of norbrydge for vi peer of gloves to way yeren at ii d ob the peer xv d

[21] A much amended entry; originally it appears to have been worded 'the roffe by the olde halle . . .' and the weight xliii pounds, with a total of vii s ii d.
[22] An earlier total is illegible.

vii° november
. . . the Smyth of norbrydge for the makyng and steelyng of a new slege for the forge x d
x° november
. . . fylpott for on new henge for a new dore in the forge vii d
viii^vo december
. . . John Sanders of horste for iiii C of weyttes for the thechyng of peter gelles howse at iii d the C xii d
Sum vii s ii d

[*73^r*] Empcions
Payd for ii quere of paper vi d
ix^no december
. . . for iiii peer of new gloves bought at norbrydge at iii d peer to way yeren xii d
Strawe
. . . Thomas Umfery for xxvi heeppe of Whett Strawe to make thathe for peter gelles howse at ii d the hepe iiii s iiii d
. . . for a new flanders pott to macke ynke in[23] i d ob
. . . for a new Shovell bought of the Smyth of norbrydge vii d
Sum vi s vi d ob

[*73^v*] Sum huius titli iiii li ii s i d

[*74^r–75^v*] *blank*

[*76^r*] Land Carriage of Sowes
. . . sclatear of dallyngton for the carryeng of xxi loodes of sowes the laste yeer and was not payd for them untyll thys yeer as Rychard marten ys wytnes unto the same reconyng at xx d the lood carr xxxv s
of this Summ ii s paid to marten for lath ix s to blacnoll for dett ii s vi d[24]
to antony norman for dett xxiii s vi d[24]
. . . Rychard reves for the carr of ii homers and on Andvyld and ii molddes from the fornes to glotyngham beyng in the wynter xxi d
Then he loste on hys oxen[25]
xxix^no marcii
Payd for the carryage of the sayd hamers and andvyld from glotyngham to the forge viii d

[23] A similar flanders pot entry has been crossed out at the head of *73^v*
[24, 25] These entries appear in the left hand margin.

. . . John aweke[26] of nethervyld for the carriage of xxi^{ti} loodes of Sowes to the forge at xx d the lod xxxv s
Sum iii li xii s v d

[*76*^{v}] Lond carriage of Sowes
. . . John Reffe of Monfyld for the carriage of lii loodes of Sowes from the fornes to the forge at xx d the tonn iiii li vi s viii d
. . . Rychard Reffe of monfyld for the carriage of vii loodes of Sowes to the forge xi s viii d
. . . Wylliam Reffs wedow of monfyld for the carriage at xx d the ton xxxiii s iiii d
. . . Thomas pocke of monfyld for the carriage of xx loodes of sowes to the forge at xx d the lod xxxiii s iiii d
Sum viii li v s
Sum huius titli xi li xvii s v d

[*77*^{r}*–*^{v}] *blank*

[*78*^{r}] Land Carriage of yeren
xii^{mo} Januarii
. . . Hawes for the carryeng of the yeren from the forge to the yeren howse on the pay day xii d[27]

[*78*^{v}*–82*^{v}] *blank*

[*83*^{r}] Hepyng of Sowes
vi^{to} July
. . . the workemen for the hepyng of xxviii ton of sowes at i d the ton ii s iiii d
xx^{mo} July
. . . xxxiii loods of sowes at ob the pece ii s ix d
iii^{o} August
. . . xxiiii^{ti} loodes of Sowes at i d the lod ii s
xvii^{mo} August
. . . xvi loods of Sowes at i d the lod xvi d
Sum viii s v d
Sum huius Titli viii s v d

[*83*^{v}*–85*^{v}] *blank*

[*86*^{r}] foren charges
Payd for the amendyng of ii colle baskettes ii d
v^{to} februarii
. . . george marshall for hys labor in goynge from robarttsbrydge to pensorst with v fesantts xii d

26 Reffe was originally entered.
27 Entire entry crossed out.

x^mo^ februarii
. . . peter gelly for hys labor in goynge from socknes fornes to pannyngryge fornes with ii moldes on for the homer and on for the andvyld with the hyer of on horse x d
iii^o^ marcii
. . . Wylliam Hadlow for hys expence in comynge from pensorst to robarttsbrydge and ther beynge v days in sekyng owt of tymber that lyeth in the woode ther and markyng of yt at ix d the day iii s ix d
Sum v s ix d

[*86^v^*] foren charge
xiii^o^ marcii
. . . george marshall for hys labor in carryeng of fysshe to pensorst xiii d
xx^mo^ marcii
Payd my expences in goyng from pensorst to Mr James gage with my masters letter be hys comandement viii d
ultimo marcii
Payd my expences goyng from robartts brydge to pensorste iiii d
vii^mo^ aprilis
. . . John arsfyld and to nycolas bottlar for the carryeng of ii molddes on for a andvyld and the other for the homer from glotyngham to socknes fornes the which weer borrowyd of Mr Welche vi d
xxix^mo^ aprilis
Payd for my expences in goyng to catsfyld ii d
vii^o^ maii
. . . my expences in goyng and comyng from Robartts brydge to london by the space of iiii days ii s
Sum iiii s x d

[*87^r^*] foren charges
xxix^no^ maii
. . . my expences in goyng from robarttsbrydge to dover with my masters letter to master Cockrell for ii tonnes of yeren that was taken with the quens comyssyon by the space of iii days iii s iii d
iii^o^ June
. . . my expences in goyng to pensorst on whytson monday iiii d
xv^to^ July
. . . my expences in rydyng from halden to batell for my soper ther that nyght and my horse mett vi d

. . . my dener and baytyng of my horse the nexte day at apeldore v d
ix^no^ August
. . . the settyng on of iii new Showes of the horse that carryed fysshe from Robartts brydge to penshorst ix d
Sum v s iii d

[*87^v^*] foren Charges
v^to^ August
. . . my expences in goyng and comyng from Robarttsbrydge to pensorst with fryshe water fyshe be my mr comandment viii d
xviii^vo^ August
. . . my expences in Rydyng to Rotam[28] be my mr comandement viii d
. . . my dener and for my horse mett at tonbrydge the same tyme vii d
Sum xxiii d
Sum huius titli xvii s ix d

[*88^r^–93^v^*] *blank*

[*94^r^*] Carpentars
p^mo^ februarii
Payd to Wylliam Hadlow for the fellyng and hewyng of xxxix tonnes of tymber lyeng in folbrock wood tymber wood and in longley sprynge at xiiii d the ton hewyng xlv s vi d
ix^o^ marcii
. . . Thomas Hamond for on days worke in hewyng of a rabett and settyng in of the same in the forge x d
xxiii^o^ maii
. . . Rychard Smyth and to Charles marshall for on day a pece ether of them in the new makyng of a great gate and hangyng of the same with new postes in brarens land at stockwood for the carr of colles xvi d
ii d charles
Sum xlvii s viii d

[*94^v^*] Carpentars
xxv^to^ Maii
. . . John Hamond for ii dayes di workyng at the forge in settyng in off skoppes in the whelles ther and shewyng of ii new rabetts makyng of a new trowe for the fynery and hewyng of a block for the chafery chemney and nayllyng of the borddes over the colle howse at xi d the day ii s iii d ob

[28] Wrotham.

. . . Rychard hamond for ii days di in workenge at the sayd forge ut supra at x d the day ii s i d
xxi^mo August
. . . John Eden Carpenter and to hys man for on days work ether of them in makyng of the chafery chemney xx d
xiiii^to September
. . . John Hamond for on days labor in skopyng of the hamer whell and mendyng of the gogen ther xi d
Sum vi s xi d ob

[*95^r*] Carpentars
xxiii^o november
. . . Thomas Hamond for iiii days working at the forge at sondery tymes as in mendyng of the skopes of the homer whell and of the chafery whell and makyng of ii new dores and nayllyng of xxi new bordes over the forge at x d the day fyndyng hym selfe iii s iiii d
. . . John Hamond and to his servannt for on days work ether of them in the settyng in of vi brasts for to hold up the wall in the forge xviii d
Sum iiii s x d
Sum huius titli lix s v d ob

[*95^v–97^v*] *blank*

[*98^r*] Sawyers
xi^mo marcii
. . . John Comber of youhorst for the Sawyng of vi C fote di of qrt bord and yench bord for the a mendyng of the forge and for skoppes for the whelles at xvi d the C sawyng viii s
. . . the sayd John comber for the makyng of a Sawstage xii d
primo June
. . . John Comber of youhorst for the Sawyng of CC fotte di of plankes for to macke the brydge in follynges land at xvi d the hondred sawyng iii s iiii d
Sum xii s iiii d
Sum huius titli xii s iiii d

[*98^v–100^v*] *blank*

[*101^r*] Lond Carriage
. . . Hawes for the carriage of on lood of bord owt of tymber wood to the forge for reperacions ther vi d
ix^mo marcii
. . . more for the carriage of on rabett owt of welhed wod to the forge ii d

xiii° aprilis

. . . Hawes for the carriage of xx loodes of fyer wood owt of welhed wood to the workemen at iii d the lood carriage vs

. . . sharvold for the carriage of a trowe for the fynery out of parke wod iiii d

xxvi^ti^ maii

. . . more to hym for the carriage of a blocke for the fynery owt of welhed wood ii d

Sum vi s ii d

[*101^v^*] Lond Carr of Synder

viii^mo^ June

. . . John bresenden for the carriage of viii^xx^ iii loodes and of synder and colle duste from the forge and leed yt in the ways to folbrocke gate and in other places at i d the lood xiiii s v d

xxii^do^ June

. . . John besenden for the carriage of vi^xx^ and iii loodes of Synder from the forge and leed yt in the wayes from stone stylle to radland brydge at ii d the lod carriage xx s vi d

viii^vo^ July

. . . Lewes hyckes for on lood carriage of whet and barley from robartts brydge to pensorst viii s

. . . John Smyth for on lood carriage of bay salte and barley to pensorst ut supra viii s

Barlye iiii qrts whet iii qrts mustard seed ii bz baysalt ii hoghedd and a barrell[29]

Sum l s xi d

[*102^r^*] xxix^mo^ July

. . . John Smyth for the carriage of iiii quarters and a halfe of wheat from Robarttsbrydge to pensorst viii s

v^to^ August

. . . Showsmith for the carriage of iii barrells of grest from the towne to the forge iiii d

. . . John Sharvold for the carr of vi loodes of yerthe and on lod of stone to make the chafery chemney at ii d the lod xiiii d

. . . hym more for the carr of on lod of planke to dodman fyld ii d

Sum ix s viii d

[*102^v^*] Lond Carriage

. . . Thomas Clerke for the carr of on lood of pavyng tylles from the oke to Robartsbrydge place xii d

xix^mo^ october

[29] Note in left hand margin.

. . . John brestenden for the carryeng of ii loodes of the forsayd tylles ii s
. . . Showsmyth for the carriage of ii loode of the sayd pavyng tylles ii s
. . . John Smyth for the carriage of CCC of pavyng tylles that was lefte at the water syd beyng many of them broken viii d
xxix^no^ november
Payd for the carryeng of a homer helve owt of cortens wood to the forge ii d
Payd for the carriage of ii rabettes and on homer helve owt of tylloste wood to the forge vi d
Sum vi s iiii d

[*103^r^*] Lond Carriage
. . . thomas shusmyth for the carryeng of ii lodes of the sayd wheetstraw from the parsonage barne to the forge xvi d
Payd more to hym for the carryeng of ii lodes of fyerwod owt of park wod to the forge for the workmen ther xii d
Payd more to hym for on days carriage of postes and raylles owt of park wod to radland walle ii s
. . . John brestenden for the carriage of ii lodes of the forsayd whett straw to the forge xvi d
. . . hym more for on days carriage of postes and raylles owt of park wod to the radland walle ii s
Sum vii s viii d
Sum huius titli iiii li ix d

[*103^v^–104^v^*] *blank*

[*105^r^*] Laborars workyng in water work
. . . marten copen for viii days workyng in mendyng of the hamer pound wall and castyng of a dychych to the same wall v s iiii d
. . . Edward cresy for vi days workyng ther on the sayd wall iiii s
v^to^ maii
. . . Atkenson for on days labor in cottyng of weeddes in the homer dych viii d
. . . Thomas hogens for ii days labour in the amendyng of radland bay xvi d
. . . John comber for iii days ut supra ii s
. . . thomas mascall for on days labour ther ut supra viii d
. . . byne for on days labour ther ut supra viii d
Sum xiiii s viii d

[*105v*] Laborars workyng in water worke

. . . Thomas Hogens for on days labor in cottyng of the weddes in the homer dych viii d

. . . John comber for on days Labour ther ut supra viii d

. . . Thomas Hogens for on days labour in cottyng of the weddes in the homer dyche beyng in the water ix d

. . . Thomas mascall for on days labour ther ut supra ix d

vi^to Junii

. . . stordygat for on days labout ther beyng in the water ut supra ix d

. . . John Crefford for on days labour ther ut supra ix d

. . . nycolas botlar for on days labour ther in the water ix d

. . . marten copen for on days labour ther in the water ix d

Sum v s x d

[*106r*] Water Worke

. . . Thomas hogens for on days labour in makyng of a dame to stope the water in bakars medow[30] ix d

viii^vo June

. . . Stordygatt for on days labour ther ut supra ix d

. . . John crefford for on days labour ther ut supra ix d

. . . Stordygatt for iii days labour in cuttyng of the wedes in the ryver from the baye to radland brydge and from thens to norbrydge ii s

. . . John Crefford for iii days labour ther ut supra ii s

. . . the pollyng owt of the weddes owt of the ryver at the bay on day ther viii d

Sum vi s xi d

[*106v*] Water Worke

xv^to July

. . . Thomas Hogens for ii days labor in makyng of a wall over the dyche in clerke medow at the end of the homer wall xvi d

. . . John comber for iiii days labour in cottyng of the sydde of the homer ryver wheras the grase dyd grow ther in the water at ix d the day iii s

. . . Robart tyrke for iii days labour ther ut supra ii s iii d

xxix^no July

. . . nycolas butlar for iii days labour ther at ix d the day ut supra ii s iii d

. . . Thomas mascall for halfe a days labour iiii d ob

. . . John collyan for on days labor ther ut supra ix d

Sum ix s xi d ob

[30] normans medow crossed out in the original.

[*107*^{r}] water worke
. . . Thomas Hogens for halfe a days worke in the amendyng of the wall at Radland bay iiii d
xviii^{mo} November
. . . Stordygat for halfe a days labour ther ut supra iiii d
. . . John a thessher for halfe a days labour ther ut supra iiii d
Sum xii d
Sum huius titli xxxviii s iiii d ob

[*107*^{v}–*127*^{v}] *blank*

[*128*^{r}] Naylles bought
. . . fylpott fot iiii C of vi d naylles ii s
xxx^{mo} marcii
. . . for iiii C of v d naylles xx d
. . . more for iiii C of iiii d naylles xvi d
. . . more to hym for the mendyng of a kay for the yeren howse dore in the forge ii d
. . . to fylpott for xviii naylles for to amend the chafery wheel i d
xxvii^{mo} July
. . . fylpott for CC of dobell x d naylles at xx d the C iii s iiii d
Sum viii s vii d

[*128*^{v}] Naylles bought
. . . fylpott for iii C of ii d nayles for the new latheng of the chafery chemney vi d
xxi^{mo} August
. . . hym more for C di of iii d nayles iiii d ob
. . . more to hym for CC of ii d nayls iiii d
x^{o} november
. . . fylpott for CC of iiii d naylles for to make a new dore in the forge and nayllyng of the bordes over the forge viii d
vii^{o} december
. . . more to hym for C of v d nayles v d
Sum ii s iii d ob
Sum huius titli x s x d ob

[*129*^{r}–*132*^{r}] *blank*

[*132*^{v}] 1555
(MS damaged) Md receved of Edmond Robartts of hawkhurst the xix day of october v M of pavyng tylles of hym bought be my mr Sir Henry Sydney Knyght at (*blank*) the thousand
[*133*$^{r–v}$] *blank*

[12] SUMMARY ACCOUNT FOR PANNINGRIDGE FURNACE AND ROBERTSBRIDGE FORGE, 1555

378/7 *U 1475 B3/7*

[*1ʳ*] Robertsbridge
The declaracon of the Iorne mynes there the ii[de]
and iii[de] yere of the regne of kyng phelyp
and quene mary anni phi and marie ii[de] and iii[tio]

[*1ᵛ*] *blank*

[*2ʳ*] A declaracon of accompte of William Blackenall Clarke of the Iorne Workes to the Ryght Worshipfull Sir Henry Sydney Knyght at his mannor of Robertsbridge in the Countye of Sussex aswell of all and synguler suche sommes of money by hym receyvyd as also all suche somes of money by the seyd William Imployd to the use of the seyd Sir Henry from the feast of the Nativity of our lord god in the fryste and seconde yere of the raynes of our sovereigne lorde and lady Kynge phelypp and quene mary untyll the same feaste of the Nativity of our lorde god then nexte ensuyng in the seconde and iii[de] yere of ther gracius Rayne that is for one hole yere ut inferius per

fryste he is charged with tharragiis of his last accompte as it appereth in the foote of the same xxx li xii s iii d q

Item he is charged with suche money as he hath receyvyd of John hawes Receyvor of the issues of his office hoc anno as it appereth by a boke of Recepte upon this declaracon showed and examyned CCClxxiiii li xviii s q

Item he is charged with money receyvyd of John Thomas as it appereth by the seyd boke xx li

Item he hath receyvyd of adryon dogen for frannces langley & [ ] langley for money owyng to my master by them lx s

[*2ᵛ*] Item he hath receyvyd of George Colefelde for one ton of Iorne solde to hym in anno primo Regni Regine marie vi li vi s viii d

Item he hath receyvyd of George Cooke for his dette of the parsonage of Salehurste dew at michelmas anno primo marie lxiiii s

Item he hath receyvyd for xiii ton xii^C^lv lli of Iorne solde ther hoc anno as the particelles doth appere by a boke therof upon this declaracon showed and examyned Cx li xviii s vii d
Item he hath receyvyd for woodde solde there hoc anno as it appereth by the seyd boke xi li ix s viii d

Sum totall of all the receptes foreseyd with arrears Dlx li ix s ii d ob

wherof

[3^r^] layd oute at Robertsbridge
In primis for Cuttynge of MMDCCxxiiii cordes and di of woodd at divers prises as it appereth by a boke therof showed and upon this declaracon examined xxxviii li xvi s viii d
Item payd to the hamermen and fyners for the makyng of Clxvi ton xii^C^ of Iorne at xiii s iiii d le ton with xi s vi d for the fyning of one ton di and iiii^C^ of olde Iorne more than is above spesified at iiii d le C Cxi li xvi s x d
. . . for the colyng of ix^C^xxi lodes of Coles as it appereth by the seyd boke lvii li xi s iii d
. . . for the caryng of ix^C^xxi lodes of Coles at divers prises ut per dictum librum xxii li iii s vi d
. . . for hepyng of Coles hoc anno xxx s
. . . for the dressyng of the belowes xiii s iiii d
. . . for Servantes wages and borde wages ther hoc anno . . . xiii li iiii s iiii d
. . . for the londe cariage of Iorne hoc anno . . . xxix s iiii d
. . . to laborers in necessarye busynes hoc anno . . . vi li ii s viii d
. . . in empcions for certen necessaries for the forge hoc anno iiii li ii s i d
. . . for the londe cariage of Sowes hoc anno . . . xi li xvii s v d

[3^v^] . . . for hepyng of sowes ther hoc anno . . . viii s v d
. . . in foren charges ther hoc anno . . . xvii s ix d
. . . to Kerpentters in workyng abowte the forge and for hewyng of xxxix ton of tymber . . . lix s v d ob
. . . to the sawyers for sawyng of bordes for the forge and for plankes for bridges hoc anno . . . xii s iiii d
. . . for the londe cariage of Serten neccessaries at Robertsbridge as also to pensehurste hoc anno . . . iiii li ix d
. . . to laborers in workyng of water worke aboute the forge hoc anno . . . xxxviii s iiii d ob
. . . for nayles bought there hoc anno . . . x s x d ob

Sum of all the paymentes foreseyd at Robertsbridge
CCiii^{xx}x li xv s iiii d ob

[*4*^{r}] And at pannyngridge
. . . for the Cuttyng of iii^{M}iii^{C}liii lodes of woodde at divers prices as it appereth by a boke therof upon this declaracon showed and examyned[1] lv li xix s xi d ob
. . . for the Colyng of Diiii^{xx}xiii lodes of Coles at divers prises . . . xxxix li x s viii d
. . . for the Caryng of vii^{C}viii lodes of Coles hoc anno . . .[2]
xxvi li xix s vi d
. . . to the fownder and fyller for xxii foundes and v dayes with the makyng of annderns and andevyles hoc anno . . .[3]
xvii li viii d
. . . for the castyng of vii^{C}lxx of smale lodes of myne at ix d the lode ut . . . xxviii li xvii s vi d
. . . for the carragine of DCxvii great lodes of myne at divers prises . . .[4] xii li xvii s i d
. . . for necessaries bought for furnes hoc anno . . . vii li xiiii s x d
. . . to laborers for the repayng of the furnes and other necessaries there hoc anno . . .[5] Cii s iii d
. . . for the rente of the woode tythe of the furnes wages and bord wages of marten and libtie Thowrow mennes grownde hoc anno . . . xxxiii li xx d

[*4*^{v}] Item in Expenses in goynge to pannyngridge at divers tymes as it appereth by the seyd boke iii s ix d
Sum of all the paymentes at pannyngridge foreseyd
CCxxvii li vii s x d ob

[1] In Glyde Wood and Snowe's Land, cut by two men only (382/6: B10/8).

[2] Some charcoal came from 'Mr. Ashburnham's land' despite the existence of his own furnace.

[3] The furnace was little used in 1555. The previous year's campaign ended on March 3rd. Charles Pulleyn was paid on April 17th for re-building the hearth and casting 6 hammers and 3 anvils, but full working only began about October 1st, running until April 18th, although a new hearth was built on December 26th.

[4] Pits on 'Snowe's land' were used, and Walter Snowe undertook the carriage 'from his own wood'.

[5] There seems to have been flood damage in the autumn: the Furnace Book has payments for the purchase of 800 bricks to repair the furnace walls, carriage of cinder, and of stone from Penhurst Quarry for the same purpose. A new charging bridge was built, the penthouse over the furnace re-boarded, and the floodgates repaired: the cause is indicated by a payment 'clensing and making clene of the Furnace by the reason of the flood'.

[*5^r^*] Sum totall of all thallownnces and paymentes aforeseyd
Dxviii li iii s iii d
and so oweth xlii li v s xi d ob

[*5^v^*] The Remaynes aswell at Robertsbridge as at pannyngridge hoc anno viz at
Robertsbridge
Cordes of wodde ther In primis the remayne anno per pced
Miii^{C}lxxiii cordes and di
Item made ther hoc anno MMvii^{C}xxiiii cordes di
Sum of all the cordes iiii^{M}iiii^{xx}xviii cordes wherof spente hoc anno MMvii^{C}vi cordes and so remayneth Miiii^{C}iiii^{xx}xii cordes

Coles ther Item the remain . . . D lodes
Item made ther hoc anno in lodes ix^{C}xxi
Sum of all the lodes Miiii^{C}xxi^{ti} wherof spente hoc anno ix^{C}lxxi lodes and so remain in lodes at storehowse iiii^{C}l

myne Item the remain . . . C lodes
Item carried hoc anno nil
Sum of all the lodes of myne C which remain

[*6^r^*] Sowes ther Item there is in sowes by tale CCxxxv
and pannyngridge Item in sowes ther by estymacon iiii^{C}xxxviii
Sum of all the sowes DClxxiii

The accompte of Iorne Item the remayne . . . xviii ton v^{C}lxvi lli
Item ther hoc anno made Clxvi ton xii^{C}
Sum of all the tonnes Ciiii^{xx}iiii ton xvii^{C}lxvi lli, wherof solde hoc anno by the seyd William Blackenall as it appere by the boke of Receptes upon this accompte showed and examyned xiii ton xii^{C}lv lli, and delyverd to the forge hoc anno as it appereth by the seyd boke v^{C}iiii lli, and delyverd to mr Roberts at divers tymes at my master his comandement viz prima vice vii^{mo} die april xxi ton, ii^{da} vice quinto die may xxi ton, iii^{tia} vice xx^{mo} die may xxi ton, iiii^{ta} vice xiii^{o} die augusti xiii ton, v^{ta} vice xiii^{o} die december xvi ton, vi^{ta} vice primo die october xxi ton, vii^{ma} vice xvi^{o} die october xii ton xii c iii qrts iiii lli, eodem die vi ton ii^{C}iii qrts v lli, viii^{va} vice ix^{o} die september xxiiii ton, eodem die iiii ton iiii^{C}xlvii lli, ultoto [ ] libru dicta William Blackenall super hunc comp examinat Clx ton, and so remain xi ton vii lli, tunc remain in the store howse prima die January anno ii^{do} and iii^{tio} Regna Philip and marie xiiii ton ix^{C} di
ther is gayned in the wayte hoc anno iii ton ix^{C} xlix lli

[*6^v^*] pannyngridge
Cordes of woode ther Item the remain anno per pceden Dlxxvi

Item made ther hoc anno MMMiii^{C}liii cordes
Sum of all the cordes iii^{M}ix^{C}xxix wherof spente hoc anno MMiiii^{C} cordes and so remain Mix^{C}xxv cordes

lodes of coles Item the remain . . . iiii^{C}xx
Item made ther hoc anno vii^{C}viii
Sum of all the lodes MCxxviii wherof spente hoc anno vii^{C}lxviii lodes and so remain iii^{C}lx

lodes of myne Item the remain . . . viii^{C}l lodes
Item caste and caried hoc anno vii^{C}lxx
Sum of all the lodes of myne Mvi^{C}xx wherof spent hoc anno vi^{C}xx and so remain M lodes

[*7^{r}–7^{v}*] *blank*

[*8^{r}*] The remayne of the Stoke at Robertsbridge and pannyngridge the xxi^{ti} day of december anno predicto
pannyngridge
In primis Mix^{C}xxv cordes of woode ther at vi d the corde xlviii li ii s vi d
Item in lodes of Coles CCClx at v s the lode iiii^{xx}x li
Item in lodes of myne M at xii d l li

Robertsbridge
Item in cordes of wood there Miii^{C}iiii^{xx}xii at vi d the corde xxxiiii li xvi s
Item in lodes of Coles ther CCCCl at v s the lode Cxii li x s
Item in lodes of myne ther C at x d iiii li iii s iiii d
Item in Sowes ther CCxxxv
Item in sowes at pannyngridge iiii^{C}xxxviii } vi^{C}lxxiii at xxvi s viii d DCCCiiii^{xx}xvii li vi s viii d
Item in the store howse of Iorne xiii ton ix^{C} di at viii li le ton Cxv li xvi s iiii d
Sum totall of all the remayne foreseyd Miiii^{C}lii xiiii s x d

[*8^{v}*] A declaracon of the clere gayne of the Iorne workes foreseyd dicto anno ii^{do} and iii^{tio} regno phi and marie
In primis the price of of Clxx ton i C xlix lli of Iorne made there hoc anno at vii li x s le ton MCClxxv li ix s
Item incressed in the stoke of woode Coles sowes and myne hoc anno nil
Sum of all the Incresse and gayne anno predicto MCClxxv li ix s, wherof to be abated of Dxviii li iii s iii d for money payd in divers

Kyndes of the seyd worke hoc anno as the particelles doth appere in a boke therof made and examined, and also to be abated of CCCxl li iiii s iii d whiche is spente oute of the stoke there hoc anno as it appereth by accompte of the same, and so remayneth clere gayned hoc anno CCCCxvii li xviii s

[*9r–10v*] *blank*

[13] SUMMARY ACCOUNT FOR PANNINGRIDGE FURNACE AND ROBERTSBRIDGE FORGE, 1556

378/8 *U 1475 B3/8*

[*1r*] Robertsbridge The declaracon of the Iorne mynes there the iii[de] and iiii[th] yere of the rignes of kyng phelypp and quene mary. Ann[i] rign[ ] phi and marie iii[tio] and iiii[to]

[*1v*] *blank*

[*2r*] A declaracon of accompte of william Blackenall Clarke of the Iorne Workes to the Ryght Worshipfull Sir Henry Sydney Knyght at his mannor of Robertsbridge in the Countye of Sussex. Aswell of all and Singuler suche sommes of money by hym receyvyd as also suche somes of money by the seyd William Imploied to the use of the seyd Sir Henry from the feaste of the Nativity of our lorde god in the seconde and iii[de] yere of the raynes of our souvereigne lorde and lady Kyng phelyp and quene mary Untyll the same feaste of the Nativitie of our lorde god then nexte ensuyng in the iii[de] and iiii[th] yere of ther graces Rayne that is for one hole yere ut inferius per

fryste he is charged with tharraragiis of his laste accompte as it appereth in the fote of the same xlii li v s xi d ob

Item he is charged with suche money as he hath receyved of John hawes Receyvor of the Issues of his officie hoc anno as it apperethe by a boke of Recepte upon this declaracon showed and examined CCClxxii li viii s iii d ob

. . . with money receyved of George Cooke Collector of the parsonage of Salehurste as yt appereth by the seyd boke xii li

Item he hath receyvyd of John Thomas at ii tymes . . . xx li

. . . for xi ton xix[C] iii quarters and xxvi lli of new Iorne solde ther hoc anno as the particelles doth appere by the seyd boke[1] . . . iiii[xx]xix li xiiii s xi d ob

. . . for x[C] of olde Iorne solde hoc anno ut per dictum librum lxx s viii d

[*2v*] . . . for one plate solde hoc anno . . . iiii s

[1] This total is made up of sales to smiths from surrounding villages, although Gebens, of Rye, who took 6½ tons, seems to have been working on a larger scale. Deliveries of larger quantities to Edmund Roberts of Hawkhurst and Mr. Clerk, ironmonger of London, are listed, but payment for these would go straight to the Receiver. (381/2: B8/8.)

. . . for olde tymber stone and woodde solde there this yere as it appereth by the seyd boke lxi s iiii d

Sum totall of all the receptes foreseyd and arrears Dliii li v s ii d ob

wherof

[3r] layde oute at Robertsbridge

In primis for Cuttynge of MMCCx cordes di of woodde at divers prises as it appereth by a boke therof showed and upon this declaracon examined[2] xxxii li xix s ix d ob

Item payd to the hamermen and fyners for the makyng of vi^xx^vi ton xvii^C iii quarters of Iorne at xiii s iiii d le ton with iiii s geven in Rewarde for the fynyng of Serten olde Iorne as it appereth by the seyd boke[3] iiii^xx^iiii li xvi s

. . . for the colyng of Mxxxii lodes of coles at xvi d the lode[4] lxviii li xvi s

. . . for the caryng of Mxxxii lodes of coles at diverse prises ut per eundem librum[5] xxxvii li xvi d

. . . for the hepyng of coles hoc anno lxi s iiii d q

. . . for the dressyng of the belowes hoc anno xii s

. . . for wages and borde wages ther hoc anno ut per dictum librum xi li ix s

. . . for the londe cariage of Iorne hoc anno ut per eundem librum vi li x s x d

. . . for the water cariage of Iorne[6] hoc anno ut per dictum librum iiii li x s iiii d

. . . to laborers in neccessary busines[7] . . . vii li x s ix d ob

. . . to laborers in water worke . . . iiii li xix s ix d ob

[2] The woodcutting entries in the Forge Book (381/2) are of interest in that they show concentration, probably 3 woods, and a long period when no payments were made (May 6th–December 19th); there is no sign of a backlog of payments on the latter date. The make-up of the labour force differs little from earlier years.

[3] John Collins operated the hammer throughout.

[4] Charcoal burning was done over a short season in 1556; payments run from May 16th to September 13th.

[5] In 381/2 (B8/8) the rates were: Parke Wood 4d, Great Morgay 9d, Stockwood 1s per load.

[6] It is clear from 381/2 that this includes Edmund Roberts' purchases, which were carried by lighter to Rye.

[7] References in 381/2 suggest considerable replacement of timber structures at the forge, with the dismantling in September of the hammer beam and wheel and the chafery wheel and 'much other work', occupying 20 man-days. The carpenters' accounts contain further references to this work: 2 carpenters spent 15 days each setting up new timbers.

. . . for neccessaries bought for the forge . . . vi li ix s vi d

. . . for the lande cariagine of sowes hoc anno ut per eundem librum xxv li vi s vii d ob

. . . for the hepyng of sowes hoc anno xxiii s i d

. . . in foren charges hoc anno ut dictum librum C s ix d

[*3*^v] . . . to the kerpentters in workyng aswell aboute the forge as also in makyng the great bay standyng at the gate[8] ut per dictum librum vii li viii s iiii d

. . . for cariage of serten neccessaries there hoc anno . . . lviii s vi d

. . . for nayles and other Iorne bought ther hoc anno . . . xxiii s viii d

. . . for Thechyng ther hoc anno iiii s ii d

. . . to the Sawyers for sawyng divers neccessaries bothe for the forge as also for the greate bay and for the stable . . . lxix s x d

Sum of all the paymentes foreseyd at Robertsbridge CCCxv li xi s viii d q

[*4*^r] and at pannyngridge

Item payd for the Cuttynge of MCxxxvi cordes of wood at divers prices hoc anno as it appereth by a boke therof upon this declaracon showed and examyned xxi li xvi s iiii d

. . . for the Colyng of DClxii lodes of Coles at divers prises hoc anno as it appereth by the seyd boke[9] liiii li xiiii s x d

. . . for caryng of DCCiiii lodes of Coles at divers prises[10] hoc anno ut per dictum librum xxi li x s vi d

. . . to the founder and fyller for xxii^ti foundes and ii dayes with v s for the makyng of a newe hathe[11] . . . xvi li vi d

. . . for the rente of the woode tythe of the furnes wages and borde wages and libertie thorowe mennes grownde hoc anno . . . xxxiii li viii s ii d

. . . for neccessaries bought for the furnes hoc anno with serten myne bought and woodde . . . xxvii li xv s v d ob

. . . to laborers in neccessarie besynes ther hoc anno . . . xii s iiii d

. . . in foren charges this yere that ys in Expenses at pannyng-

[8] Repairs to the Great Bay(dam) in July took 71 man-days.

[9] Five colliers are recorded in 382/7 (B10/9), none working consistently over the year, probably a reflection of a widening local demand for charcoal with the construction of Ashburnham furnace, which was first mentioned in 1555.

[10] The carriage entries also suggest the need to take up any available supply, for charcoal was brought from 8 woods, more than in any other year, and the highest charge yet (1s 2d) is recorded.

[11] The furnace was again under-used, being blown out on April 18th, not to work again until December 6th.

ridge and for martens expenses comyng to London at divers tymes to knowe my master pleasure . . . xxvi s ii d

[4^{v}] . . . for castyng of MC smale lodes of myne at ix d the lode . . . xli li v s

. . . for the cariage of DCCiiii^{xx}ix greate lodes of myne hoc anno . . . super hunc comp examnat xvi li viii s ix d

Sum of all the paymentes at pannyngridge aforeseyd CCxxxiiii li xviii s ob

[5^{r}] Sum of all thallowances and paymentes foreseyd Dl li ix s viii d ob q

and so oweth lv s v d ob q

[5^{v}] The remaynes aswell at Robertsbridge as at pannyngridge hoc anno viz at Robertsbridge

Cordes of woode there

in primis the remayne anno p[er] preceden Miii^{C}iiii^{xx}cii cordes

Item made ther hoc anno MMCCx cordes di

Sum of all the cordes iii^{M}DCii cordes di wherof spent hoc anno iii^{M}Cxxi corde and so remayneth iiii^{C}iiii^{xx}i and di

Coles there Item the remayne . . . iiii^{C}l lodes

Item made ther hoc anno Mxxxii lodes

Sum of all the lodes Miiii^{C}iiii^{xx}ii lodes wherof spente hoc anno viii^{C}iiii^{xx}ii lodes and so remain vi^{C} lodes

myne there Item the remain . . . C lodes

Item caried hoc anno nil

Sum of all the lodes of myne C which remain

[6^{r}] Sowes ther and pannyngridge } Item there is in sowes by tale iiii^{C}li
Item in sowes there by tale Ciii

Sum of all the sowes Dliiii

The accompte of Iorne Item the remayne xiiii ton ix^{C} di

Item made there hoc anno Cxxvi ton xvii^{C} and iii qtrs

Sum of all the tonnes Cxli ton vii^{C} qrt wherof solde hoc anno by the seyd William Blackenall as it appereth by his boke of receptes upon this declaracon showed and examyned xi ton xix^{C}iii qrts and xxvi lli and delyverd to diverse persons within the tyme of this accompte viz prima vice xii^{mo} die february to mr Roberts xxv ton ii^{da} vice xvi^{mo} die martii to mr Clarke xx ton iii^{tia} vice xvi^{to} die martii to mr Roberts iii ton iiii^{ta} vice xi^{de} die April to mr Roberts x ton v^{to} vice viii^{vo} die July to mr Roberts xx ton vi^{ta} vice ultima die october to mr Roberts xxi ton and vii^ma^ vice vi^to^ die december to mr Roberts xx ton in toto p[ ] per librum predictum Cxix ton and also delyvered to the forge and other plases as it appereth by the seyd boke vii^C^ and one qrt and so remain x ton xxx lli tunc remain in the Storehouse primo die january anno iii^tio^ Rigno p[ ] philip and marie xi ton i C di

And so gayned in the wayte hoc anno i ton i C and xxvi lli

[*6^v^*] pannyngridge

cordes of woodde there   Item the remaine anno p[er] preceden Mix^C^xxv

Item made there hoc anno MCxxxvi cordes

Sum of all the cordes iii^M^lxi corde wherof spente hoc anno Mviii^C^xxxi cordes and remain xii^C^xxx cordes

lodes of Coles   Item the remain . . . CCClx

Item made there hoc anno DCClxii

Sum of all the lodes MCxxii wherof spente hoc anno DCxxii and so remain D lodes

lodes of myne   Item the remain . . . M lodes

Item caste and caried hoc anno MC lodes

Sum of all the lodes of myne MMC wherof spente hoc anno M and so remain MC

[*7^r^*] *blank*

[*7^v^*] *blank*

[*8^r^*] The Remayne of the Stoke at Robertsbridge and pannyngridge the xxi^ti^ day of december anno predicto

pannyngridge In primis MCCxxx cordes of woodde there at vi d the corde xxx li xv s

Item in lodes of Coles D at v s the lode Cxxv li

Item in lodes of myne MC at xii d the lode lv li

Robertsbridge   Item in cordes of woode ther iiii^C^iiii^xx^i corde and di at vi d the corde xii li ix d

Item in lodes of coles there DC at v s the lode Cl li

Item in lodes of myne ther C at x d the lode iiii li iii s iiii d

Item in sowes ther iiii^C^ li }Dliiii at xxvi s
Item in sowes at pannyngridge Ciii } viii d the sowe
DCCCxxxviii li xiii s iiii d

Item in the store howse of Iorne xi ton i C di at viii li le ton iiii^xx^viii li xii s

Sum totall of all the Remayne foreseyd MCCiiii li iiii s v d

[*8v*] A declaracon of the clere gayne of the Iorne workes foreseyd dicto Anno iii^{tio} and iiii^{to} rigno p[ ] phi and marie

In primis in the price of Cxxvi ton xvii^{C} iii qrts of Iorne made ther hoc anno at vii li x s le ton DCCCClii li ii s

Item incressed in the stoke of woode Coles sowes and myne hoc anno nil

Sum of all the Increse or gayne anno predicto DCCCClii li ii s wherof to be abated of Dl li ix s viii d ob q for money payd in divers kyndes of the seyd workes hoc anno as the particelles dothe appere in a boke therof made and examyned And also to be abated of Cxlviii li x s v d whiche is spente oute of the Stoke ther hoc anno as it appereth by accompte of the same and so remayneth clere gayned hoc anno CCliii li xxii d q

[14] SUMMARY ACCOUNT FOR PANNINGRIDGE FURNACE AND ROBERTSBRIDGE FORGE, 1558

378/9 *U 1475 B3/9*

[*1r*] Robertsbridge et Pannyngridge The declaracion of the Iron works and myne there for one hole yere ended at the feaste of the nativitie of our lord god in the yere of the reigne of our Soveraigne Ladie Qwene Elizabeth the first[1]

[*1v*] *blank*

[*2r*] A declaracion of Accompte of William Blacknall Clerk of the workes to the right worshipfull Sir Henry Sydney knight at his manor of Robertsbridge in the countie of Sussex aswell of all and Singler soche Somes of money by him Receyved As also of all soche Somes of moneye by the seid william imployed to thuse of the seid Sir Henrye his master from the feaste of the natyvitie of our Lord god in the iiii[th] and v[th] yeres of the reygnes of Kynge Phylypp and Qwene marye untill the seid feaste of the nativitie of our Lord god in the first yere of the Reigne of our Soveraigne Ladie Elizabeth by the grace of god of England frannce and Ireland Qwene Defendor of the faythe etc That is to say for one hole yere.

first he is charged with tharrerages of his last accompt as appeareth in the fote of the same	xxxii li iii s v d ob q
And for the price of wood by him solld oute of fulham wood and Ebdens wood as by his booke appereth besydes v lodes asshe price xx s owynge by cypryane ferely	xvii s viii d
And for xvii lodes of olde Stone of the walls solld to dyverse persons at dyverse prices	xv s
And for the price of xxii Tonn Iron xiiii c iii quarters by him solld and delivered at diverse prices from the ii[de] of Januarye Anno 1557 untill the xiii[th] of decembre Anno 1558	Clxix li xvii d ob
And for money by him receyved of Mr John Thomas the ii[de] of Februarye Anno 1557	xx li
. . . of John Hawes receyvor at Diverse tymes within this accompte of thissues of his Office	iii[C]lviii li xix s vii d ob
. . . of Mr Carrells Servant xx[mo] Septembris Anno 1558	xiii s iiii d

[1] This account is in a hand not previously seen.

[*2v*] .... of the proffits of the Corne mill there this yere remaining in the Lords hands vii li xi d

Sum of Thole chardge Clxxxix li xi s v d ob q

Payments made by the seid William Blacknall within the tyme of this Accompte

Robertsbridge viz[2]

Woodmakers for Cuttinge of ii^M^ii^C^iiii^xx^vii cords wood di felled and cut there at diverse prices with toppinge of certen Okes Ryvynge of logges as by the booke of payments appeareth at Lardge with x d for taling of wood xxxv li xv s xi d ob qu

Colliers for Colinge of vi^C^lxviii lodes coles at xvi d every lod except one lod xx d with ii s for carynge of ii dusts as by the said boke appeareth xliiii li xiii s

Cariage of The said Coles by land in waynes at diverse prices to the colehouse with xxxvi s xi d paid for repairinge the waynes besides lxvi lib Iron bestowed upon the said waynes as by the boke appeareth xxiii li ix s xi d

heapinge of coles viz Caryinge of Dxxx lodes coles and layinge them in howse beneth the beames at ob qu the lode as above i d qu xlvi s v d qu

[*3r*] Wood bought Mr morgayn xii li x s besides iii^C^ cords paid by John hawes iii^rd^ February Anno 1557 and besides xvi li paid by the seid John to Richard Shetter and William his Sonne and John Ebden iii^C^ cords as by the seid booke appereth xii li x s

Chardges of the Sowes Caryinge of Ciiii^xx^ii Ton from the furnes to the forge at xx d the Ton xv li iii s iiii d and of Clxii Ton xxxiii s iiii d with iii s iiii d for the Tale makinge xvii li

Iron makers viz to The hammermen and fyners for makynge of Cxxviii Tonns xvii C di Iron at xiii s iiii d the Ton iiii^xx^v li xviii s iiii d

Chardges of the Iron betwene the makinge and delyvery viz for Cariage of all the seid Iron made this yere from the fordge to the Iron house, viz by land Cv ton or lods and by watter vi ton, vi li ii s vi d, cariage to the watter iiii s viii d, wainge Iron with xviii d ob for breade and drynke to the laborers xi s x d ob, bearinge Iron to the waynes ix s viii d

[2] No Forge Book survives.

xxxiiii paire of gloves gyven to the Iron weyers vii s i d, with a lock and ii hooks for the bote x d, as by the seid booke appeareth viii li xvi s vi d ob

fierbote for the workmen Cariage of iiii^xx^xv lodes wood delyvered the seid workemen for there harthe to burne with there Coles the yere xxxi s ob

Repairinge the forgehouse and cokhouse with the appertenances in Setting up a new Tymbre chimney, repairinge the forgehouse forge wheles and stertes and the colehouse vi li xiiii s xi d, ii hides for the bellowes xxii s and repairinge the same xviii s i d and diverse necessaries bowght for the forge iii s ii d ob with vii s for hewynge of Tymber ix li v s ii d ob

[*3*^v^] Watter worke Clensinge the River, the hammer diche and ponde, with repairinge the walles and other lyke worke there xliii s viii d ob repairinge the vawe[3] over the greate Ryver xxiii s and the baye v s lxxii s viii d ob

Repairing for cariage of cole and wood viz for makinge of v gates with the Iron worke besides xxxviii lib iron di, i bridge in Estmedowe and i called Cressesbridge and repairinge the ways with Synder lxvii s ii d ob

Cariage of Tymber and Borde viz of Tymbre out of the Springe and to the sawe pitt xlix peces and i lod vii s ii d and ii lodes borde to the Storehouse called the priorye house vii d vii s ix d

Reparing of howses there The corne mill in Walls and Tymbre worke xii s xi d the Storehouse xvi d xiiii s iii d

hedginge and Brusshinge The growndes and ralinge for Safegard of the Springe this yeare xix s iii d

Wages paid to William Blacknall for thole yere with his boord and xix s v d for his rydynge costs to London and there with his retorn x li vii s v d Peter Gelley xx s and Sambert Sheringe xx s as by the booke appereth xii li vii s v d

foren payments viz for Money bags ii d and Tramell nett xviii d, and Statute booke xii d, a hooke to cutt wedes in the garden ii d, a cock [b]lade corde xviii laths vi d, i lib of packthrede to amend the drag nett vii d, a lyne iii d ii quaires of paper vii d, and cariage of a Letter iiii d v s i d

Sum CClxii li ii d ob

[3] Vault.

[*4r*] Panningridge viz

Woodmakers for the Cuttinge of ii^M^iiii^C^lxvii cordes wood di there at diverse prices with vii li x s parcell of xv li, and viii li xvi s parcell of xi li vi s over and besides the residewe part of allowed the last yere and paid for cuttinge of vii^C^iiii^xx^ix cords of Logges whereof was made in cole ii^C^lxiii lodes as appeareth by the booke[4] xl li xix s iii d

Collers for Colinge of vii^C^iiii^xx^ix lodes coles at diverse prices with lvi lodes coles and owynge for to Lawrence Reynollds and for the price of xli lodes redie caried bowght of the wydowe hankes at vi s the lode lxv li xiii s ob

Cariage of DCCCiiii^xx^xi lodes coles by land to the colehouse at diverse prices with ii s v d abated for ii lodes excesse as appeareth by the booke xxxi li iii s i d

myne bowght[5] [ ] stone not digged iiii li iii s iiii d iiii^C^ lodes at ii d ob ye lode and iii^C^xx lodes at iii d the lode iiii li as appeareth by the seid booke viii li iii s iiii d

drawing of Diiii^xx^xix lodes myn at ix d the lode as appeareth by the seid booke[6] xxii li ix s vii d ob

Carriage of DCC lodes of myn by land at v d the lode as appeareth by his booke[7] xii li ix s xi d

Ironne fownders fowndinge of xxxviii lodes at vi dayes to the Fownde at xiiii s viii d for everye Fowndie and fillinge and Fowndinge with iiii s for casting iii hammers and xviii s for makinge a Butterye to the Forge[8] xxix li xvi d

Necessaries bowght furnace to repaire the same and the bellows with vi d x d for greise as appereth by the Booke[9] xxx s vi d

[4] The Furnace Book (382/8: B10/10) gives an incomplete record, ending with payments on May 24th, for a total of 1708 cords.

[5] 382/8 records 370 loads bought from Mr. Egleston of Nenvyld (Ninfield).

[6] On Snowe's land only.

[7] This entry relates to carriage, done largely by Walter Snowe.

[8] The furnace was in blast at the end of 1557, for which records are lost; it was blown out on April 6th 1558, after casting plates for the forge (probably to line a hearth). Work began again on July 1st, but the furnace was stopped on the 9th for repairs, requiring Charles the founder, who made a new 'bottews'. Apart from a break from October 5th–18th, when no relining was done, smelting continued between August 10th and the end of the year.

382/8 later confirms that the scarcely legible 'bottews' or buttress was in fact the pillar of the furnace, the stonework separating the casting and blowing arches: 6 loads of stone were dug in Panningridge wood for the 'pillar' of the furnace. The source of stone for the hearth is identified as Mr. Barnwell's quarry. Barnwell was vicar of Penhurst.

[9] The item for grease should read vi s x d.

Laborers at the furnace with xii s x d for weyinge of vii ton Sowes as appereth by the booke viii s viii d

[*4ᵛ*] Tithe of the fornace paid to the vicare of Asshebornham with xii d for [taske] of the same paid to the Qwene as appereth to the books vi s

Wages paid to Richard Martyn ix li viii s Ransell xiii s iiii d Lawrence Reynolld xiii s iiii d and for the seid accomptants costs payinge the workemen this yere iii s ii d as by the seid booke playnly appeareth x li xvii s x d

Castinge and Carying of sand and stone with the price and cariage thereof this yere xxxiiii s viii d

ferm of land paid to Sir John Baker Knight xx li, the parson of penhurst xx s, John aweke vi s viii d, wydowe hawkyns iii s iiii d xxi li x s

Sum CCxlvi li vii s iii d

Sum Total of all the payments aforeseid Dviii li vii s iiii d ob

And he oweth lxxi li iiii s i d q whereof there is allowed him for the bordage of John Williams Gentilman from the xxiiii[th] of Aprell Anno 1557 untill the xxv[th] of Marche Anno 1558 as by a booke thereof particlerly appeareth and upon this accompt examined x li iii s i d ob. And allowed him xx s in rewarde gyven to Thomas hugons for kepinge of the Corne millne at Robertsbridge at Sundry tymes within the tyme of this accompte as by a booke of the profitts thereof and upon this viewe examined appeareth

And so he oweth lx li xi d ob

whereof

[*5ʳ*] Upon George bigge of fordiche nere Cantorburye for the price of vi ton Iron to him solld payable at Our Ladies daye next to come after this accompte xliiii li

The seid accomptant of the clere arrerages of his seid accompte this yere xvi li xi d ob q

The accompte of the Iron worke The remain per pced xxi ton vii[c]iii qtr xxiii lib And made hoc anno Cxxviii ton xvii[c] di

Sum total of the Iron Cl ton v[c] li libr whereof solld this yere by the seid William as by his booke appereth xxii ton xiiii[c] iii qtr iiii lib. And he hath delivered to the forge and furnace for Anno as by his booke appereth iii[c] di xiiii libr. And delivered to Mr. Roberts mense february Anno 1557 xxx ton. xviii[mo] mcii iii ton. xviii[vo] Avril Anno 1558 iiii ton xviii[vo] novembres eodem Anno xxx ton. And to Mr Bacon xiiii[to] maii eodem Anno xx ton, et xvi[to] Augusti eodem

Anno xxi ton, in all Cviii ton. And remain in the Storehouse primo Januarii dicto Anno primo divine Regine xviii ton xviii^{C} di. Et deficit DCCC di v libri

[*5v*] Robertsbridge The declaracion of the remaynes there taken by the seid William Blacknall and Thomas hogan upon new yeres evening Anno primo [ ] Elizabeth Regine [ ]

Cords of wood The last yeres aremain ix^{C}lxv cords di
And made this yere MMii^{C}iiii^{xx}vii cordes di
Sum of the seid cordes MMMii^{C}liii whereof made in cole this yere ii^{M}iiii cords And so remain in sundrie woods there as by a booke thereof particlerly apperethe Mii^{C}xlix cords

Coles there The last yeres remain iiii^{C}l lodes
And made there this yere DCiii^{xx}viii lodes
Sum MCxviii lodes whereof spent this yere at the forge DCxliiii lodes after the rate of v lodes to the ton of Iron And remain iiii^{C} lodes so deficit lxxiiii lodes

Myne there The last yere of the remain left in Anno [ ] 1556 which remain there yett C lodes

Sowes there and at panyngridge The last yeres remain there with Cl at panyngridge as the accompte appeareth iiii^{C}xl
And made in the fornace at panyngrydge iii^{C}xli

Sum of the seid Sowes vii^{C}iiii^{xx}i Sowes whereof made in Iron by the hammer men and finers after the rate of iii Sowes to the ton and one over iii^{C}iiii^{xx}vi Sowes
And Remain there ii^{C}lxv Sowes and at panyngridge Cxxix Sowes So deficit i Sowe

[*6r*] Panyngridge
The declaracion of the remain there taken die et Anno predicto

Cords of wood there The last yeres remain ix^{C}xl cords
And made there this yere MMiiii^{C}iii^{xx}vii cords

Sum of the cords MMMiiii^{C}vii cords whereof made in cole this yere ii^{M}iii^{C}lxvii cordes after the rate of iii cordes to every lode cole And remain in diverse woods there this yere as by a booke thereof appeareth iiii^{C}lxx cords So deficit Dlxx cords

Lodes of coles The last yeres remain iii^{C}l lodes
And made this yere with xli lodes redie caried and by thaccomptant bowght viii^{C}xxx lodes

Sum MCiiii^{xx} lodes whereof spent at the furnace this yere for the meltinge of Sowes viii^{C}lii lodes And remain iii^{C} lodes So deficit xxviii lodes

Myne The last yeres remain MC lodes
And cast this yere Diiii^{xx}xix lodes
Sum of lodes of myne MCiiii^{xx}xix wherof Spent in the furnace vii^{C}iiii^{xx}xix lodes And remain ix^{C} lodes

[*6^{v}*] Robertsbridge and Panyngridge The valewe of the re maynes there taken the daye and yere aforesaid

Robertsbridge
Of Mii^{C}xlix cordes di wood at vi d the cord xxi li iiii s vi d
iiii^{C} lode cole at vi s the lod Cxx li
C lodes myne at x d the lode iiii li iii s iiii d
ii^{C}lxv Sowes at xxxiii s iiii d the ton CCxx li xvi s viii d
xviii ton xviii c di Iron in the storehouse at vi li xiii s iiii d the ton Cxxvi li iii s iiii d
Sum DCC li vii s x d

Panyngridge
Of iiii^{C}lxx cords at vi d the cord xi li xv s
iiii^{C} lodes coles at vi s the lode iiii^{xx}x li
myne ix^{C} lod at xv d ob the lode lviii li ii s vi d
Cxxix Sowes at xxxiii s iiii d the ton Cvii li x s
Sum CClxvii li vii s vi d
Sum of thole valewe of the remaynes aforeseid is DCClxix li xvi s vii d

[*7^{r}*] The declaracion of the clere gaynes of Iron works aforeseid predicto anno unto [ ] natalis d[ ] Regni [ ] Elizabeth Primo first in the price of Cxxviii tons xvii^{c} di made hoc Anno at vi li xiii s iiii d the tonn DCCClix li iii s iiii d
And encreassed of the Stock of wood coles Sowes and myne there nil
Sum of the valewe aforeseid DCCClix li iii s iiii d
whereof to be abated Dvi li vii s iiii d ob for money disbursed and paid in and aboute diverse kynds of workes and necessaries provided in and for the making of the seid Iron as by the fornace and forge books upon this declaracion examined particulerly doth appere. And also to be abated of l li ix s x d ob which is spent oute of the Stock there hoc anno as upon the dewe examinacion thereof appeareth. And so remain there gayned hoc Anno iii^{C}ii li vi s i d

[7v] The valewe of the deficients which the lorde loseth this yeare and is not answered of

Coles at Robertsbridge	lxxiiii lods	xxii li iiii s
Coles at Pannyngridge	xxviii lods	viii li viii s
Cords of wood at panyngridge	Dlxx cords	xiiii li v s
Sowes at Robertsbridge	i	xvi s viii d
		xlv li xiii s viii d

[15] SUMMARY ACCOUNT FOR PANNINGRIDGE FURNACE AND ROBERTSBRIDGE FORGE, 1563

378/10–4 *U 1475 B3/10*

Anno 1563

[*1r*]

[*1v*] *blank*

[*2r*] Com Sussex

The declaracon of Thaccompte of wyllyam Blacknall Clarke of the Iron workes to the Right honorable Sir henry Sydney Knight Lorde President of the Quenes highnes Councell in the marches of wales, As well of all such Sumes of mony as he hath Receyved to Thuse of the said Sir henry, As of the defraying, payeng and disbursing of the same in and about the said workes, from the firste daye of January in the fyrste yeare of the Reygne of our Soverigne Lady Quene Elizabeth unto the said firste daye of January in the Sixthe yeare of the said Quenes heighnes Reigne That is to saie for one holl yeare

firste he is chardged with tharrerages of his laste Accompte, as in the foote thereof appereth xlvii li xiiii s v d ob

And in the price of woode by him solde this yeare, As by one booke of the Receptes of the saide Accomptannte for this yeare made appereth vi s

[*2v*] And of the price of v Tonn CCCC di ii pounde Iron by him this yeare solde at diverse prices besides lxx [ ][1] Tonn v^c^ Iron, delivered Mr Edmonde Robertes Marchannte, CC iii quarters delivered for necessaries to the forge and fornace, and for libertie of Carriage, one Tonn to Pensehurst and xii^c^ i quarter xvi pounde delivered to halden, As by the said booke particulerly appereth lviii li viii s iiii d

And with Redy mony by him Receyved, Aswell from the lordes coffers at too Severall tymes Cl li As of the said Mr Robertes Clxxi li vi s viii d And of John hawes the Lordes Receyvour within the Counties of Sussex, Kent, and Southampton within the tyme of this Accompte CCC xix li xix s x d, As by the said booke of Receptes particulerly appereth vi^c^xli li vi s vi d

[1] *ms* is very faint; there appears to be a missing figure.

Sum of the holl
chardge aforesaid DCCxlvii li xv s iii d ob

wherof

[3r] Paymentes made by the said Blacknalle within the tyme of this Accompt as foloweth at Robertsbridge, as to say to and for

woodemakers videlit for felling and cutting of MMCCCiiii^xx^v Cordes di of woode theare, wherof in hurnewoode DCCiii Cordes di, Andrewes lande xxi Cordes di,[2] Chettilbrech CCCCix Cordes di, Cottrell woode CCCCiiii^xx^ Cordes, parke-wood CClvii Cordes di,[2] Dunkens Lande xxiii Cordes di, Knell woode Cl Cordes di, Clarke Lande Cxvi Cordes di, Wyners Lande Cviii Cordes di, partriche Lande Cxv Cordes di, As by the booke of paymentes of this yeare particulerly appereth xliii li iiii s vii d

Colliers for Coling of xi^C^iiii^xx^ix lodes coles at diverse prises there wherof in hurnewoode CCCiiii^xx^xviii lodes, Chettilbrech Clxxi lodes, parkewood Clvi lodes,[3] Clarkeslande and Knoll liii lodes, welland xxiiii lodes, Cottrell woode Cxxxvii lodes,[3] Potters lande xviii lodes, hucksteppes land xli lodes, Davies woode xiii lodes, Jarvis lande Cxl lodes, mattheis woode xviii lodes, and Knolleslande iiii^xx^xviii li vi s x d

[3v] xx^ty^ lodes, with iiii s paid for Carrage of Duste, and ii s for Cordes, As by the said booke appereth

Lande cariage viz of The said Coles to the forge and Colehouse at diverse prises by this Accomptannte paid besides li li iiii s vi d owing for the lande Carriage viz [of] viii^C^lviii lodes alredy caried with iiii li x s viii d ob for the prise of wheles, Amending and making of waynes, and xviii s for libertie to passe thorough mens groundes, As by the said booke appereth xxvi li xv s xi d ob

heaping of coles Cariag of xi^C^ii lodes of the said Coles into the Colehouse and heping them there at i d the lode, As by the said booke appereth iiii li xi s x d

Wood bought videlit of John Holmes viii Acres Standing

[4r] xvi li, Thomas Eves one percell that made viii^C^iiii^xx^xiii Cordes x li v s, John Dunke Clxxiiii Cordes in Knell woode

[2] The Andrewes and Parkwood entries are later insertions.
[3] The Parkewood and Cottrell entries are later insertions.

vii li v s, Thomas partriche Cxv Cordes di, Ci s ob, Edward Dunke Dxxi s Cordes in Chettilbrech xxii li x d, John Bernes iiii^xx Cordes iiii li xiii s iiii d, and Thomas Clarke Cxvi Cordes iiii li xvi s viii d in full payment of all the said woode bought ex Recognicio dci Compnte coram Auditore lxx li xii d ob

Cariage of Sowes, Shott and Iron with Lading, heping and waying, as to say for Land carrage of Clx Tonn of Sowes and other Iron from the fornace to the forge at sondrie prises xviii li v s viii d, liiii Tonn Shote at viii d Tonn xxxvi s lxxiiii Tonn to the Oke lxxi s, from the forge to the Iron house xiii s vii d, lading and bering of Iron, with heaping of vii^xx xi Tonn Sowes at the forge xvi s xi d, keping the skore for Recept of sowes the holl yeare iii s iiii d, and weying of Iron xii s x d, As by the said booke appereth xxv li xix s iiii d

[*4^v*] Iron makers as to say to the hamermen xxv li viii s viii d, and fyners xl li vi s iiii d, for making and fyning of lxxvi Tonn CCCC and iii quarters Iron at Sondry prises this yeare made, As by the said booke appereth lxv li xv s

Sowes and Iron bought And in the prise of lx Tonn l^C of Sowes bought and Receyved of John Morrys at lxvi s viii d Tonn and xl s over in the holl CCii li iii s iiii d, in full payment of lxi Tonn bought of wyllyam Relfe and Bartilmewe Jeffery, and Receyved at midsomer within the time of this Accompte besides xxxv li Allowed in the laste Accompte xxxv li, and i m Cordes of woode uncutte, in parte of payment of lxi Tonn of Sowes bought at like prise of heughe Collins to be Receyved at midsomer nexte as by Bill appereth xl li xiiii s ix d ob q. In perte of payment of lxii Tonn of Sowes bought of the said Relfe and Jeffery at there said former prise, to be Receyved at Midsomer nexte (in like prise of v Tonn Sowes iii qrters bought of Mr Gardiner xvi li xv s x d[4]) as by Bill appereth xxxv li and for CC I qtr Iron bought of James Berdon (xx s[4]) As by the said booke appereth CCCxxx li xiii s xi d ob q

[*5^r*] Necessaries for workmen Diverse necessaries for workmen, viz Rakes, Skeppes, Dishes, i Stone Bottell, and Russhes for Thatch, and repairing Peter Jellies house this yeare xiiii s iii d

Chardge of Repairing the fornace and forge as to saye to Sondrie Artificers as to saye, Carpenters, Sawiers, Masons

[4] Inserted in *ms.*

and Laborors, in newe making, amending, and Repairing the Sydes of the fornace, the Chafery and fynary wheles and Chymneys, the Baye and Jettey at the forge, and laieng too newe Guttes, Too Rounde Beames, Too Roodes, one penstocke and Repayring and Amending the bellowes, Together with Carriage of Necessaries for the same, As by the said booke particulerly appereth xvii li xii s v d ob

Making
[5^v^] Waterworkes Amending of Cariage waies with hedging and ditching of weyes and Gates for Cariage of cole and Sowes xxx s i d, Sondry water workes in the hamerditche and other Cxix s ix d, Raling Ciiii^xx^vi Roddes at weste Derne at sondry prises li s v d, Ditching and hedging CClxi Rodd xxxi s vi d, As by the said booke appereth xi li xii s ix d

Wages paide for Tholl yeare ended at Christmas within the tyme of this Accompte, As to saye to Wyllyam Blacknall with his Bourdewages ix li viii s, Peter Jelly xxvi s viii d, James Barden xx s, Peter Bartilmew xxvi s viii d and Thomas Glede xl s As by the saide booke appereth xv li xvi d

foreyne payments And for diverse foreyne paymentes, As to say for vi qwaier paper xxiii d, Tackes for Sowes xii d

[6^r^] Riding Costes of this Accomptante xi s ii d, Too Ropes for lading and unlading Tymber, ii s viii d, Cariage of a Tonn Iron to Pensehurst x s, Necessaries for Repayring the Lordes mannor howse at halden this yeare with iiii li xiii s iiii d for cariage of lyme, xxviii s ix d for lathe, xx s, x d for Stone, vii s iiii d making Iron barres, xv s iiii d for hewing and squaring Timber for Borde, Cxi s ix d for Sawing and carrage of Borde, in all xiiii li iiii s ix d, as by the said booke appereth xv li xi s vi d

Sum DCCxxvi li xx d ob

like Paymentes made by the said Blacknall within the tyme of this accompte, as foloweth

[6^v^] Pannyngridge videlit for
Woodmakers as to say for felling and cutting of liii Cordes woode in Rownden with ii s iiii d for Topping of xxv Okes, as by the fornace booke of this yeares paymentes appereth xxvii s x d

Colliers as to say for Coling of Cxviii lodes coles at xx d the lode with xvii s ii d for carriage of woode and duste, to the pytte, As by the saide booke appereth x li viii s vi d

Cariag by lande of The saide Cxviii lodes coles from the pitte to the fornace with iii s x d for Amending of Cariag waies and gates, xii s x d for heaping coles, and xvi s viii d for libertie to passe thoroughe other mens Groundes As by the said booke appereth x li iii s iiii d

[7r] Lyme burning, As to saye in Digging and Setting Stone for too Kilnes lx s Cariage therof v s iiii d, Cariage and Cuttinge of woode for the Kilne xxxv s x d As by the saide booke appereth Ci s ii d

foreyne paymentes Seking of mynne vi s iii d, weying Sowes bought x s ix d, Cariage Lyme ii s v d and Expences of this Accomptannte xi d, As by the saide booke appereth xx s iiii d

Sum xxvii li xiiii s

Sum of all the said Somes of Money paid by the said Accomptannte this yeare DCCliii li ii s x d ob, And so he oweth nil, because he is in Supplussage Cvii s vii d, And is Allowed him by force of my lordes warrante Dated xxvii^mo^ martii in Anno iiii^to^ [dic] divine Regine for money by him lente to Too Colliers that rann away xlii s, And then his superplussage is (xl li i s i d)[5]

[7v] Against which he is to be chardged with xxiii li xv s iiii d for mony by him Receyved of heugh Collins for the Cutting of xi^C^xxii^ty^ Cordes woode, whereof dewe to the saide heughe by Bill x^C^ xxii Cordes, besides i C delivered him in parte of the nexte yeres payment, And so he oweth xvi li v s ix d

[8r] Roberts Bridge

The declaracon of the Remaynes there taken by the saide William Blacknall Secundo die January in Anno Sexto Regni Divine Regine Elizabeth

Iron The Remayne of the laste yeare DCCCC and di

And made within the time of this Accompt lxxvi Tonn iiii^C^iii quarters

Sum of all the saide Iron is lxxvi Tonn di iiii^C^ I quarter, wherof sold this yeare by the saide Accomptannt to sondry persons v Tonn iiii^C^ di ii pounde, And delivered by him for diverse necessaries for the forge and fornace this yeare CC iii quarters, And by him Delivered to my lordes workes at pensehurste i tonn and halden xii^C^

[5] Indecipherable in *ms*: calculated from next entry.

i quarter xvi pounde this yeare i Tonn di CC i quart xvi pound And delivered to Mr Edmond Robertes Marchant within the tyme of this Accompte in full payment of the olde warrante of the last yeare xx Tonn v^c^. By a newe warrant this yeare in full payment thereof xl Tonn And since that without Warrant x Tonn, in all lxx Tonn v^c^ And so is clerely gayned in weying this yeare

x^c^xlvi li poundes

[*8^v^*] Cordes of woode The last yeares Remayne

MMCiiii^xx^ix Cordes di

And made this yeare as by the saide booke of paymentes appereth

MMiii^C^iiii^xx^v Cordes di

Sum of all the saide Cordes iiii^M^v^C^lxxvi Cordes wherof be made in cole this yeare at the Rate of iii Cordes to every lode coles MMM Dlxvii cordes and Remayneth cutt in the woods there, As to say in hurnewoode CCiiii^xx^xv Cordes. Grete Cottrell CCx Cords. Andrewes lande xxi Cords di. John Dunks land als Knell woode Clxxiiii Cords. Pertrich land als knoll woode xxx Cords in all DCCxxx Cords di. Et deficit CClxxvii Cords di, which is supposed by Thaccomptannte to be consumed in the smalnes of the woode.

Coles there The last yeares Remayn iiii^xx^ lodes
And made this yeare there xi^C^iiii^xx^ix lodes

[*9^r^*] Sum of all the saide coles xii^C^lxix lodes, wherof spente this yeare at the forge after the Rate of v lodes for every Tonn of Iron CCC iiii^xx^ii lodes. And remayne in the colehouse there by estimacion DCCCiiii^xx^vii lodes.

Sowes and Shott at Roberts Bridge and pannyngridge The laste yeares Remayne with xxxi Tonn at Pannyngridge Clxxix Ton xi^C^ And with Sowes bought and this yeare Receyved, as in the said booke of paymentes in the Title of Sowes bought appereth

vi^xx^vi Tonn i^C^iii Quarters

Sum of all the saide Sowes of Iron iii^C^v Tonn di [i]^C^iii quarters wherof made in Iron this yeare by the hamer men and finers after the Rate of Thre Tonn of Sowes to Too Tonn of Iron Cxiiii Tonn vii^C^ di, And Remayneth at Roberts Bridge in Sowes and Shott vii^xx^xi Tonn v^C^ i quarter, And at Pannyngridge in Sowes xxv Tonn and at Fowlbrooke nere Roberts Bridge [ ]

[*9^v^*] Pannyngridge
The Declaracon of the Remaynes there taken by the saide William Blacknall the saide seconde daye of January dico Anno Sexto pd Divine Regine

N

Cordes of wood The Remayn of the laste yeare MDxlii Cordes
And cutt this yeare liii Cordes
Sum of all the said Cordes MDiiii^{xx}xv Cordes wherof there is delivered heugh Collins in parte of payment of a Bergeine of Sowes not yet Receyved, As by his Bill appereth xi^{c}xxii Cordes And made in Cole this yeare at the Rate of iii Cordes to the lode of Colles CCCliiii Cordes. And Remain Cxix Cordes which ar supposed to be consumed in burning more than is allowed because it was smalle woode

Coles The Remayne of the laste yeare none
But there is made there this yeare Cxviii lodes

[*10*^{r}] Sum of the saide Cole Cxviii Lodes which all Remayne the Seconde day of January Anno Divini 1563

Mynne Md Richarde Baker Esquier oweth my Lorde for mynn Lent him from Pannyngridge Cviii Lodes, and Bartilmew Jeffrey likewise there Lent xxvii Lodes Cxxxv lodes
Sum Cxxxv Lodes

[*10*^{v}] Robte Bridge and pannyngridge
The valewe of the Remaynes there taken the day and yeare aforesaid

Roberts Bridge
DCCxxx Cordes di of woode, at xiiii d the corde xlii li xii s iii d
viii^{c}iiii^{xx}viii Lodes Coles at viii s the lode CCClv li iiii s
vii^{xx}xi Tonn v^{c}i quarter in Sowes and Shotte at lx s the Tonn iiii^{c}liii li xv s ix d
Iron olde broken in Brayes and Sow Irons not here chardged because the weight is not knowen
Sum viii^{c}l li xi s v d

Panningridge
Cxviii Lodes Coles there at viii s the Lode xlvii li iiii s
xl Tonn of Sowes with xv Tonn at Fowlbrooke at lx s the Tonn Cxx li
Mynn remaining Cxxxv lodes ix li
Sum Clxxvi li iiii s

[*11*^{r}] Sum of the holl valewe of the Remaynes is Mxxvii li xv s v d
The declaracon of the Clere Gaynes of the Iron workes aforesaid for the saide yeare ended the said Second day of January in the said

Sixte yeare of the Reigne of our Souvereigne Lady Quene Elizabeth first in the prise of lxxvi Tonn xv^{c} xviii lib Iron made this yeare with x^{c}xlvi lib gayned in weight at xi li the Tonn
viii^{c}xxxviii li vi s vii d

And encreased of the Stocke of woode and cole this yeare cleare CClix li xii s

Sum of the said valewe Miiii^{xx}xvii li xviii s vii d

wherof ther is to be (abated) for

[*11*^{v}] mony by this Accomptannte paid in and about diverse kinds of works and necessaries bought and provided in and for the making of the said Iron, As by the fornace and forge bookes upon this declaracion examyned particulerly appereth v^{c}xiiii li xix s x d. And abated for prise of the Stocke of Sowes and Shott this yeare Spent, As by due examynacion therof appereth CCl li xviii s iiii d And so remayneth clere gayned this yeare CCCxxxii li v d

[16] SUMMARY ACCOUNT FOR ROBERTSBRIDGE FORGE, 1568[1]

378/10–9 *U 1475 B3/10*

[*1r*] William blacknall anno 1568
Robertsbridge
Thaccompte of the Iron workes these for the yere Ended primo die January 1568

[*1v*] *blank*

[*2r*] Robertsbridge in Sussex. The declaracon of Thaccompte of William Blacknalle Clerke of the Iron workes there to the Right honorable Sir Henry Sydney of the noble Order of the Garter, Knight, lord president of the Quenes majesties Counsell in the marches of Wales and deputye to hir highnes of the Realme of Irelande, as well of all such Somes of moneye as he hath Receyved to thuse of the said Lorde, as allso of the defrayinge payinge and disbursinge of the same in and about the said workes, from the first daye of Januarye in anno x^mo^ Regni Divine Regine Elizabethe untill the same first daye of Januarye anno xi^mo^ eisdem divine Regine, That is to saye by the Space of one holle yere

Arrerages first he is Chardged wyth arrerages of this last accompt as in the foote therof appereth xviii li v s i d q

wood solde And wyth the prise of woode by the said accomptannt this yere to sondry persons Solde as by his Book as this yeres Receptes apperethe xvii s viii d

Sale of Iron at the forge And wyth the price of xx^tie^ Tonns xvi^c^di x libri Iron by him this yere solde and delivered as diverse prises, besides xx^ti^ Tonns delivered to

[*2v*] Mr Edmund Robertes Marchannt xx^ti^ Tonns to Mr Webbe, di Tonn to Thomas Whytton for repacon of lamberhurst, and besides xlv Tonns del by Mr Bluntes warrannt to be sent into Irelande to Mr Cosgrave Merchannt, xii Blomes to laye under the Andvilles weyinge CCCC libri, 1 Gogeon xxviii libri, i Barre for the Chafery Chymney Cix libri i Trevett sent to penshurst xxiiii libri and for libertie of

[1] The accounts from 1568 onwards are in a different hand from their predecessors.

cariage xxviii lib as by the said Book of Receptes at large apperethe Clxxvi li xvi s viii d

Redy mony received by the lordes appoyntment And wyth readye moneye by the said accomptannte wythin the time of this accompt receyved as well from the said Mr Edmund Robertes lvii li x s, as from John hawes the lordes particuler Receyvor within the Counties of Sussex and Southampton at sondry times Cxl li ix s iii d. And in parte of payment of John Coggers dett of Goodhurst besides vii li yet owinge xlvi s viii d as by the said booke of this accomptanntes receptes particlerlye apperethe CC li v s xi d

Sum of thole Charge aforesaid is CCCiiii^{xx}xvi li v s viii d q

[*3*^{r}] paymentes made by the said William Blackenall wythin the time of this accompte as followethe

Charges of the forge paid to and for

Wood cutters videlit for fellynge and cuttinge of Mvii^{C}liii Cordes of wood this yere at sondrye prises wherof in Chytcomb iiii^{C}iiii^{xx}ii Cordes di, Courtlag v^{C}xx Cordes di, Shethers wood iii^{C}lix Cordes di, Badland lix Cordes, Benegrotten iiii^{xx}v Cordes di, and in homan wood of Mr Tuftons CClvi Cordes, wyth lxii s vii d ob for Toppinge of Okes as by the Booke of this accomptanntes paymentes for this yere made appereth xxx li xi s x d ob q

Colliers Colynge of viii^{C}viii lodes of Coles at Sondry prises wherof in Chytcombe CClvi lodes, Courtlodge iii^{C}lviii lodes, farlow woode Cxxv lodes, Bene Grotten xxii lodes, and in Jervys Land and in hurst wood xlvii lodes as by the said Boke of paymentes particlerly Appereth lxvii li x s vii d

[*3*^{v}] Lande cariage of The said Coles from the woodes to the Colehouse at diverse prises wyth xi s vi d for amendinge the Cole wanes and ii s for cariage of duste out of the Colehouse lxii li x s

howsinge and heping of Coles videlit Cariage of parte of the said Coles and hepinge parte wythin the Colehouse parte wythout as by the said Boke of paymentes appereth lxv s xi d

Caryage of Sowes and Iron with heping and weying viz of Land Cariage of CCvi Tonns Sowes this yere videlit from Neytherfeld of Mr wekes xl Tonns xl s, Sockneys of heugh Collyns lxi Tonns iiii li xi s vi d, and from the newe furnace of Mr Wekes with xii Tonns paid for by Raffe Knight and ii Tonns of hammers and andevilles [iiii^{xx}xii] Tonns[2] Cviis and for caryage of Ciiii Tons Iron to the Oke Cvs for Caryage from the forge to the Iron house uppon the paye dayes xis for caryage of l Ton from the Oke by water to Rye and to Appildore iiiili vs and for hepynge

[*4*^{r}] of Clxxi Tonn Sowes xiiiis viid for weyinge Iron and Sowes xxxiiis xd and for helpinge to laye them and lode them iiis xid as by the said Boke of paymentes at large appereth xxiiiili xis xid

Ironmakers viz to The hamer men and fynors for makinge and fyninge of Cxvi Tons ix^{C} libri i quarter Iron this yere at sondrye prises wyth vis in Reward to James Barden as by the said Boke apperethe iiii^{xx}ii li xixs

Sowes and Iron bought of heugh Collyns lxi ton besides M Cordes woode burnt Cxviiili viiis iid and CC Rawe Iron vs lxviiili xiiis iid

woode bought Of Mr. Sakfeld xxvii Cordes in Chytcombe at xixs vd ob And of John Davys Clii Cordes di then iiiili iis viid as by the said Booke of payments apperethe Cis viiid ob

dyverse necessaries
for the said workemen videlit iiii Rakes xiiiid, i Shovelle xiiiid, i skoppett xiiiid

[*4*^{v}] One hooke to cutt wedes wythall vid, one Spade xid, ix Baskettes viis vd, v Buckettes xviid, i whelebarrow mendinge iiiid, disshes iiid, x gallon pottes xxd, and fellynge and Caryage of lxvi lodes fyrewoode for the xxxs iiiid as by the said Booke of payments appereth xlvis iiiid

Repacons Bestowed this yere viz upon makinge a newe Iron howse besides the Timber xlvis viid ob, the Coole howse besides timber xlvis xd, the forge xxiiis iiid ob, makinge the furnes pond Baye vili viiis vid, the olde Baye at Baybroke meadowe iiis, the grete Baye xxd, makinge the wall at the olde Rever vis, castinge up the hamer dyche Banckes vis ixd, Reparinge the vawte of the Rever xxxvis vid, the hamerdyche and hamer pond walle lis iid ob, the Colehouse dyke iiiis, Radland water drawinge and wedinge xxxs viid, the hamer wheles and chafery wyth Armes

[2] This is scarcely legible and appears to have been substituted for Cvii.

[5r] and andevylles[3] for hammers xxxvs iid, castinge and makin of x hammers iii awndvilles xix Brasses or plates wyth Carryage therof xviiis viiid, reparing the Bellows lxvis ixd ob, and of the workemens howses xviis vid as by the said Boke paymentes particlerly apperethe xxvi li iis ob[4]

Charges of caryage and wayes and springe Makinge and amendinge of wayes for Caryage of Iron Sowes and Cooles wyth xi Gates throughe groundes xvis vd ob Castinge a dytche iiiis libertie of Caryage besides iis iiiid of the price of one Share mold iis and for hedgynge of iii^Cl rodd for savinge of Springe xxiis id as by the said Booke of paymets appereth xlvis xd ob

Wages with ridinge costes for the holle yere ended at xpemes wythin the time of this accompte viz of this accomptannte lxvis viiid, for his borde wages vi li xvid, and for ridinge costes ixs xid, Peter Jelley wyth xs to bye him haye ls,

[5v] James Barden xxs, Phillipp hill xiiis iiiid, And of Peter Gawnett xiiis iiiid and paper xvid as by the said Booke of payments apperethe xiiii li xvs xid

forren paymentes Made and paide by this accomptannte wythyn the said time viz for Caryage of one lode lyme to Salehurst iis iiiid, (Ryding Chardges ixs xid)[5] fyshing and Sowinge the hammer pond xs vid, Caske iiiis id, Sawinge of Borde laid in the Storehouse wyth makinge pyttes drawinge squarynge and caryage therof lxiiiis, and pytching the Bote viiid as by the said boke of paymets apperethe iiii li xixd[6]

Sum of all the said Somes of money this yere paid CCCiiii^xx xiiii li xvis xid ob

Et debet xxviiis iiiid ob wherof ys allowed the said William for money paid to Thomas Clerke in full payment of Cordinge C Cordes di wood the last yere and before this no Allowance therof demanded xxs Et Sic debet viiis iiiid ob

[6r] Robtesbridge

The declaracon of the Remanes there taken by the said William Blacknall ultimo die decembris predico Anno xi^mo dico divine Regine Elizabethe videlt

[3] 'And helves' crossed out in the original.

[4] Originally written xxvi li xiis iid.

[5] Crossed out.

[6] Originally written iiii li xis vid.

Iron The last yeres Remayns in the Iron house in good newe Iron weyedd xxxvii Tonn xviii^{C} libri and in cracked Iron vii^{C} libri xxxviii Ton v^{C}[7]

And is made in Iron wythyn the tyme of this accompt as by the said Boke of paymentes appereth Cxvi Ton ix^{C} libri i qtr

Sum of all the said Iron is Cliiii Ton xiiii^{C}[8] libri i qtr, wherof solde this yere by the said accomptannt as before xx Ton xvi^{C} di x libri and delivered to the forge this yere for diverse necessaryes v^{C} I quarter ix libri and to Thomas Whytton for Repacons at Lamberhurst di Ton for libertie of Cariage xxviii libri and sent to pensehurst i Trevett xxiiii libri and delivered to Mr Edmund Robertes xx Ton and to Mr Webbe xx ton and delivered by Mr. Bluntes warrannte which was sent into Ireland to Mr Cosgrave merchannt xlv Tonn as by the said Booke of this accomptanntes Receptes apperethe Cvi Ton di CCi qtr xv libri and remayneth in the Iron howse

[*6v*] Weyed the said daye and yere in good newe Iron xlviii Ton di iii^{C} di And in olde Iron xiiii^{C} libri And so is made of Blomes and Gunstons the Supplussage of the said Remayn one Ton v hundred di[9] xv libri

Cordes of woode The last yere Remayne Miiii^{C}vi Cordes

And Cutt this yere in sondry woodes as before appereth Mvii^{C}liii Cordes

Sum of all the said Cordes ys MMMClix Cordes wherof ys made in Coles this yere in Courtledge MCl Cordes, Chytcombe viii^{C}xxvii Cordes, Shethers land wyth Badland iiii^{C}vi Cordes, Benegrotton and Normans land lxxii Cordes, and in Jervys land and hurst wood Cliiii Cordes as by the said Booke of payments appereth MMDlx Cordes and Remain in Chytcomb Clx Cordes di and in Mr Tuftons wood called homan wood felled CCxlvi Cordes and unfelled xiiii acres iiii^{c}vi cordes di xiiii acres Et deficit Ciiii^{xx}xii Cords di xiii Acres and Sic deficit ultimo xxiii Cordes in Remain supplus suponat Clxix Cordes di

[*7r*] Cooles there The last yeres Remayne at the Colehouse Cxvii lodes

And made this yere as before viii^{C}viii lodes

Sum of all the said Coles ys Miii^{C}xxv lodes wherof Spente this yere at the said forge at the Rate of v lodes for every Ton Iron Ciiii^{xx} lodes and for makinge of three Ton Blomes at

[7] Originally written viC. [8] Originally ixC. [9] iii qters di crossed out.

three lodes to the Ton ix lodes And Remain in the Colehouse the said daye and yere viii^C^xxxvi lodes[10]

Sowes and Shotte The last yeres Remayne in Sowes at the forge xliiii Tons iiii^C^ at vynehalle xxiii Tonns xvii^C^ xiiii libri in Blomes v Ton di and in Shotte x Ton

iiii^xx^iii Tons di Cxiiii libri

And in Sowes and smale Iron bought and receyved this yere as before apperethe Ciiii^xx^i Ton CC libri

Sum of all the said Sowes Blomes Iron and Shotte ys CClxiiii Ton di CCCxiiii libri wherof made in Iron this yere by the hamer men and fyners at the Rate of Three Ton Sowes to ii Ton Iron Clxxiiii Ton xiii libr iii Qrt di and remain at the forge in Sowes

[7^v^] the daye and yere abovesaid Cxxvii Sowes estemed at lxxvi Ton iiii^C^ (at xii C the sow)[11] and Remain in Blomes there viii Ton di and in Shott v Ton di

Robtes Bridge
The valewe of the Remaynes there taken the daye and yere above written

As to saye in vii^C^xxxvi lodes Coles at ix s the lode	iii^C^xxxii li ii s
lxxvi Ton iiii^C^ Sowes at l s the Ton	Ciiii^xx^x li x s
v Ton di Shotte at xl s the Ton	xi li
xlviii Tonn di iiiC di good new Iron in the Iron howse at viii li vi s viii d the Ton	iiii^C^v li xii s vi d
xiiii^C^ libri olde Iron at v s the C	lxx s
viii Ton di of Blomes at Cvi s viii d the Ton	xlv li vi s viii d
[8^r^] iiii^xx^x lodes myne at xi d the lode	iiii li ii s vi d
iiii^C^vi Cordes di woode at xiiii d the Corde	xxiii li xiiii s iii d
And xiiii acres fallable woode in Mr Tuftons wood at lxiii s iiii d the acre	xliiii li vi s viii d
Sum of the valewe of the said Remaynes	Mlx li iiii s vii d

The declaracon of the Clere Gaynes of the Iron workes aforsaid for the said yere ended the said last daye of december in the eleventh yere of the said Quene hir highnes Regne

first in the prise of Cxvi Ton ix^C^ libr i quarter Iron made this yere videlit of lxxi Ton ix libr i qrt solde and remayninge in

[10] xlii loads crossed out. [11] Inserted.

Englande at viii li vi s viii d the Ton and xlv Ton sent into Irelande at xi li the Ton Miiii^{xx}vi li xiiii s i d q

Sum of the said valewe is Miiii^{xx}vi li xiiii s i d q wherof ther is to be abated as well for money by this accomptannte paid for sondry workes

[*8*^{v}] as for neccessaries bought provided and spent in and about the makinge of the said Iron by the Boke of defrayng of the same herupon examyned particlerly appereth DCCii li xvii s i d ob q And for parte of the price of the Stock of wood and Shotte this yere likewyse spent lxxviii li ix s x d And so remain Clere Gayned this yere CCCv li vii s i d ob

[*9*^{r}] Md the said William Blackenhall hath delivered to the duchmen to the use of the Stele workes iiii^{C}iii qtr xxvi libri Iron at viii s iiii d the C xli s vi d

Md allso that besides the Remayn of Sowes before expressed yt is agreid by wrytinge that Mr Wekes shall deliver before Michelmes next at the forge as the workmen shall stand nede CCx Ton Sowes the moytie of the Cariage to be borne by my lord, The said Mr Wekes to have for the said Sowes lxx Ton Iron to be delivered him at the forge aforsaid and my lord to have the Rest.

[*9*^{v}] *blank*

[17] SUMMARY ACCOUNT FOR ROBERTSBRIDGE FORGE, 1572–3

378/10–13 *U 1476 B3/10*

[1] Robertsbridge
Thaccompte of the Iron workes there for the yere endyd the xvi[th] of May 1573

[*1v*] *blank*

[*2r*] Robertsbridge in Sussex
The declaracon of thaccompte of william Blackenall clerke of the yron workes there to the Right Honourable Sir Henry Sydney Knight of the most noble order of the garter lord president of the quenes maiesties counsell in the marches of walles aswell of all suche somes of money as he hath receyvyd to thuse of the seyde Sir Henry, as also of the defrayenge paying and disbursinge of the same in and aboute the seyd workes frome the fyrst daye of may in A[o] xiiii[to] Elizabeth Regine untill the xvi[th] daye of maii in A[o] xv[to] eiusdem Regine, as to say by the space of one whole yere and xvi dayes viz

arrerages first he is Charged with tharrerages of his laste accompte as apperethe in the foote of the same xx li xii s iii d

Coles solde and wood And with lvi s for vii lodes of Cole by him sold out of the Colehouse at Beckherst to sundrye persons at viii s the lode
And xii d for the pryce of three lodes of Olde Beche motes sold frome the Coppylands of Barnes heires as apereth by his boke of Recept lvii s

Sale of yron at the fordge And with CCxlvi li xviii s x d for the pryce of xxiiii[or] Tonnes xvii[C]xii libri of yron by him solde unto dyverse persons at the fordge within the tyme of this accompte as by his booke of Receiptes appereth. Besyde xi[C]ii libri by him delyvered as well for dyverse necessaries about the fordge as for one longe spytt

[*2v*] and one fyer panne delyvered to my lords use to halden, and ii fyer pannes and ii peles to penshurst. And iiii[xx]viii Tonnes of Iron delyvered unto Richarde Wekes in full payment and discharge of all the Iron due unto him at the first

daye of may last past for sowes. And xlii Tonnes xv^c^iii quarters ii libri of yron delivered unto william webb at sundrye tymes within the tyme of this accompt in parte of payment of fiftye Tonnes of yron to him solde by William Blountt gent the lords generall Receyver wherof xx^ti^ Tonnes were solde at ix li the Tonne and xxx Tonnes at viii li[1] the Tonne CCxlvi li xviii s x d

note v tonnes of this yron delyvered to Mr Webbe was in full payment of a bargayne of xl tonnes solde to hym and Mr [harry] the yere before and The xxxvii Tonnes xv^c^ iii quarters ii libri remain ys in parte of payment of ii bargaines of xxx tonne and xx tonne, made this yere by Mr Blount with him to the full payment wherof Mr Weston hath delyvered to Webb xii Tonne iiii^c^xxvi libri, of the xii Tonne di which he owed my lorde, and so mr Weston now oweth v^c^iii quarters ii libri and my lord ys even with all the rest.[2]

And with iiii s ii d receyved of gabriell Gebons, l s of william hudson, iiii li x s of Walter ferbye, ii s iii d of mr Horden, xiii s vi d of William fryer of Rye, ix s of martyn of Sandhurst lx s of Fryere of Rye, iiii li x s of the Smythe of Brensett, xiii li v s of gabriell Gebon, xl s vi d of goodgrome of Redyng, all which somes were sett in supra on this accomptantes last accompt as may appere by the same xxxi li iiii s v d

[*3^r^*] Redye money Receyved by the lords appointment And with iiii^xx^ix li vi s iii d by him Receyvyd at sondrye tymes of John Hawes the lords Receyvor within the Counties of Sussex and part in Kent as may appere by his book of receipts iiii^xx^ix li vi s iii d

Summe of all the saide Receiptes and arrerages iii^c^iiii^xx^x li xviii s ix d

Wherof woodcutters viz for In payments made by the saide william Blackenall within the tyme of this accompte as followeth viz for fellinge and Cuttinge of ii^c^iiii^xx^vi Cords iii quarters in Beckherst, MMCCCiii Cords di in fowlbroke, iiii^xx^xv Cords in little marlinge, CCxvi Cords di in the shawes in morgyefeldes, at sondrye pryces as may appere by the book of paymentes of thys accomptant xlix li iiii s

[*3^v^*] Collyers for Colynge v^c^xxvii lodes at xx d the lode, viz in Berkeherst iiii^c^ xvii lodes, In downlande Cxvi lodes,

[1] Gap left in *ms.*

[2] This note appears in the margin.

In felbroke iiii^{xx}xiiii lodes, as may appere by the sayde book of payments within the tyme of this accomptant liii li v s

Caryage of Cole for iiii^{C}xvii lodes of Cole frome berkherst to the fordge at xviii d the lode, Cxvi lodes frome downelands at viii d the lode, iiii^{xx}xiiii lodes frome fowlbroke at vi d the lode, as appereth by the sayde booke of paymentes within the tyme of this accompt xxxvii li viii s

Laborers in necessarye workes with caryage of yron and stoke To dyverse laborers at sondre tymes aswell for weighing of yron digginge of earth and synder, mending of hedges against Tymberwood springe, caryeng yron (and sand) to the oke, felling wood in Berkherst before the Cutters mendyng the Bellowes, Cutting of fyerwood for the fordgemen, setting of postes in Downland spring, weighing of Sowes, makeng a herst for the hamers, one new yron Rake, mendinge the tymber [ ], mending the lane at hodesbarn, mending the way at the fordge, skowring busshes in the dyke, mending the bridge in the west medowe, Curryeng ii hydes for the Chafery Bellowes, mendinge the walle in long broke, mendyng of ways, casting ii andvyles one hammer, mendinge dykes and the Ryver, casting iiii^{or} new hammers ii plates vi payre of Andyornes, making of hedges about the springe and diverse other necessaries as may appere [ ] ix li viii s vi d

[*4*^{r}] Emptions of dyverse necessaryes For one skovell to cast the dykes, Bukettes Shovells Baskettes Ropes hokes to cutt wedes, Byll, spade, gloves to weighe iron, grese leather for the bellowes, with xx s iiii d for nayles and with v s for a tramell of Five fedome at xii d the fedom and dyverse other necessaryes for the workes as may appere by the sayde booke of payments within the tyme of this accompte iiii li xi s x d

Land caryage with liberties of wayes for xxvii lodes of wood for the fordgemen Caryadge Synder frome the fordge to amende the wayes in west medowe, caryage of earth to the forge drawing of Tymber to the Sawpytt, Caryage of pyles for the furnace ponde for caryedge of iiii new hamers, caryadg of pyles and post to mende the Ryver at norbridge, one lode of Russhes to thache petyr Jellys house, Clay to the gret bay, framed Tymber from the sawstage to the Valte under the Ryver, drawing of old tymber out of the valt, dust to the Collyers earth to mende the Ryverwall in the lords mede, hamers and plates with vi payre of Andyerns frome the furnace to the fordge, Bords for the Cole house, caryedge of Mr wekes weights borowed and weayeng the same. with ii s for liberty of ways to Richard Sander as may appere by the sayde boke of payments within the tyme of this accompt vi li xiiii s vii d

[*4*^{v}] Carpenters daubers and charges for Repacons of the workes and houses
For dressing the bellowes iiii^{or} sevrall tymes vi s viii d. To Carpenters for mendynge the bridge in west medowes for the better caryadge of Coles ix s iii d for bording a parte of the Colehouse and setting iii new shores. Mending the bridge at norbridge the fludgate there, for a new pynstoke for one of the fyners. for framynge and setting a new slewes under the Ryver. repayring one of the fyners whele and gutt, repayring the hamer whele, ii new gates for fowlbroke wood and hanging the same, for sawinge of Bords and plankes for the Colehouse and sawing of Tymber for the new gutt and valt for hewing of xxi Tonne di xiiii foot of tymber of fowlbroke and iii Tonne in badlands at xiiii d the Tonne with dyverse other necessaryes workes and repacons (with xxxiiii s iiii d for making a new bote)[3] as may appere by the sayde booke of paymentes within the tyme of this accompt
xvii li ix s iiii d

forren charges For the sayde accomptantes expenses aswell in ryding to London at ii severall tymes and dyverse other wayes xviii s iiii d In rewarde to dyverse men at sondry tymes comyng to view the repacons of the workes to be done toward the defrayeng of their charges iiii s, for the xvth of the quenes maiestie for your lords wood in Berkherst xv d, for the expenses of your lordship officers coming to deliver your wood and workes at ii severall tymes xiiii s as appereth by the boke of payments afforeseyd within this accompt
xxxvii s vii d

[*5*^{r}] water workes For Cuttinge of wedes in the Ryver and hammer dyche at sundrye tymes and for repayringe of bankes and walles aboute the workes with iiii li xii s iii d for the Charge in makinge a new dyche to cary the backe water frome the fordge. And xlix s iiii d for makinge a dich to bringe the water frome the furnace ponde to the fordge. And x li xv s i d to dyverse laborers in Stopping the Ryver and

[3] Inserted.

laying the new gutt under the Ryver, besyde the Carryadge and Carpinters work as may appere by the sayde book of payments within the tyme of this accompt xx li vii s vi d

yron makers viz to The hamerman and fyners for making of Cl Tonns xiiii^C^iiii^or^ pownds of yron at sondrye pryces within the tyme of this accompt as may appere by the seyde booke Ci li iii s ii d ob

heping of Coles and sowes To dyverse persons for hepyng of Coles lvii s i d and for hepyng of Sowes xv s as appereth by the seyde booke within the time of this accompt iii li xii s i d

wages and Bordwages To Peter Jellye for bothe the fyneres in full discharge of all his wages due at the last of may beinge then discharged iii li iii s iiii d, To Anthony Pullen for his wages for like tyme xxiiii s iiii d, To Phillip [hilles] for his wages for like tyme xviii s iiii d, To the sayde accomptant for his wages for one yere and one quarter endyd mydsumer 1573 iiii li iii s iiii d, And for his bordwages for the like tyme at ii s iiii d the weke vii li xi s viii d as may appere by the seyde booke xvii li

[5^v^] Redye money payde To Hercules Raynsforde gent at your lordship last beinge at Robertsbridge to your use and by your lordship comandment x li, And to Arkinwalde Parkins to deliver your lordship xxx li as (which xxx li was delyvered to Walter)[4] xl li

Sume of all the saide paymentes CCClxi li xix d ob

And so the saide accomptannt owith uppon this accompte xxix li xvii s i d ob

William Blountt gent for money by him Receyved of walter fyrsbye for the pryce of halfe a Tonne of yron within the tyme of thys accompt as may appere by his byll Under his owne hande dated the xi^th^ of October 1572 C s

(Thys is set over to paswatertone care)[5]

And uppon the sayde accomptant for his clere dett due unto your lordship uppon this accompt xxiiii li xvii s i d ob

(Thys as the next before)[6]

wherof the sayde accomptant is allowed for Cuttinge of wood and other necessaries heretofore delivered to the stele works, and ys to [lend] my lord ageine by Edmund Roberts xlii s viii d

4 Different hand.

5 In the same hand as in n. 4; written in the margin.

6 In the same hand as in n. 4; written in the margin.

And then the saide accomptant owethe Clerelye uppon this accompt xxii li xiiii s v d ob[7]

[*6*^{r}] Robertsbridge

The declaracons of the Remaynes there taken the xvith of may in the xvth year of our soveraigne Ladye quene Elizabeth

Iron The laste yeres Remayne in the Iron house at the fordge viii Ton xviii^{C}iii quarters xiii libri

And ys made in yron within the tyme of this accompte as by the sayde boke of paymentes apperithe Cl ton xiiii^{C} iiii^{or} libri

Sume of all the sayde yron Clix Tonnes xii^{C}iii quarters xvii libri

Whereof

Solde to dyverse persons by this accomptant xxiiii^{or} Tonns xvii^{C} xii libri. And xi^{C}ii libri delyvered for reparacons and dyverse necessaryes as may appere in this accompte. And iiii^{xx}viii Tonnes delyvered unto Richarde Wekes in full payment of hys complement aswell for the yere laste past as for the tyme within thys accompt for the halfe due unto him. And xlii Tonnes xv^{C}iii quarters ii libri delyvered to william webb uppon dyverse bargaynes as may hereafter appere. And so in deficient iii Tonnes ix^{C} one pownde of yron Where unto this accomptant answereth that he was over Charged In his last accompt in the title of Remaynes of yron ii Ton and a halfe. And yett deficit xix^{C} one pownde yt semyth that this deficient was lost this yere in the drawght or over waight for that this yere there hath byn muche solde by reteyle to smythes

[*6*^{v}] Cords of wood The last yeres Remayne Mix^{C}xxii Cords

And cutt thys yere in sondry woods as before particlerly appeareth MMix^{C} one corde iii quarters

Sume of all the said Cords iiii^{M}viii^{C}xxiii cordes iii quarters wherof ys made in Coles this yere MMCli Corde at the rate of iii Cords iii quarters to every lode. And allowed to the Collyers for makinge of bridges to Carye of whelbarowe one Corde, iii quarters. And delyvered Michaell weston for hys Coplement thys yere and in part of the next yere MMvi^{C}lxxi Cords

And so remayneth nothinge

Coles The laste yeres remayne C lodes

And Coled thys yere vi^{C}xxvii lodes

Summe of all the sayde Coles vii^{C}xxvii lodes whereof spent within

[7] Originally written xv s v d.

the tyme of this accompt at the sayde fordge for the makinge of vii^{xx}x Ton xiiii^{C} iiii^{or} libri of yron, all the sayde Coles which ys under the Rate of v lodes of Coles to every Tonne of yron, as hath byn accustomed to allow by xxvi lode iii quarters

[7^{r}] Sowes The laste yeres Remayne at the fordge in sowes lxvi Ton iiii^{C}xvi libri

And receyvyd of Richarde Wekes within the tyme of This accompte Ciiii^{xx} Tonne

Sume of all the said Sowes CCxlvi Tonnes iiii^{C}xvi libri whereof wrought into Yron for the makinge of Cl Tonnes xiiii^{C}iiii^{or} libri of yron after the Rate of one Ton and a halfe of sowes to make a Tonne of Yron CCxxvi Tonnes one hundred vi libri. And so remainith xx Tonnes iii^{C}x libri, where unto ys to be added xxx Ton of sowes defalked on the Remayne at the last yeres accompt for to make xx^{ti} Ton of yron for mr Wekes due for his full coplement the last yere, Because the same yron was made within the tyme of thys accompt. And then Remaynith l Tonnes iii^{C}x libri whereof delyvered to the saide Michaell Weston to be worked to halfes xxxvii Tonnes one hundred vii libri. And so shoulde remayne xiii Ton iii^{C}iii libri, which ys in deficient and supposed to be wasted in plats aboute the fordge and harthes.

[7^{v}] *blank*

[8^{r}] The declaracon of the Clere gaynes of the yron workes for thys one yere xvi dayes ended the xvith of May 1573

firste in the pryce of xxiiii^{or} Tonnes of Iron xvii^{C}xii libri solde by thys accomptant to sondry persons for CCxlvi li xviii s x d. And solde to Mr Webbe xx ton at ix li the Tonne Ciiii^{xx} li.[8] And v Tonne solde to Mr Bacon and Mr Webbe at viii li the Tonne xl li. And xvii Ton xv^{C}iii quarters ii libri delyvered to Mr Webbe in parte of payment of xxx^{ti} Tonnes solde for viii li xiii s iiii d the Tonne Cxlvii li xiii s iiii d. Besyde xi^{C}ii libri delyvered for dyverse necessaryes. And beside xxviii Tonne delyvered unto Richarde Wekes in full payment of his Coplement for sowes the laste yere. And lx Ton for sowes receyvyd of him within the tyme of this accompte vi^{C}xiiii li xii s ii d

Summe of the saide value vi^{C}xiiii li xii s ii d whereof there ys to be abated aswell for money by this accomptant paide for sondrye workes done there as for necessaries bought as before may playnlye

[8] This first entry conflicts with 149 (U 1475 A4/4), the Receiver's Account, which shows 20 tons sold for £190.

appere with the [ ] of the Stocke spent likewise v^{c}iii li ii s vii d ob

And so remain Clere gayned this yere Cxiii li ix s vi d ob

Shoued as a Just accompt and the accomptant a Just honest man

by me H. Sydney[9]

[9] In Sir Henry Sidney's hand.

[18] STEELWORKS ACCOUNTS, 1566[1]

384 *U 1475 B4/1*

[*1r*] The Book of the Generall Acompte of the Stelle workes 1566

[*1v*] *blank*

[*2r*] 1566 In primys paide John Frolycke and John Bowde for there expencys lynge longe by the waie mor then they Receavede of my Mr Sarvante in flanders nett 01–04–0 1

Item paid a Duchman that came from London to be an intarpretor betwene my Mr and them and was here the space of [4] daies 01–10–0

. . . for ther expencys here and conveinge the Duchmene to London and for his horse hyer 00–10–0

. . . John frolycke and John bowde at ther departure to beare there charges to Andwarpe 02–00–0

. . . for John Bowdes orden[ar]ys in London and other 3 Duchmen the 28[th] of June 1565 at ther goinge into Walles 02–09–0

. . . John Bowde in his purse then in London nett 01–10–0

. . . the Caryare that Caryed them to Bristowe nett 01–06–8

. . . for the Cariars charges in London taringe for them nett 01–06–8

. . . John Bowde the 25th of July 1565 at his goinge over 01–00–0

. . . for his orden[ar]y and John Witherdens Ridinge to Dover and for horse heier 00–08–0

Item the 4th of october 1565 paid Ralfe halle for bringinge over the Duchemen 02–00–0

Item paid Swettinges wife of Rie for ther meate the same daie 00–06–0

. . . mor for meate they dide eate aborde Ralfe halle 00–02–0

Item the 5th of october 1565 to the Stele workes 3C of 10d Naylles nett 00–02–6

Item the 1 daye paid 2 men that Brought Gervase and his company from Caunterbury 00–10–0

[1] This account is in poor condition. The ink has soaked into the paper making entries on the reverse difficult to read, particularly on the upper half of the page. There is also damage to the bottom corners of pages, and the microfilm available in the Library of Congress shows that some deterioration must have taken place since 1942, when the record was made.

Item to the workes a C of 10d nailles 00–00–10
Item paid frinde of dressynge of 6 hides for the belowes the 13th of october 1565 00–12–0
Item the 14 daie paid for 4 quartes of wine for the duchmen 00–01–1[0]
Item the 17th a C of 3d nailles and on C 4d naills 00–00–07

£16–[ ][2]

[*2v*] Item the 18 of October 1566 paid for i thesell 3 axses an on [ ] for the duchmen 00–05–7
Item more to the workes on C of 10d nailles 00–00–10
Item paid alborne for bordinge of 5 men 01–00–00
. . . ashomaker for bordinge of 4 men 00–15–00
. . . [ ]ade for bordinge of 4 men 8 daies 00–16–[0]
. . . for 5 C of bordes at 3s 4d the C 00–16–8
. . . coulgate for caringe a lode of bordes from Selscome to Robertsbrige 00–03–00
. . . Jeames barden for carringe of colles at [to]rise in parte of payment 00–13–00
Item to the workes a C of 4d nailles and ½ a C of 5d nailles 00–00–6½
Item paid mor for bordes net 01–02–0
Item to the workes ½ a C and 5li of yrone to make hoppes for the belowes nett 00–05–6
Item the 23rd 2 C priges 2 C 4d nailles and ½ a C 10d nailles 00–01–03
mor 2000 of priges at 00–01–8
Item paid the sawiers for [7] daies sawinge of belowe bordes the 25th with ther borde 01–01–0
. . . John dowrke for 16 hydes hade of him for the belows at 6/8 the pece 04–16–0
Item the same with ½ a C of 10d nailles and 3C 4d nails 00–01–5
Item mor a ¼ and 10 li of yron for the workes 00–03–4
Item the 26th 200 of 3d nailles 00–00–6
Item paid sander gilbarde for 11 daies worke for 3 of his men at 5d the daie 00–13–9
Item the 29th ½ a C of 10d nailles a C 4d nailles and a C 3d nailles 00–01–[0]
mor 300 of 2d nailles and 40 10d nailles 00–00–[ ]
Item paid Mr Williams to paie the sawiers 00–05–[ ]
. . . Rich gilbarde for 14 daies worke at 7d the daie 00–08–[ ]

[2] The totals are also written in the left margin, several are illegible or damaged.

. . . for carringe of the canvas *and* for 2 mallinge cordes for the duchmen	o[ ] o [ ]
. . . for the Duchmens ordenry in London	o –[ ]
	£13–[ ]

2

[3ʳ] Item the 3rd of November 1566 paid Mr blacknowle for carringe of earth and powles at divers tymes	00–14–0
Item paid John husson for 55 li of belowe nailles at 4d[½]d the li	01–00–6
Item ½ a C of 10d nailles ½ a C 4d nailles and a C of 3d nailles at	00–00–10
Item paid for 2 gallons and a quarte of traine	00–05–2
mor 23 li of tallowe at 3d the li	00–05–10
Item paid Ric gilbarde for 7 daies worke at 7d the daie	00–04–1
. . . for a matoke for the worke men	00–01–0
Item the 17 of November 1565 william renolde for 16 daies worke at 6d the daie	00–08–0
Item paid William Weller for 20 daies worke	00–10–0
. . . sander Robens for 12 days worke	00–06–0
. . . Jeames barden for 26 daies worke about the makinge the belowes at Robertsbrige	01–16–0
. . . him more for drawinge the belowe pipes and for 2 li of candell	00–06–8
Item the 18th paid a coriare for to helpe Dresse the belowes and for 2 shets of lead spent aboute them then	00–02–2
Item paid the tinker for mendinge the copper at Robertsbrige	00–03–6
Item the 19 of november 1565 paid coulgate for caringe of 20 corrdes of woode to the Duchmen	00–18–0
Item paid for fraight of Gervases chest and for charge over Lande	00–03–8
. . . for bringinge of the Duchmens canvas from London to flymwell	00–03–0
. . . John apese for bringinge the plates from chinglye fornes at Robersbrige	00–07–4
. . . for 2 bordens ¾ of stele for the Duchmen to make the tolles withe	00–18–0
. . . Richard Vousden for 17 days worke about the makinge of the belowes	00–10–7
	£09–04–5

[3^v] . . . Edwarde Renett for worke done about the said belowes 00–04–8
Item the 25th of november 1565 paid Richard gilbarte for 14 daies worke on of his men and on daie a boye at Robersbrige 00–07–3
Item for 11 C $\frac{3}{4}$ and 21[li] of yron delyvered per Mr Blacknowle for the stele workes 00
Item paid thomas butcher for 8 plates for the stele workes nett 04–06–8
. . . brisindon for bringinge of nessesaris to Robersbrige 00–07–4
. . . for fraighte of 21 tonnes of plates from Cardife [in] Walles to Rie and paid in december 1565 033–00–0
Item the 10 of December 1565 $\frac{1}{2}$ a C 10d nailles 000–00–5
Item paid Richard gilbarde for on daies worke 000–00–7
. . . for a beame in London to waie the Stele 000–01–10
Item the 30th of december 1565 for 2 dayes worke about the belowes 000–00–10
Item paid Smythe for tillinge at Robersbrige 000–02–6
. . . for sackes to carrie the Stele in 000–02–0
. . . Jeames barden for caringe of 109 loodes of colle into the house and for 39 lodes hade of John mathewe 000–16–0
. . . him mor for makenge of hamers and anvells for the Duchmen 000–05–0
. . . for 2 hogges geven to Gervase 000–05–0
. . . collman for worke don by him at Robersbrige in tillinge and dabinge 00–14–6
Item the 27th of January 1565 a thousande of priges 00–01–0
mor a C of 3d nailles 00–00–3
mor 20 10d nailles 00–00–2
Item paid Richard gilbarde for 3 daies Worke at Robersbrige at 6d the day 00–01–6
Item the 3 of february 1565 a C of 3d nailles 000–00–3
Item paid coulgate for carringe of a loode of corde wood 00–01–[6]
mor for fechinge on loode of bricke at Ewhurste net 00–01–8
mor for caringe 2 grinstones to the place 00–00–6
mor for caringe of hamer blockes and trowghtes 00–04–0
mor for 21 loodes of plates to the place from the ocke 01–01–0
mor for on daies caringe dobinge earthe 00–02–0
mor for a shovell lente the duchmen and broken 00–00–10

£42–08–9

3

[4r] Item Paide William Blacknowll for bordinge of the duchmen before they [went to worke] 02–19–6
mor for bordinge other duchmen besides 00–08–4
Item mor for caringe and worke don by him about the stele work 001–01–8
Item paid for [ ] for John Frolycke at his beyng here 000–14–0
. . . unto Lade alborn [ ] and sharpe of Salhurste and Robersbrige for bordinge of certayne of the duchmen before They begane to worke 006–05–1
. . . for lightrege of 22 tonnes of plates from Rie to the ocke 001–16–8
. . . for [ ] 2 grinstons for the workes 000–08–0
. . . for the [sartifycathe] for the plates 000–01–8
. . . to Gervas for so mych geven him in consideration of his great travell paynes and charges taken upon him in governinge the men in ther worke 200 dallers at [4s 4d] the daller nett 043–06–8
Item mor for the Charges of the said Garvas him selfe and 17 men more from holantyde tyll christmas 025–04–0
Item mor for his wage of a dalar and ¼ the weke and a daller for every on of his men from the 13th of auguste 1565 unto the 10th of october folowing 254 dallers at [s 4d] the daller 033–07–8
Item paid for 10 beedes and bolsters bought of Mr [ege] and for canvas bought of Mr gamage with elles as apereth 23–03–0
. . . Mr [ ] for bordinge of carpentors tillers and other workmen the sume of 03–07–8
. . . him mor for buter chese and bere for the duchmen beinge before halantide at the makinge of chimneys harthes and elles 003–15–8
. . . for cuttinge of cross brases for the belowes 15d and makinge a saw pitte 6d and for 2 loodes belowe long tymber and 2 great loges to the stage 000–03–9
. . . the Sawiers for sawinge of timber for the belowes and tables 000–
. . . clarke of euhurst for ½ a 100 of brickes 00–03–4

£146–06–8

[*4*ᵛ] . . . for the charges of Gervase his worke and [expensys] here at the leaste 14 dayes [ ] about 25 or 26 parsons before they went to worke at 6d the daie wyth lodginge 006–00–0

. . . henery Sheafe for 16 halfe barrells to put Stele in at 10d the barrell 000–13–4

. . . hym mor for [ ]ynge of an old barrell to put stele in net 000–00–8

. . . John frolycke to paie a gide that brought him from Andwarpe 000–18–0

. . . Gervase with the reste of the Masters and men at the new contracte made with them the 22nd of february 1565 for longer [ ] 000–17–6

. . . John frolycke at his departure onto flanders the 24th of february 156[5] 002–00–0

. . . for 4[ ]th [ ] which my Mr gave Gervase 001–12–0

. . . John [ ] and 4 men for 3 days worke at Robersbrige 000–03–0

. . . for a spade for the workes 000–01–0

. . . [a gide] that brought 2 duchmen from Rie to hawkhurst and for ther breckfast ther 000–02–4

. . . coulgate and blacknowle for cariage of 10 half barells of stele from Robersbrige to the ocke the 22nd 00

. . . John the yntarpretor upon his wages 001–00–0

. . . thomas moris for lightrage of 3 halfe barrells of stele from the ocke to Rye 000–02–0

. . . Robert awinter for lightrege of 7½ barells of stele from the ocke to Rie 000– 2–6

. . . John gillians for fraight of 10½ barells stele from Rie to london for 2 tons ½ at 4s 4d a ton 000–10–10

. . . John husher at his goinge [into] Walles to colliar 000–10–0

. . . Mr Knyght and is for Smyth as he paid for the makinge the Lyverie and for the great seale for the Stele workes the 16 of marche 1565 006–00–0

. . . for the duch founders wages and John hushers in London at ther goinge into Walles 000–19–6

. . . for 12 yardes a ¼ and ½ of new color for the duchmen in Walles at 8s the yarde 004–19–0

. . . Richard gilbarde for 8 daies hewinge of timber findinge him selfe at 14d the daie 00–09–4

£26–11–0

4

[5r] . . . Wyllyam for [ ] for 8 daies hewing belowe bordes finding himself at 12d the day 000–08–0
. . . Richard Gilbard for [2] daies hewinge timber for the brige at Robersbrige 000–01–9
. . . william weller for 3 days hewinge timber ther also 000–01–6
. . . Ralfe halle upon his fraight into walles for plates the 25th of marche 1566 002–00–0
. . . for John Ramsdens charges then in Rie 000–01–0
. . . Robart [croge] and his partenor for 7 days ½ sawinge of belowe bordes beyonde flymwell at 14d the day 000–08–9
Item for Duchmens pasage and for bere and bread they had in the shipe 000–17–0
Item paid them at their comynge from London to hawkhurst 001–00–0
. . . for ther ordenary in London 000–03–4
. . . on that brought them from London to hawkhurse the 7th of Aprell 1566 000–08–0
Item my mr ought to be alowed for the meat drinke and brede of the 5 duchmen that came hether the 7th dito and taried for that nyght had ther drinkinge soper beede and breckfast 000–03–6
Item paid Mr Keltrege for 3 beedes more for the duchmen 003–00–0
. . . Robart barker for bringinge those 3 beedes from London to flymwell 000–08–0
. . . mudells wyffe for the sawiers borde that sawed the bellowe Bordes 000–09–0
. . . thomas Bericke for 20 li belowe nailles for the belowes 000–07–6
. . . Edmond wenor for 7 hides for the belows at 6s 002–02–0
Item the 11th of Aprell paid gorge Moris for Caringe 14 tons of stele plates from Rie to the ocke 001–03–4
Item the 12th paid Robart[e]rige and his partenor for 3 days sawinge belowe bordes at 14d the day 000–03–6
Item paid for ther borde these 3 day 000–03–0
Item the 13th paid for makinge of 2 colle weanes 001–01–7
Item paid for pailles for the duchmen 000–02–0
. . . christofer for his halfe yers servis at his goinge awaie 001–04–4
Item more for his halfe yere borde nett 03–00–0
Item paid mor for pailles for the duchmen 00–02–8
Item the 24th paid for caringe of 9 verkins stele from the ocke to Rie 000–03–9

£019–03–6

[5v] Item paid for a C 2d nailles [ ] 00–00–3½
. . . william fyndall for fraight of [9] verkins of stele from Rie to London acounted for 2 tymes 00–10–0
. . . the [searcher] for the coket nett 000–00–4
. . . Ralfe halle upon his fraight into Walles for the stele plates 020–00–0
. . . for bringinge a hogshed of trayne oylle and settyng 8 [hoppes] in yt [00]–00–8
. . . thomas moris for caringe of 20 tonnes of stele plates from Rie to the ocke 00–16–8
. . . gorge moris for caringe 12 tonnes stele plates from Rie to the ocke at [20d] the tonne 001–04–4
. . . for [ ] charges at bodiam and for help to unlode them 000–00–10
. . . collman for 4 daies worke at Robersbrige 000–04–0
. . . for 2 mallinge cordes for the beedes in London 000–01–4
. . . for caringe them into southworke 000–00–8
. . . for helpe to Lade 2 halfe barrells of stele sent to Mr Winches 000–00–2
. . . for carringe ½ a barrell into woodstreat and for help to Lade it 000–00–6
Item geven the osteler to se it convaied unto Coventrie 000–00–4
Item the 7th of maie 1566 to the workes 6 gallons of trayne at 18d the gallon 000–09–0
Item paid for the charges of 28 men for contynewing her before they went to worke divers and sundrie daies per the particulers to be sene for Mr John and all his company at Robersbrige with other of Gervases men 005–17–6
. . . thomas drew for charges and expenses of 9 duchmen and him selfe from Andwarpe to hawckhurste over and besides 7 li paid him in Andwerp per Mr Marklen 004–06–6
. . . John dewke for 6 hides for the belowes at 6s pece 001–16–0
Item spent per [nyc] unladynge the stele plates 000–00–6
Item paid xpofer in part of his heier for bringinge over the Duchmen the 12th of maie 1566 000–06–0
. . . for a sartificate for the stele plates at Rie 00–02–2
Item geven Mr John a potell poot pris 00–00–4
Item the 14th paid John Ducke for 3 hides mor at 6s pece 00–18–0

£36–13–1½

5

[6r] Item paid for plates at Robersbrige and for nailles at Boxhurste 000–0[ ]–1

. . . for 4 gallons of trayne for the belowes at 18d the gallon 000–06–0

Item more for 18 li of tallowe hade of Gervase 000–03–9

Item paid for 6 C ½ of 2d nailles 000–01–1

Item the 18th of maie 1566 a C 4d nailles and a C 3d nailles at 000–00–7

Item paid thomas fylpote for 5 Lambe skynes for the Duchmen 000–02–1

. . . thomas Moris for carringe 4 verkins of stele from the ocke to Rie 000–01–8

. . . for caringe of 6 yron poots to battell 000–00–3

. . . for bringinge of this 6 pootes from London to hawckhurste 000–01–0

Item the 21st dito paid Edmond wenor for on hide for the belowes 000–06–0

Item spent by mr John Davison[3] when I went to staie the 4 duchmen which went awaie at Rie 000–00–10

Item paid the sargante for arestinge them 000–01–4

. . . the searcher for his fee of John hilles coket at his goinge into Walles 000–00–6

Item the 22nd dito spent per John Ramsden in sendinge John Gilles awaie 000–03–0

Item paid for my Mr charges aboute the duchmen which wer goinge awaie the 25th maie 000–05–0

. . . for 2 basketes to carry colles in 000–02–0

. . . mathew wood for bere the 9 duchmen hade abord him and for that he was trobled with them 000–05–0

. . . the sargante at Rie for the charges of the duchmen which wer goinge awaie the 27th 000–15–8

. . . for Jno Ramsdens ordenry and horsmeat at Rie about yt 000–01–8

. . . for caringe of 3 yrone pootes from the[r] syde to [dise] keye 000–00–3

. . . bells wife for the 2 duchmens charges that went over the first of June 1566 000–02–4

. . . wibley and the other carier upon a compte of caringe stele plates 001–00–0

£04–01–1

[3] Replaces *me*.

1566

[6v] ... [ ] John Cre[ ]r in a Reknynge made with him the 4th of [Jun] 000–18–0
... [henery sharpe] for makinge of 12 ferkins to put the stele in at 000–10–0
Item to the workes the 10 of June 1566 500 of priges 000–00–6
Item paid for thomas dans and Mr John horsmeat in London the 13th 000–01–10
Item the 18th paid for caringe of dustes to the forges 000–04–6
Item paid thomas moris for caringe of 4 verkins of stele from the ocke to Rie 000–01–8
more for 4 verkins from Bodiam to Rie 000–01–6
... for 2[2] elles a $\frac{1}{4}$ and $\frac{1}{2}$ of canvas to make 3 beedes and bolsters therto and for 20 stone of floxe at 8d the stone and for makinge them 002–07–6
... Mr clarke of Sandwich for fraighte of 8 verkins of stele from Rie to London at 4s 8d the tonne 000–09–4
... for nailles to mend the steel barrells in London 000–00–7
Item the 12 of July 1566 paid John hilles in part of payment of 34 li dewe to him for his fraight into walles 020–00–0
Item paid him mor in full payment of this 34 li 014–00–0
... for lightrege of 50 tonnes of plattes from Rie to Bodiam at 18d the tonne 003–15–0
mor for carringe them to boxhurst 20d and 4s over in the holle 004–07–4
... Ralfe halle per thomas dan in Walles in full payment of 28 li dewe to him for his fraight thether for Stele plates 006–00–0
... for 2 yardes $\frac{1}{2}$ of clothe for Gervase which was promysed him at 10s the yarde 001–05–0
... vowsden of goudhurst for worke don by him about the belowes 000–08–0
... for his Borde the same tyme 000–03–6
... Jeames barden for drawinge of 12 paier of belowe pipes for Boxhurste 000–12–0
mor for 8 paier of belowe pipes 000–08–0
mor for 5 andvells at 000–01–8
... frinde for dressinge of 16 hiddes for boxhurst 000–08–0

£056–03–11

6

[7r] ... Thomas fytzegefory for his charges about the stele and takinge of corde woode 000–04–2
... for a C 2d nailles [ ] for the belowes 00–00–7

. . . to fylpote of [ ] 000–00–5
. . . henery [ ] for the makinge of 60½ barrells for stele made befor the primo of September 1566 at 10d the barelle wherof theis 16 writen [ ] and her 44 I saie 001–16–8
. . . longe Jacobe for caringe of colles into the colhouse at Robersbrige nett 000–04–0
. . . thomas standen for yron workes to the collewean 000–07–0
. . . mor for 2 paier of whelles net 001–02–0
. . . for caringe in of colles and synder awaie to make the place even 000–02–4
. . . for 100 of ii d nailles to naille the stele barrells 000–00–2
. . . for lightrege of 69½ barrells stele shiped to London and into walles befor the 12 of september 1566 at 20d the tonne 001–07–11
. . . for fraight of the saide stele excepte for 4½ halfe barrells sent into walles which is a compted for 16 tonnes ½ at 5s the tonne 004–01–3
. . . for carringe of 11 verkins of stele from boxhurste to bodyame per wibley and enerye 000–05–0
Item le 8 of august 1566 paid Renold lye for flotage of 50 tonnes of stele plates at Bodyame and for 2 tonne ½ of stele and 2 chaldron of coles 000–12–0
Item paid for 4 chaldron of colles carried to Robersbrige from boxhurste to make ther colles at 16s the chaldron net 003–04–0
. . . for 2 grindstones for the workes 00–06–0
. . . for carringe of the saide colles to Robersbrige and boxhurste and lightrege up nett 00–18–0
Item spent per thomas fizgefery at his Ridinge into walles as per his bille of particullers alpereth 01–16–6
Item paid for Jno davisons charges Ridinge to seeke after the duchmen at dover Rie hethe net 000–03–7
Item spent mor per John Ramsden Ridinge to london about them nett 000–08–0
Item paid a surgant in part of payment of curinge duchmen 000–10–0

£17–09–7

[7ᵛ] . . . for [Lyley] to Lade 34 loodes of colle at the old fornes at Robersbrige 000–01–4
. . . thomas [ ] for [ ] and Roodes 9 daies at vi d the daie 000–04–6

. . . for carringe 2 verkins of stele into the Storehouse in London net 000–00–4
. . . on man 5 daies ladinge colle at 12d the daie 000–05–0
. . . mr Keltrege for canvas floxe and makinge of beedes for the duchmen 003–10–0
. . . [a colliere] in parte of paymente of carringe colles 000–06–4
. . . Jeames barden in part of payment of makinge of belowes and such lyke 000–10–0
. . . Mr Burcokes man for letinge the duchmen bloud 000–06–0
. . . old peter for caringe of 7 loodes of colle to the colle nett 000–00–9
. . . for 2 baskettes to carre colles nett 000–01–8
. . . a coper for worke done aboute the Stele barells in London the 27th of august 1566 000–06–0
. . . help to lade 20 verkins of Stele in London 000–00–8
. . . for carringe of a verkine of Stele to send to yorke and for wharfage and to the water balye 000–00–8
. . . Mr Burcoke for letinge the duchmen bloude and for medcins for them 001–04–0
. . . a boot to feet the stele from oxney verie to Rie 000–02–0
. . . for John Ramsdens ordenry at Rie Shipinge of the Stele 000–02–0
. . . for caringe of colles into the house 000–01–0
. . . for a paier of shoes for John Bowde 000–01–3
. . . Mr John the surgant for mynystringe of medcines to the duchmen in part of payment 000–10–0
. . . wiblis wife for a barell of bere for the duchmen 000–02–8
Item to the workes at boxhurst a C 4d nailles 000–00–4
Item paid old peter and others for carringe in of 20 lodes of cole into the house at Robersbrige 000–02–0
Item a C ½ of 2d nailles for the Stele barrells 000–00–3
Item paid Mr John the surgant as full payment of all surgerie done per him to the duchmen 001–00–0

£8–18–9

7

[8r] . . . for the Charges of John Bode and John frolycke [ ] John bern[ ] and Jno [ ] the begynynge of them until this present 24th of september 1566 nett 015–00–0
. . . mr adolf [ ]incke and is for so myche geven him in consideration of his great travell in gettinge the men yett 004–09–0

. . . him [asketh] geven him in Andwarpe upon like consideration as is foresaid 00
. . . henericke and his brother and [ ] and his wiffe of vitaills hade at Blacknalls for them 000–07–4
. . . barden for ladinge 84 loodes colles and bearing them 000–05–4
. . . Rouse for carringe in 2 loodes of colles 000–00–4
Item spent per them as [for] gefferie beinge a daie and a nyght with the workemen 000–00–10
Item paid old peter for caringe of colles 000–01–0
. . . for a C ½ of bordes for the workes 000–06–0
. . . for a C of nailles for the workes 000–00–6
. . . harmon for carringe of colles 000–00–4
. . . symon morell for carringe 16 loodes colles and bredinge of walls with Roodes 000–02–4
Item the 5 of september 1566 spent per thomas takinge of corde wood and felles 000–00–3
Item paid pawle for cuttinge of 12 powles 000–00–3
. . . on that brought them out of the wood 000–00–4
Item spent more per thomas nett 000–00–2
Item the 12th of september 1566 paid for canvas and floxe to make abeede for the duchmen 000–10–0
Item more for thryde and makynge the bede 000–01–0
Item to the Duchmen 12 elles of canvas to make sheets at 9d ½ thelle 000–09–6
Item paid and geven 3 duchmen that went a waie 000–04–0
Item geven them mor to beare ther charges to Andwarpe 000–13–0
Item paid for ther ordnry in Rie and myne and for my horsmeat and for on that cared them in to the [ ]dell 000–04–2
Item to make a bolster 2 nailles of floxe at 16 the naylle 000–02–8

£22–18–4

[*8v*] Item the 8th of september 1566 paid peter for filling 3 Lodes of [ ] 000–00–4
Item paid symon [ ] for [ ]inge of colles 000–00–8
. . . [Renie for makinge] 14 lodes of colles at the olde fornes 000–00–8
. . . for thomas expenses goinge about the woodes taken of colles 000–00–3

. . . on for gatheringe 9 bordens of loodes 000–01–4

. . . [fryth] for settinge up a fornese and brekinge[ ] a stone wall and makinge [ ] 000–06–8

. . . symon and gelles colliars for carringe 13 loodes of colles 000–0[ ]–0

. . . [henrey] for carringe of 12 loodes of olde [colles] 000–01–6

. . . harmon for carringe of colles 000–01–0

. . . coulgat for carringe of plates and stele wood and elles as per the particullers by his bille apere 002–05–5

. . . [ ] for the caringe of all the olde colles savinge that carride before from the old furnes 002–00–0

. . . for helpe to waie the plates at boxhurste 000–00–6

. . . for 15 li of tallowe for the belows at 2d $\frac{1}{2}$ le lib 000–03–1$\frac{1}{2}$

. . . mor for 2 gallons of traine at 18d le galon 000–03–0

. . . for a gallon of flower for the belows 000–00–4

. . . henery sheafe for makinge 2 barells for Mr John at 3s and on at 16d 000–07–4

. . . for a paille for the workes 000–00–8

. . . for a yarde of canvas and for 4 li of fether for to make a pillows for them 000–02–8

Item the 24 of september 1566 paid for 2 gallons traine 000–03–0

Item paid mor for 6 li of talowe at 2d $\frac{1}{2}$ le li 000–01–3

. . . for 2 C of 2d nailles for the workes 000–00–4

Item the 29 daie paid brisinden for carringe of a C xl loodes of synder and yearth from the place net 000–08–0

Item paid him for carringe 6 loodes of Lomes 000–01–0

. . . him for fechinge of 5 cortes secolles from the place 000–02–4

. . . and spent then per thomas net 000–00–3

. . .per enrys sonne of caringe in 4 Loodes of colle 000–00–6

£6–13– $\frac{1}{2}$

8

[9r] . . . holte for bearinge of 12 loodes of olde colle into the house nett 000–01–6

. . . Rouse for bearinge of 16 loodes of colle into the house nett 000–01–4

. . . pawles servante for carringe in of 4 loodes of colles into the house 000–00–4

. . . and spent then by thomas for gefery 000–00–3

. . . wybleyt for caringe of the workmens stufe from Robersbrige to boxhurste 000–02–4

... vinsnols man for bearinge in of 9 lodes colle into the house 000–01–0
... and spent per thomas 000–00–4
... for 5 plattes for the belows 000–01–3
... for 400 of nailles 000–00–8
... on fortrimynge of the belows 000–00–4
... to Ger vase Krisker Mr of the workes at boxhurste per accompte made with him for makinge 34 barrells and a halfe of stele at 3 li the barrell amounteth to 103–10–0
... unto John verderbecke Mr of the workes at Robersbrige upon accompt of all suche stele as he and his company hath made sithens ther comynge into the countrie 36–02–6
... Gervase per so mych as he remayneth in debte per accompte made with him this present 29th of September 1566 over and above his Rewarde and the stele which he hath made deducted the some of 96–10–0

£236–11–10

Item mor per so mych paid for the buildinge of the worke house at boxhurste on dwellinge house and parte of another with 2 great colle houses which wille amounte unto at the Leste a hundreth poundes to be syne per the particulers
... as remaineth unto John bowde by contracte in fulle of 2000 dallers dewe unto him to be paid in such order as we shall beste agree ether the holle or rebatinge of part therof yf by any meanes yt maie with him be broughte to pase I saie fower hondreth and therty poundes

[*9v*] Some totallis of all the somes before wryten amounteth unto vi^C^lxiii li ii s besydes the charges for buildinge the houses and work houses at boxhurst and the money to be paid unto John Bowde some 663–02–0

9

[*10r*] Charges dysbursed in flanders
Item paide unto [ ] in Emden and [ ] at divers tymes for the procuring of John frolycke and Jno Bowde for the Tryalle of the myne for the stele in charges giftes and elles as per the [said] starkys accompte maie apere wrytten 034–10–0
... mor to the saide frolycke and bowde the 24th of marche 1566 at ther first comynge unto Inglande for ther wages by contract made with them 007–10–0

P

. . . for ther charges [ ] in Andwarpe for passage and for makinge aparell promysed them 002–11–10

. . . unto Mr peter [ ] hawgat for clothe hade for ther aparrell 009–18–8

. . . mor to them in money to paie for ther charges thence at ther first comynge net 003–15–0

. . . to the said frolycke and boude at ther retorne the 21st of aprell 1565 out of Inglande againe for the procuringe of Masters and men and for ther charges 060–00–0

. . . for John Bowdes charges in Andwarpe at his Retorne out of duchlande with the myners and Berghe Knighten for 7 or 8 daies 001–15–7

. . . him in money at his goinge with them into Inglande to paie ther charges 008–02–2

. . . for postage of letters out of duchlande and Inglande to Andwarpe 000–03–4

. . . John Boude the laste of July 1565 at his Retorne out of walles with the myne to Andwarpe 002–15–0

. . . for bowdes Charges at Andwarpe 000–14–10

. . . for charges of him and frolycke at ther goynge into duchlande Laste before which is not writen in the other charges afore 000–18–4

Item the 10 of september 1565 paid for postage of letters out of duchlande to Andwarpe upon occatyon nett 000–1[3]–2

Item paid Jno Bowde to paie unto Gervase the master of the workes for anvells formes and elles provided by them in duchlande 026–05–0

£159–12–11

[*10v*] . . . [ ] at his goinge out of the high countrie wyth the duchmen to be [ ] for 004–00–1[0]

Item spent per Edward [ ] goynge and comynge out of holande [ ] Relfe [howle] to take [ ] Gervase and his company 00–15–0

Item paid frolycke the 24th of September 1565 00–07–0

. . . budde the same day and to be acompt [ ] for 02–00–0

. . . the tayller for makinge aparrell for Gervas Budde and frolycke with other and for [ ] to the saide aparrell 07–04–10

. . . for the Chardges of Gervase budde frolycke and ther company at Andwarpe tarringe upon the passage and to make them aparell 15 li 16s 6d besyde that which Jno Budde paid ther also and his accompte aperinge 015–16–6

. . . John frolycke to paie his charges Gervases and Companye from Andwarpe to hawkhurste which was spent per them which appere some 018–09–2

. . . for [openyng Shergatte] at Andwarpe when Gervases wife and here company cam thether 000–00–8

. . . harman Budde at Andwarpe to paie for the charges of Gervases wife [powle] and his wife children and companye 008–01–8

. . . John budde at his going unto utrichte in holande the 3 of october 1565 for the formes and other nessaris providede in duchlande 005–04–7

. . . for pasage of frolycke garvase and company from Andwarpe into the Charges in the shipe and upon the waie and at ther a Rivalle at mydelborowe 005–08–6

. . . for hoppinge abarrell that came with Gervases mens aparrell from utrichte 000–00–3

. . . John Budde and in charges at his retorne out of holande in Andwarpe 000–08–2

. . . to him then the 19 of october 1565 at his goinge to collene him for mo masters and men 000–17–6

. . . to him the 24 of december 1565 in Andwarp at his retorne out of duchlande and goinge into Inglande with 2 or 3 men 003–04–4

£71—19

10

[*11r*] . . . Christopher at his goinge into duchlande [ ] for the procurement of mo masters and men to [ ] 02–00–0

. . . Roger Ramsden's wiffe for the charges of John frolycke and [ ] frolycke and John budde at divers tymes and for ther lodgynge for a month or vi weekes 011–16–8

. . . John frolycke for his full satisfacion of 2000 dallers dewe unto him by contracte the some of 860 dallers at 5s the daller 215–00–0

. . . unto him for his charges at andwarp with [ ]s Receaved before at his last goinge into Inglande which was for his charge [ ] 003–19–8

. . . unto christofer the 15 of January 1565 at his retorne out of duchlande to Andwarpe to beare his charges into Inglande 001–09–2

. . . for John Cromers charges at Andwarpe the [ ] of february 1565 000–15–3

. . . mor to him and on man mor to paie for ther charges out of Andwarp into Inglande 002–18–4

. . . unto John tayller for so mych spent by John frolycke John Budde and gorge starkie at ther first comynge to the Inglysshe house in Andwarpe 007–16–2

. . . to John [quakenberge] the 2 of aprell 1566 at his comynge to Andwarpe with 5 men from John Budde for his wages 000–07–7

. . . for all ther charges at Andwarp with an overplus spent by them on the waie mor then budd gave them in duchlande 002– 7–6

. . . unto Rogius smede semper van Loue hårmon trine and Jacobe to bye them hose 000–19–7

. . . to them to beare ther Charges into Inglande from Andwarpe 002–12–6

. . . John Budde in parte of paymente of that dewe to him by contract vide 2900 dallers 097–00–0

£343– 2–5

[11^v] . . . unto John [Budde] at divers tymes after his retorne out of duchlande into andwarpe from the [ ] and his companye [ ] men in [

] 467 dallers 7 [ ] about the charge of the [ ] there [ ] in duchlande] of the wages as they [do agree] the same 116–16–2

. . . for the charges of Master John verderbecke and his company at andwarpe tarringe for passage and [ ] to be made for them 08–07–11

. . . for hose for them and for making the cost by promys agreede 001–09–2

. . . for vittalls tarrie aborde the shipe 000–10–6

. . . geven 3 hamermen at ther comynge into Inglande and [ ] backe againe from andwarpe nett 000–10–0

. . . thomas drewe to paie for the charges of John verderbecke and his company from Andwarpe unto hawkhurste 007–00–0

. . . unto peter Krisker for [ ] of Master and men and bringinge of them out of duchlande unto hawkhurst and for all ther charges with his rewarde 27– 6–8

. . . John quakenbroughe the poste le 17 of maie with John Budde sent with letters to andwarpe for his charges and wages 000–13–5

. . . Ro[t]us smede at his retorne out of Inglande to Andwarpe to bring him to his countrie againe 000–05–0

. . . for a gide and his charges to bring Gervases wiffe out of Andwarpe into Inglande 001–10–0

. . . to Wm [alger] in Andwarpe and to harmse the free hooste for so mych as the duchmen at divers times hade spent ther and for abarrell of besse geven John frolycke 003–12–6

£168– 1–4

[*12r*] . . . of the charges which harman and peter of brekefillde the last Master wer at with ther Companye in Andwarpe and for vittalls ashipe borde and the rest was paid by Budde 001–02–8

. . . for 2 stoves for the Duchmen at Andwarp 005–16–0

paid to W[ ]meter varhager for clothe hade of him for John frolycke by promyse over and above his rewarde 005–16–1

£012–14–9

Some totallis of these paymentes before writen amounteth unto the some of vii^c^lv li x s v d besydes sertayne money paid by my Servant in Andwarpe the accompte wherof not presently Receaved nor charged in this Accompt but shall apere in the nexte some 755–10–5

[*12v*] *blank*

[*13r*] Le 14 of october 1565
Wood and Colles Boughte
of John mathewe and John hewson which [1565
for the stele workes folowynge

In primis paid to John mathewe for 226 lodes of colles at 7s the loode [7]9–02–0

Item to John mathewe and John hewson for [23] lodes of myne at [ ] the lode 04–17–4

Item that I carryde to salhurste to the workes of my owne [109] loodes of colles at 9s the loode amounte 049–01–0

Item paid to Ric Bishope of wattlyngton for 1000 cordes of woode bought of him 042–00–

. . . for 20 cordes of bornynge woode for Gervase and Com-

panye at salhurst at 14d the corde 001–03–4
. . . [ ] and others for caringe the [ ] woode 001–00–0
. . . John Williams for 6 loodes of burnynge wood and for caringe the [ ] woode 000–07–8
. . . John Mathewe and John hewson for 492 cordes of woode in alfforde at selscome Redie made at 14d the corde 028–14–0
. . . him mor for 160 cordes of wood in a wood of Mr Toftons at 14d the corde redy made 009–06–8
. . . Mr alexsander Coulpeper for 2000 cordes of woode at xii d the corde to be felled and utred within 3 yeres some 100–00–0
. . . for cuttinge of 270 cordes of wood parcille of the 1000 cordes bought of bishope 004–16–6
. . . to Edward howbarde for 60 cordes of wood at 12d the corde redie made wherof ther was 9 Loodes carried to the plase for burnynge wood and the rest made 16 Loodes of colle and was cared to the stele workes at the place 003–00–0
. . . to coulgate for carringe of 96 loodes of colle out of alfforde wood in selscome at 18d the Loode 07–04–0
. . . for makinge 96 Loodes of colles of the wood aforsaide out of alfforde at 20d the Loode 008–00–

£338–12–6

[*13^v^*] Item paid for makynge of 16 Loodes of colles of the wodes hade of hobarde at 20d the lode 001–06–8
. . . for carryinge of this 16 loodes of colles 000–18–8
. . . for carriage of 9 Loodes of fyer woode to the place 000–09–0
. . . John tailler for 400 cordes of woode bought of him at 12d the corde 020–00–0
. . . John [Bratell] for [ ] Loodes of colle bought to boxhurste at 8s the lood 27–12–0
. . . for 340 Loodes of colle delyvered at boxhurst per the great weane at 9s the Loode 153–00–0

£203– 6–4

Some totalis of all these paymentes before wrytene amounteth unto the some of v^c^xli li xviii s x d 541–18–10
Item paide for makinge of [*blank*] lodes of colle in bishops woode of the 270 cordes afore wrytten at 20d the Loode
. . . for the carringe of [*blank*] Lodes of colle to the saide bishops at 15d the Loode

. . . for makinge of [*blank*] Loodes of colle out of the 160 cordes of woode hade of John Mathewe out of Mr toftons wood at 20d the Loode

. . . for carage therof to the plase to witte for [*blank*] Loodes of Colle at

[*14^r*] Somma Totallys of all the paymentes befor wryten in this booke amounteth unto the some as per the particullers dothe apere at Lenght the some of £1960–11–3 besides the 100 li for buldinge the worke houses at boxhurste and that paid in Andwarpe which is not written in this Accompte as also the 403 li dewe per arest of the contracte to John Budde net £1960–11–3

[*14^v–16^r*] *blank*

[*16^v*] per Contra Received of William Chepman Le 24th of aprell 1566 nett £07–08–6

. . . of William week Le 20 of Marche 1656 for the stele on the other side £07–00–0

. . . of Mr Winche Le 10th of auguste 1566 per myne [este axstone] £14–00–0

. . . Le 20 of June 1566 of Mr fysher of London for this verkine stele £07–10–0

. . . of Mr Winche Le 10th of auguste 1566 per myn este axston £14–00–0

. . . of Mr fysher Le 23rd of Auguste 1566 and 26th dito nett £15–00–0

. . . of Mr Chepmane Le 19th of august 1566 in money net £04–11–4

mor Received of him per yorn pootes bought of him £02–08–8

£7–00–0

[*17^r*] 1566

Solde unto william Chepman of London the 20th of Marche 1565 a verkine of stele £007–08–6

. . . william weebe of London the 20 of Marche 1565 a verkine of stele at £07–00–0

. . . Mr winche of London le dito 2 verkins of stele at £014–00–0

. . . Mr Bright Le dito on verkine of stele at £07–10–0

. . . Mr fysher of London Le 2nd of aprelle 1566 on verkine of stell £07–10–0

. . . Mr winche of London Le 2nd of Maie 1566 2 verkins of stele £14–00–0

. . . Mr fysher Le 3rd of Mair 1566 2 verkins of stele at £015–00–0
. . . Mr Chepman Le dito on verkine of stele at £07–00–0

[*17v*] Per contra received of thomas dalbye Le 2nd of Maie 1566 for this verkine of Stele £7–10–0
. . . Mr Penefather Le 27th of august 1566 for this verkine £06–13–4
. . . Mr winche le 23rd of august 1566 nett £46–13–4
. . . Gilles gerton le 28th of June 1566 upon accompt £14–00–
. . . him le 27th of august 1566 £07–00–0
£21–00–0

. . . of thomas dalbey le 20th of auguste 1566 for this verkine of stele £07–00–0
. . . Robart Richardes le 27th august 1566 upon accompte 6–13–4

[*18r*] Solde unto Thomas dalbie le 2nd of Maie 1566 on verkine of stele at £07–10–0
. . . Edward borows of Coventrie Le 3rd Maie 1566 on verkine of stele
. . . Mr penefather of London le dito on verkine of stele at £6–13–4
. . . Mr winche Le 27th June 1566 7 verkins of stele at 6 li 13s 4d le verkin £46–13–4
. . . gilles gerton le 27th June 1566 3 verkins of stele at 7 li le verkin £21–00–0
. . . thomas dalbey Le 27th June 1566 on verkine of stele at £07–00–0
. . . thomas fysher Le 27th June 1566 on verkine of stelle at £07–00–0
. . . Robart Richardes Le 27th June 1566 on verkine of stele at £07–00–0

[*18v*] . . . of gorge bige Le 16th of July 1566 for this verkin of stele £6–19–0
. . . mr chepman le 22nd of august 1566 nett £12–10–0
. . . of mr winche Le 23rd august 1566 nett £03– 6–8
Received mor of him le 27th of august 1566 upon accompte £40–00–0

[*19r*] Solde unto Gorge bigge Le 16th of July 1566 on verkine of stele at £06–19–0

. . . mr chepman Le 19th of August 1566 2 verkins of stele at 6 li 5s verkin £012–10–0

. . . thomas fysher le 20 of August 1566 2 verkins of stele at £13–10–0

To paie at holantid

. . . mr winche Le 20th of August 1566 12 verkins of stele at 6 li le verkin £72–00–0

. . . Thomas dalbye Le dito on verkin of stele at £06–10–0

Thomas fysher le 27th of August 1566 2 verkins of stele at £13–00–0

to paie at xpmas

. . . Wm webe Le dito 27th of august 1566 on verkine of stele at £06– 6–8

. . . John Bakker of Ipswiche Le dito on verkin of stele at £06–13–4

[*19v*] *blank*

[*20r*] Sold unto Thomas Dawson of Yorke le 27th of august 1566 on verkine of stele and sent him per Edwarde Cooke £06–15–0

To paie at Ladie daie next

Sold in the house per the burden and Sheafe from the 15th of december 1565 unto the 26th of september 1566 129 borden 3 sheafe for the some of £38–17–0

Shipd upon

Some totalis of all the money that hath bene Receaved upon the stele befor the 29th of September 1566 amounteth unto the some of ii^c^lxix li ii s x d besydes 21 verkins shiped upon Ralfe halle to London and not ther aryved and 15 verkins solde in London and the money not yet Received as apereth in thys booke befor written as also 4 verkins shiped into walles to thomas dane the 18 of Maie 1566 last paste which he must be accomptable for and savith xx barrells to gether £269–01–2

[*20v–21v*] *blank*

[**19**] STEEL WORKS ACCOUNTS, 1567–8

385 *U 1475 B4/2*

[*1*^{r}] The Steele Workes in the Countie of Kent

A declaration of the Reconing of the Steele Workes in Kent belonging unto the right honorable Sir henry Sidney of thorder of the Garter knight Lorde president of wales and Lorde Deputie of Irelande; Edmunde Robertes of Hawkhurste in the said Countie gent; and Jone knight of London Widowe the Late wife and Administratrix of the goodes and Cattells of Raffe knight. Owners and Copartners of the same Workes of which the saide Edmunde oweth the one halfe Aswell of all such monie as hath bene receaved as disbursed in and aboute the necessarie uses and furniture of the same which Monye was receaved and disbursed and the Reconing therof kept by the saide Edmunde Robertes and his Substitutes Viz from the xth daie of December in the xth yere of the raigne of our soveraigne Lady Elizabeth by the grace of god of Ingland frannce and Irelande Quene defendor of the faithe and Untill the xviiith daye of Aprill then next ensuing Stiz by the space of fower Monithes and od Daies

The Chardge

First the saide Edmund Robertes is chardged with somuch mony depending uppon diverse persons in the last Accompt as by the same aperith with xvii li therof by him receaved as by a particuler Booke of this Reconing doth appere CClxxviii li iiii s iiii d

Also with somuch Mony growing of the price of xvii firkins one burden v Sheef di of Steele solde of which xlv li xiii s iiii d as yet unreceaved as by the saide particuler Booke doth appere Cv li xiii s

} CCCiiii^{xx}iii li xvii s iiii d

Wherof Uppon

The particulars after named for somuch Mony by theme Due for Steele solde them and depending in the last Accompt and not yet receaved Videlt. Thomas fisher parcell of ii firkins besides C s receaved vi li Thomas Porter of London for one firkin solde him the xxviith of August 1567 vi li. Robert winch of the same for one firkin at vi li another at C s solde the xxviii^th^ of October 1567 xi li. Thomas Page of the same for one firkin of vi li, another of C s solde the xxvi^th^ of November 1567 xi li. Robert Richardes of

[*1^v^*] Lethered for one firkin to him solde the xxviii^th^ of November 1567 vi li. and Thomas Dawson of yorke for one firkin to him then solde vi li in all xli li

John Ferderbeck late Steeleman John Cromer and Jacob Scult his Suerties for somuch mony imprested to him and depending uppon the last Accompt yet unpaide xlv li xiiii s vi d

Gervas kriskan steelmaker for somuch imprested and depending uppon him in the last Accompt Clxxiiii li ix s x d

Diverse persons after named all of London for Steele to them solde since the last Accompt and yet unpaide Videlt Robert winch for ii firkins sold the xii of December xii li and other ii the xxii^th^ of february in all xxii li. Thomas fisher for one firkin solde the xvii of January vi li. John Emmes for one firkin solde the xxii^th^ of february vi li. Richard Davies for one firkin solde the xxii^th^ of february vi li. And [ ] Penyfather for one firkin solde the xxii of february Cxiii s iiii d in all xlv li xiii s iiii d

Sum of the saide Debtes CCCvi li xvii s viii d

And then Remayneth lxxvi li xix s viii d

for and against which some

[*2^r^*] Payde and disbursed to and for

Wood bought at sundry prices viz redy made lxi Cordes Cii s vi d and unmade CCCxxi Cordes xvi li xii d xxii li iii s vi d

Woodcutters for cutting viii^C^iiii^xx^x Cordes of Wood at sundry prises xv li xv s viii d

The Making of lvii firkins of Steele at xxxi s the firkin iiii^xx^viii li vii s

Making of firkins for Steele Bellowes and other necessaries bought for the workes iiii li xiiii s ix d

Lande carriadg of Plate and steele and other necessaries for the workes lxvii s x d

Fraight Lighterage for plates and Steele and other necessari Water cariage xxx li x s iiii d

Wages with C s for the Auditors Reward for the Last Accompte xvii li xxi d

Rentes for houses xl s

Foren Charges viz ryding chardges Rewardes to workmen Dockettes and such Like with C s iiii d for chardges in surgery and answer to the Lanegrave of hess xii li vii s x d

CCv li viii s viii d

And so the saide Edmunde is in A Supplussage uppon this Accompt Cxxviii li ix s

[*2v*] The Declaracion of the Reconing of Steele plates wood and Coles According to A Remaynte taken the saide xviii[th] daie of Aprill 1568

Wood uncutt There remayned uppon the Last Accompt MMMC Cordes

Bought this yere CCCxxi cordes MMMCCCCxxi Cordes

wherof Cutt within the tyme of this Reconing

DCCCiiii[xx]x Cords di

And so Remayneth standing in sevrall places MMDxxx Cordes di

Wood cutt There remayned uppon the last Accompt CCCClxxv Cordes Cutt within the tyme of thas Accompte DCCCClii Cordes

MCCCCxxvii Cordes

Coles There remayned uppon the last Accompt

CCCCxxiiii Lodes

whereof Spent to make lvii firkins of Steele at iii Lodes to a firkin Clxxi Lodes

And so Remayneth CCliii Lodes

viz

Lent to Blacknall my Lordes Clerke xxiiii Lodes

Remaining by estemacion CC Lodes

In [deficient by burning] and by [ ] of steele made [there] is [noted] [xxix] lodes CCliii Lodes[1]

Plates for Steele Remayning uppon the Last Accompt xxix ton di CC di Receaved in the tyme of this reconing xxxix ton vii[C] di

Lxix Ton

wherof Spent in making lvii firkins of Steele after DCCCC di [or theraboutes] to a firkin xxvii Ton C di

And so Remayneth by estimacion xxli Ton di C di

[*3r*] Steele Remayning uppon the last Accompt with ii firkins sent by Raff Knight into Ireland and vi firkins sent to Thomas Dan

x firkins di v burdens

Made since the Last Accompt lvii firkins

lxvii firkins di v burdens

wherof Solde within the tyme of this Accompt with v firkins

[1] The *ms* is faded.

solde by Thomas Dan		xvii firkins i burden v Sheaffe di
And so Remayneth		l firkins di iii burdens di sheaff
Therof Delyvered to Thomas Dan	of olde ii firkins, more iiii: vi firkins	l firkins di iii burden di sheaff
Delivered by Raff Knight in to Ireland	ii firkins	
Remayne more	xlii firkins di on burden, di sheaff	

The value of the Remayntes	
Wood uncutt MMDxxx Cordes di at xii d a Corde	Cxxvi li x s vi d
Wood cutt MCCCCxxvii Cordes at xvi d ob a Cord and xx s over [ ]	[ii]^{xx}xix li ii s i d ob
Coles CCxxiiii Lodes at viii s vi d the Lode	iiii^{xx}[x]v li iiii s
Plate xli Tons di C di at iiii li a Ton	[Clxvi li vi s]
Steele l firkins di iii burden di the [a firkin]	CCliii li ii s viii d
	DCCxl li v s iii d ob

[*3*^{v}] A Brieffe Estimate of the value of all Debtes and Remayntes both of Iron and Steele worke viz

At the Iron Workes	
Debtes in that Accompt besides huggettes Respite and Nevettes overplus	CCCxxviii li vi s iii d
The Value of the Remaintes in thende of that Accompt	DCCClxiii li ix s v d
The Landes and Tenementes belonging to the forge and furneis purchased in fee simple cost	CCCC li
The farme of the Rather having one yere to come	vii li
Horses viii at xvi s a peece and a Bull xx s in all	vii li viii s
Synders to wash by estimacion lx ton besides xx s a ton wasshing	lx li
Olde Iron with Anviles hammers and other Tooles	xii li
	MDClxxviii li iii s viii d
At the Steele Worke	
Debtes in that Accompte	CCCvi li xvii s viii d
The Value of the Remaintes in that accompte	DCCxl li v s iii d ob
The Tooles of those Workes	xx li
Twoo Stoves	Cxvi s
Bedding by estimacion	xx li
	Miiii^{xx}xii li xviii s xi d ob
Sum Totalis	MMDCClxxi li ii s vii d ob

[*4*$^{r-v}$] *blank*

[20] GLAMORGAN IRONWORKS ACCOUNTS, 1564–5

386 *U 1475 B17/1*

[*1r*] The vewe of the Accompte of Edward Nevet for i yeare ended at the feast of the Annunciation of our Lady 1566

[*1v*] *blank*

[*2r*] A briefe vewe of the Accompte of Edward Nevet, Clarke of the Iron workes within the Com of Glamorgan begyning the Laste of Aprill 1564 exclusive and ending the xxviith day of february 1565 inclusive

The Chardge

Firste the saide Edwarde is chardged with sundry somes of money parcell of a bill of preste or remaynt to him delivered at his entry over and besides sundry somes in his severall bookes charged and over and besides divers other somes otherwise cut of and allowed, as by the said bill of prestes more particulerly it dothe and maye appere Clvii li xii s viii d

Also he is charged with sundry somes of money by him receaved aswell parcell of the said bill of prestes as otherwise to the use of the Masters besides money receyved for Iron as by his forge booke of the yere 1564 particulerly apperethe Cxli li x s v d ob

. . . money receyved of sonndry persones to the use of the Masters for the price of iiii^{xx}i tonne xvii^{C}iii q xvii lli weight of Iron by him sould at sundry rates as apperethe in his forge booke of the said yere 1564 ix^{C}xx li iiii s viii d q

. . . sundry somes by him receaved aswell parcell of the said bill of prestes as otherwise to the masters use as appereth by ii forge bookes for the yere 1565 xxxix li

. . . money receaved of sundry persones for the prise of lxxiii tonn CCC iii q xv lli weight of Iron by him sold at sundry rates as apperethe by the said ii forge bookes 1565 DCCiiii^{xx}xiiii li iii s ob q

[*2v*] . . . so much money by him receaved at sundry tymes of John stone of bewdely and margaret his wief uppon a Reconing of xiiii tonn D weight of Iron by him alledged to be sent them as appereth by the Laste forge booke of the yere 1565 Cxxxi li iii s iiii d

Sum Totles of the said charge MMCiiii^{xx}iii li xiiii s ii d ob di

wherof Allowances

The said Accomptant is allowed for sundry somes of monie by him paied to diverse and sondry persones aswell for Rentes and wages as for thinges bought and besides xxxiii s iiii d after respited unto him as appereth by his fornes bookes of 1564 Ciiii^{xx}xiiii li xix s x d

Also for the like monye by him paied to sundry persons besides lxvi li xv s xi d after respited as appereth in his ii fornes bookes of 1565 iiii^{C}lxvi li xv s i d ob

. . . Cii s ii d after Respited and besides xl s delivered in preste after in supplus as appereth by his forge booke of 1564 iiii^{C}xv li xxiii d

. . . ix li v s ii d after respited as appereth by his ii forge bookes of 1565 CCxxxii li iii s i d q

Sum of the said allowances MCCCviii li xix s xi d ob q

[*3*^{r}] Sondry money Also he is allowed for so much money by him paied by wey of lyvery monie that is to saie to Sir henry Sidney Knight as for di tonn of Iron by him geven to Thomas blont and bought by this Accomptannt Cxii s vi d. To Edmond Robertes by thandes of his servannt Roger morrey lx li and to the said Edmund more by thandes of Mr pepwall to be paied to nicholas more Cvi li xiii s iiii d in all as appereth by his forge booke of Anno 1564

Sum Clxxii li v s x d

Sum of all the said allowances Miiii^{C}iiii^{xx}i li v s ix d ob q

And so he owth DCCii li viii s iiii d ob q di

therof Respited To him for sundry somes of money by him demed to be receaved of the parties undernamed parcell of the prest bill delevered him at his entrye which the Masters alledg he covenanted to have taken up for them uppon payment of thies parties severall wages viz Lambe the Collier xvii li x s Owli minion the Collier Cxvii s and Owbrey and michell Cxi s in all xxviii li xviii s

Also respited unto him for so muche by him alledged (but not proved) to be lesse receaved of Mr pepwall of Bristowe for yron then is charged in his bookes and contrary to a bargaine made betwixt them, which in monie he saithe Mr pepwall ought yet to paie but Mr pepwall voucheth An undoing of that bargaine by his consent, here Respited and not allowed till it may be understand what the Latter willeth in this case xv li

[*3v*] Also Respited unto him for sundry somes of mony by him demanded in his severall bookes of paimentes aforesaid but not allowed untill examinacion be hade of the assured disbursement of them without frawde as by a speciall bill of the particelles particulerly apperethe iiii^xx^ii li xvi s vii d

Sum of the Respite Cxxvi li xiiii s vii d

And so he oweth besides Dlxxv li xiii s ix d ob q di

Wherof uppon diverse persones for sundry somes of mony mencioned in the bill of prestes delivered him at his Entrye viz John mynion xl s, Richard Bachelor lvi s viii d, The same Richard lviii li, llm Jones xxxii li viii s, Jenn mercill xvi li, Lewes Rees xl s, william welles xii li, and the Colliers lxx s in all Cxxviii li xiii s viii d

William minion for so muche Receaved of the said Edward for his wages aforehand which shalbe due for a yere to be ended at middsomer 1572[1] as by his forge booke 1564 appereth xl s

The said Accompt CCCCxliiii li xix s i d ob q di

(Md this later part of the reconing was taken at the workes in may 1566 and extendeth till our Ladie daie 1566)

Wherunto There is to be added Chardge

furste for iii tonn of Iron sold by hobald parcell of the remainder delivered by Nevet in writing of his Accompte as a appereth by a bill xxxvi li v s

Item for D iii qrt xxiiii lli sold by nevetes man parcell of the same Remaint at xii s the C as appereth by the same bill lxxi s vi d

Item for i tonn di CC di iii lli parcell of the said remaint sold by Nevetes wief and otherwise chardged to him at xii li a tonn as appereth by another bill xix li x s

[*4r*] Item for so muche chardged to him for Bachelers[2] Abatement after C s a quarter for michelmas Cristmas 1565 and our Lady daye 1566 xv li

Item for so muche he before Respited parcell of the bargaine of the farme bought of Morgan Jones because the marsters cannot enjoye the bargaine xviii li xviii s iiii d

Sum of this newe chardge iiii^xx^xiii li iiii s x d

which being ioyned to the aforesaid some uppon the said Accomptannt dothe Amount in the whole to

Dxxxviii li iii s xi d ob q di

[1] There is no obvious explanation for this date. See also *387* (p. 240, below).

[2] The word *wages* has been crossed out.

therof Allowance Allowed unto him for sundry somes discounted uppon reconing with sundry persones of the prestes by him demanded and by them confessed as appereth by A brief booke therof Remaining with Thomas Danne

Ciiii^xx iii li viii d ob

Item for so muche more allowed unto him for paymentes made by his wief and hobald out of the yron laste sold as appereth by iii bylles therof [all], besides the impreste in the same billes after [set] off from him and be my entred in the said brief booke, and besides xxvi s viii d for the rest of morgan Jones paiment for the farme disallowed and besides money delivered to Thomas Danne after allowed xiii li xvi s xi d

Item for his wages for Christmas 1565 not before Allowed x li

Item for so much monie delivered to Thomas Danne at ii tymes by gobale xxi li xi s v d

Sum of thies last allowannces CCxxviii li ix s ob

And so he oweth CCCix li xiiii s xi d q di

[*4^v^*] therof Respited for so muche by him alledged to be [allowed] in prest to llan Jones besides the stocke xxxi li xvi s x d and for the like to John Powes lvii s

In all Sum xxxiiii li xiii s x d

And yet he oweth CClxxv li xiii d q di

Imprestes Remain Uppon John mynion and great John besides xxxiii li ix s iii d discounted xxix li xxi d

The same uppon Coling by lode iiii li xix s v d

Clement the Collier xxiiii li x s viii d

Gilbert xl s

Owbery besides viii li vi s vii d ob discounted lxxviii s viii d ob

Michell the Collier xxviii s iiii d

Morgan Jenkin Cutler xxviii li ii s ii d

Evan the Collier xviii li xiii s iiii d

Griff Melyn lxi s viii d

Bacheler besides xxxii li x s discounted and besides other imprestes by danne vii li xvi d ob

Hoell ap hoell xiii li xvi s

Edward Nevet himself clere Cxxxviii li vii s viii d q di

Md his bookes are so disorderly made as no man is able to make any particuler declaracion of his Chardge or dischardge, Again he had at his coming to his Accompt in february iiii^c li [allowed] in prestes and was to Accompt with sundry of the workmen for midsomer michelmas and Christmas as before, which Reconinge Raff Knight and I were forced to finishe at the workes in m[a]y last because we wold have his Accompt to determine at our Lady Daie last, for order to be the rather had herafter. The Respites are to be examined by Thomas Danne no figure will best Serve him. Which being once perfect this vewe shall be finished

[Ex per]Robt[ ] Davy

[5^r–6^r] *blank*

[6^v] Edward Nevettes accompt
24 August 1566

[21] GLAMORGAN IRONWORKS, 1567–8

387 *U 1475 B17/2*

[*1*^{r}–^{v}] *blank*
[*2*^{r}] The County of Glamorgan
The Accompte of Thomas Danne Clerke to the right honourable Sir Henry Sydney of the Order of the Garther Knight Lord President of Wales and Lord Deputie of Ireland, Edmund Robertes of Hawkehurste in the countie of Kent of gent and Jone Knight of London widowe Administratrix of the goodes and Cattells of Raffe Knight decessed, Owners and coparteners of certein Iron workes within the said Countie of Glamorgan (of which the said Edmund oweth the one half) Aswell of all such monie as he the sayd Thomas Danne hath receaved or otherwise standes chardged with As also howe the same are Defrayed disbursed or otherwise imployed in and about the necessarie use of the said workes or otherwise That is to say frome the feast of Easter in the ixth yere of the raigne of our Soveraigne Lady Elizabeth by the grace of god of England frannce and Ireland Quene Defendor of the faith or Untill the feast of Easter in the xth yere of her majesties raign As by A particuler booke Delivered by the said Thomas Danne it may and doth appere viz

The Chardge
first the said Accomptannte is chardged aswell with iiii^{xx}iii li viii s iii d for his owne arrerages uppon his last accompte as with iii^{C}iiii^{xx}iii li vii s vi d di q for divers other arrerages in the same Accompt respited and depending with lviii li x s vi d thereof by him Levied as in his said and particuler booke appereth CCCClxvi li xv s ix d di q
Also with so much monie by him Receaved for the price of iiii^{xx} tonne di ix^{C} v lli weight of Iron by him sold at sundrie prices as by his said particuler booke appereth besides xx li in the same booke defalked for so much overchardged the last yere viii^{C}xlii li xix s viii d
Also with so much monie growing of the price of Iron by him sold to be paid for at dayes to come viz to william Wele of Gloucester ii tonne at xxi li and to John Taylor of the same di tonne Cv s amounting togethers to xxvi li v s
Also with somuch due for the rent of Morgan Jenkins land due at thannunciacion last xl s
MCCCxxxviii li v d di q

[*2*^{v}] The dischardge

First the said Accomptannte is Allowed for mony by him paid for thinges bought workes don Rentes wages and other chardges concerninge onely the furneis as by the said particuler booke appereth viz to and for

Woode bought at sundry prices some by nombre of Cordes and some in grosse xxviii li ii s ix d

Woode Cutters for cutting and making of v^{M}DCCClx cordes di at sundry rates Cii li iiii s vi d

Colliers for Coling MCCxxxix load vi Sackes of coles at ii s the lode with x s viii d for xvi Sackes of coles bought Cxxiiii li ix s viii d

Carriage of coles by the loade at sundrie prices DCxxxix lode viii sackes xxiii li vii s vi d ob and by the tonne so many as made Ciii tonne sowes and plates xxv li xv s in all xlix li ii s vi d ob

Myners for drawing of Myne by the weeke with li s for digging of Marle and with li s for cutting of wood for the myne pittes iiii^{xx}ii li ii s xi d

Founders and fillers working by the weeke with ix li xiiii s viii d for burning breaking wasshing and bearing myne to the furneis and with xii li vii s for washing xiii tonne di of Iron out of Sinders lxxviii li vii s iii d

Repayringe the furneis Colehouses and other buildinges there xii li v s i d ob

[*3*^{r}] Necessaries bought with xii li viii s i d for the price of tenne horses and one bull with shoing of horses and with xiii li xvi s i d for newe making and Repayring of Bellowes xxxviii li iii d

Rentes for landes hired by the Coparteners for their necessarie use about the workes with l s nowe pourchased xxxii li xi s vii d

Wages paid to divers workemen hired by the yere with Cxi s for lyveries xv li xii d

Sum for the furneis Dlxii li vii s vii d

Also for mony by him paid for the like chardges concerning onely the forge as by the said particuler booke appereth viz to and for

Woode bought of Jem Griff in grosse Cxiii s iiii d

Woode Cutters for cutting and making iii^{M}viii^{C}lxxv cordes of woode at sundrie rates lxii li xii s x d

Colliers for coling so many coles as made in cleane Iron iiii^{xx}vii tonne at xi s a tonne xlvii li xvii s

Heapinge bearing and housing of Cxl loade of coles xi s viii d

Forgemen for fyning and hammering iiii^{xx}vii tonne of Iron at xx s a tonne iiii^{xx}vii li

Repayringe the forgehouse Colehouses and other houses there xv li iiii s vii d

[*3*^{v}] Necessaries bought, with lxxii s i d for repayring of Bellowes and vi li xiii s viii d for hammers and Andviles sent out of Sussex xi li iii s vii d

Rentes paid for landes hired by the Coparteners for their necessarie use about the workes lxvii s i d

Wages paid to divers workemen hired by the yere with C s for lyveries xli li xiii s iiii d

Sum for the Forge CClxxv li iii s v d

And also for monie by him payd for causts not properly apperteyning either to furnas or forge but generally to them both or otherwise forrein to both viz to and for

Chardges and expenses in Journeying of the Coparteners and others by their Appointment coming to the workes for the viewe and oversight of the same at sundrie times vii li. And the Clerkes chardges in Riding to dyvers places for Sale of Iron iiii li ii s viii d in all xi li ii s viii d

Carriage and fraight of Iron betwixt making and delivery uppon Sale xi li ii s vi d ob

Reparacions done uppon the house in Cardiff with hedging and ditching of landes at the Rather and elsewhere vii li iii d

Wages and Rewardes viz the Clerkes wages x li. The Auditors Rewarde C s. The generall Carriers wages lxx li and Rewardes given to dyvers workemen by the Coparteners appointment for sundry respectes xvii li vi s xi d in all Cxxii li vi s xi d

[*4*^{r}] Forreyn Paymentes besides as Inke paper chardges in Lawe writing of Instrumentes or specialtes with iiii li for A fine of land taken by lease this yere x li xii s viii d

Sum of forrein paymentes Clxii li v s ob

ix^{C}iiii^{xx}xix li xvi s ob

The Remaynder

There Remayneth due to the Coparteners parcell of the said Chardge CCCxxxviii li iiii s iiii d ob di q

thereof Respited

To Edwarde Nevet uppon his Accompt for so much monie by him alledged to be payd to Huget for an old debt due to him by the Coparteners by a bill not brought in and therefore Respited and not allowed xliii li xvi s i d

To the said Edwarde for so much by him alledged uppon his Accompt (but not proved) to be more chardged in his said bookes then receaved of Mr Pepwell of Bristowe for Iron sold him for that Mr Pepwell (as he saith) paid him lesse then his bargaine was which Mr Pepwell denies therefore here also Respited untill the matter be better examined xv li

lviii li xvi s i d

And yet Remayneth CClxxiv li viii s iii d ob di q

whereof uppon divers persons undernamed for monie by them due parcell of a bill of debtes delivered to Nevet the late clerke at his entrie to have bene discounted viz Lambert xvii li x s. Old Mynion Cxvii s. John Mynion xl s. Richard Bacheler

[*4v*] for hay xxx s. Obery and Michaell Cxi s. llan Jones besides viii li xiiii s x d discounted this yere xxiii li xiii s ii d.[3] Jem apinall besides iiii li discounted this yere C s. Lewes Res xl s. William Welles xii li. And certein colliers at the furnes lxx s. in all as appereth by the said bill and Nevettes Accompt

lxxviii li xi s ii d

William Mynyon for so much Receaved of Nevet before hand for wages for a yere to end at midsomer 1572[4] xl s

Divers persons undernamed parcell of a booke of imprest delivered in Nevettes time and in his Accompt depending besides sundrie somes discounted this yere and before, viz John Mynion and great John xxviii li x s vii d. Great John more xxxix s v d. Clement xxiii li x s viii d. Oberye xxviii s viii d ob. Michaell x s iiii d, and Gilbert xx s. In all as appereth by the booke of imprestes and Nevettes Accompt

lvii li xix s viii d ob

Richarde Batcheler for parte of his old stocke depending of iiii^xx^ li besides x li discounted the laste yere as in Thomas Dannes accompt and besides x li discounted this yere lx li

The same Richard for so much by Thomas Danne payd to Mr Mathewe for his rent this yere xvii li x s and for corne and other provision of houshold bought for him in Aprill 1567 lx s iii d in all xx li x s iiii d

Edwarde Nevet for his Arrerages uppon his Accompt besides lx li paide the last yere lxvii li x s ob di q

William Wele of Gloucester for two tonne Iron to him this yere sold to be paid for at Pentecost 1568 xxi li

[3] Originally xxxiii li xiii s ii d.

[4] This date appears in *386*.

[5r] John Taylor of the same for di tonne Iron to him this yere sold to be paid for as before Cvs
William Welles of Cardiff for monie due by him for Iron uppon Accompt with Thomas Danne vi li
Morgan Jenkin for so much lent him this yere by the Copart-eners xx li and for the rent of his land bound for the assurance thereof due at our Ladie day last 1568 xl s in all xxii li
Sum of all debtes hitherunto CCCxl li xvi s iii d di q

The said Accomptannt uppon the determinacion of this Accompt nil for that he is in
Supplussage lxi li vii s xi d ob

[5v] *blank*

[6r] The declaracion of the Reconing for the Iron Sowes Plates for Steele Myne Marle wood and Coles according to A remayne taken the xviith of Aprill 1569

Myne There Remayneth of myne at the furnes by estimacion l lodes, and at the myne Pittes CCCl loades CCCC loades

Marle There Remayne at the furnes xvi lodes

Woode cut for the furnes Remayning uppon the last Accompt
iiiMDCCl cordes di
Cut this yere vMviiiClx cordes di ixMDCxi cordes

whereof Made in Coles at iiiior cordes di to a lode MCCxl lodes and sackes vMDiiiixxiii cordes
And so Remayneth cut in sundrie places
iiiMiiiCiiiixxii cordes di
And deficient DCxlv cordes iiiiMxxviii cordes

woode uncut there There Remayneth more for the furnes uncut in sundrie places by estimacion vMviiiC cordes

Coles at the furnace Remaining uppon the last Accompt C lodes
Made this yere MCCxl lodes x sackes
MiiiCxl lodes x sackes

Whereof Spent for making Clvii tonn di C di in Sowes and lxvii tonne viiC di in plates blowen at xxxi foundies after xxxiiiior loade to a foundie Mlv lodes
Remayning at the furnes C loades
And in deficient by theft and spoyle and burning
Ciiiixxv loades x sackes
CCiiiixxv loades x sackes

[6v] Sowes and washed Iron Remayning uppon the last Accompt with ii tonne di of wasshed Iron and with one sowe of xii^C weight ix tonne CC weight Ciiii^xx tonne iii^C di
Blowen this yere with xiii tonne di
wasshed out of the Sinders Clxxi tonne C di

Whereof Made into wrought Iron after iii tonne
Sowes to ii tonne Iron Cxxx tonne di }
Made into tooles C di xxvii lli } Cxxx ton di C di xxvii lli

And so remayneth xlix ton di C di Ciii q i lli
thereof [allowed] to Mr Robertes of old one Sowe of xii C
To him more by thandes of Mr xpofer in rawe Iron
i tonne iiii^C weight
xlvii ton Cxiiii lli
Remayning with ii tonne of washed Iron xlv tonne Dxiiii lli
And so in deficient by reason the xiii tonne di of washed Iron yeldes not as the rest doth viz iii tonne to make ii ii ton x^C di xv lli
Md that is a lack of weight by a fault in the Beame at the furnes by CC di in ech tonne this notwithstanding the Sowes yeld after iii tonne to ii tonne in Iron

Plates for Steele Remayning uppon the last Accompt besides one tonne di C qrt cut of for lack of weight as before
x tonne viii^C iii qrt
Cast this yere in good weight lxviii tonne viii Ciii qrt
lxvii tonne di C qrt
All which are allowed to Mr Robertes viz before Christmas xxxviii tonne iii^C iii quart And since xpemas xxxix tonne vii^C di And so remain nil

[7r] Woode cut for the forge
Remayning uppon the last Accompt MCCiiii^xx x cordes
Cut this yere iii^M viii^C lxxv cordes
v^M Clxv cordes

whereof Made into Coles after v lodes to A tonne of Iron for iiii^xx vii tonne after iiii^or cordes di to A loade Mix^C lvii cordes di
Remayneth cut in sundrie places iii^M iii^C xlviii cordes di
And so is saved in Cordes after this rate Cxli cordes
Woode uncut there There Remayneth in sundrie places in great parcells sums as by estimacion will make x^M cordes

Coles at the forge Remaynyng uppon the last Accompt iiii^xx lodes }
Made this yere for iiii^xx vii tonne of Iron at v loades to A tonne iiii^C xxxv loades } Dxv loades

whereof Spent in making iiii^{xx}vii tonne Iron iiii^{C}xxxv lodes
Remayneth xx loades
And in deficient by occasions aforesaid lx loades } iiii^{xx} loades

Iron Remaynynge at the forge the xxix of march 1567 with ii tonnes [allowed] to Mr Robertes uppon accompt xi tonnes
Made this yere iiii^{xx}vii tonne
More in wrought tooles [allowed] as foloweth Cxviii lli weight
iiii^{xx}xviii ton Cxviii lli weight

[*7^v*] whereof Solde to sundrie persons iiii^{xx}iii ton ix^{C}v lli weight
[allowed] to diverse workemen for tooles xviii^{C} di xxvii lli
Geven in Reward for sundrie respectes xiii^{C} qrt viii lli
And so
iiii^{xx} v tonne Cxii lli
Remayneth of this Chardge xiii tonne vi lli
[allowed] to Mr Edmunde Robtes with ii tonne in the last Accompt
iiii tonne
To him more by thandes of Mr xpofer with Cxviii lli in Tooles
ii ton iii^{C}iii qrt xxii lli
Remayninge at the forge with one tonne CCCiii qrt xvi lli weight gayned in waight uppon Recept and delivery viii tonne
xiiii ton iii^{C}iii qrt xxii lli

[*8^r*] The valewes of all the Remayntes
At the furnes
Myne at the furnes fiftie lodes at v s the lode and at the pittes CCCl^{ti} lodes at ii s vi d a lode lvi li v s
Marle xvi lodes at xvi d a lode xxi s iiii d
Woode cut iii^{M}iii^{C}iiii^{xx}ii cordes di at x d the corde Cxl li xviii s ix d
Woode uncut by estimation v^{M}viii^{C} cordes at iiii d the corde
iiii^{xx}xvi li xiii s iiii d
Coles C loades at vi s viii d a loade xxxiii li vi s viii d
Sowes at lx s a tonne xliii ton di vii^{C} Rawe and wasshed Iron at xl s A ton iii Ton iiii^{C} weight Cxxxvii li xix s
Plates for Steele nil
iiii^{C}lxvi li iiii s i d
At the forge
Woode cut iii^{M}iii^{C}xlviii cordes at viii d a corde Cxi li xii s
Woode uncut by estimation x^{M} cordes at iii d a cord Cxxv li
Coles xx lodes at vi s the Lode vi li
Iron to Mr Robertes at xii li the tonne iiii^{or} tonne and at x li x s a tonne x tonne iii^{C}iii qrt xxii lli Cliiii li xiii s iiii d
iii^{C}iiii^{xx}xvii li v s iiii d
Sum totalis viii^{C}lxiii li ix s v d

[*8^v*] Thinges to be Accompted uppon not before valued
Houses and land in fee simple

Leases of houses and lande
Houshold stuff
4 Plates to be accompted for by Mr Robtes
Workehouses with their necessaries
Horses xxii[ti]
One Bull
Synders yet to wassh
Old Iron and plates at the forge
Tooles of Iron at the furnes and forge
All manner of Debtes and Arrerages

[9^{r}–^{v}] *blank*

[22] GLAMORGAN IRONWORKS ESTIMATES FOR MAKING IRON, 1568

388 *U 1475 B17/3*

[1^r] *blank*

[1^v–2^r][1] An estimate of one wh[ole yere] at the fornes and forge in the countie of Glamor[gan] the charge of a tonne of plates for steele and a tonne of Iron redie[ ] that each tonne standethe the owners in severallie proporcioned into xx[f]owndies at vi daies to every foundie viz for

[1^v] Plates x foundies wherin is cast comonlie one foundie with another viii tonne amountinge in the whole iiii^{xx} tonne

Which asketh in

Coles CCCl Loades accomptinge xxxv Loades to eache foundie that is to saie everie Loade havinge in wood iiii cordes di at ii d ob the cord standing xi d q Cutting of the same at iiii d the cord xviii d Coling of the same ii s Cariage of the same ii s ob q Howsinge of the same i d So is the loade vi s vii d which ammonteth for the same CCCl Loades Cxv li iiii s ii d

Myne CC Loade accomptinge ii loade di to everie tonne that is saie digginge and drawinge of eache loade ii s Cariage of the same from the pitte to the furnes xii d Expence of Iron charge of Smithes worke with wast of wood to burne in the pittes vi d So is the loade iii s vi d which amonteth for the same CC Loades xxxv li

Marle xl Loade accompting iiii load to every foundie that is to saie digginge and drawinge of eache loade iiii d Cariage of the same to the furnes xvi d So is the Loade xx d whiche amounteth for the same xl Loade iii li vi s viii d

Lymestones x loade accomptinge one Loade to every foundie that is to saie digginge and Carynge of each loade to the furnes vi d which amonteth for the same x loades v s

founders wagis for viii wekes di being iii persons in nombre that is to saie the Master havinge ix s vi d the weke iiii li ix d his fellow viii s the weke iii li viii s the man vi s the weke li s The Master also havinge wagis for breaking of Myne at the

[1] This heading is set across the top of facing pages, which are damaged at the spine.

pittes for xi wekes at vii s vii d the weke iiii li iii s v d So amonteth all to xiii li xv s ii d
fillers wages at vi s the foundie for the saide x foundies iii li. Washers and burners for the like at iii s the foundie to each of them iii li, is in all vi li
Clerkes wagis for one quarter and ahalf of ayeare he havinge xl li by the yeare amounthe to the Somme of xv li
Cariage of thesame iiii^xx tonne of plates from the furnes to Cardife at iii s iiii d the tonne amountes to the Som of xiii li [6s 8d]
Rentes for the furnes and landes belonginge to the same for one quarter di of the yeare the Somme of xi li iiii s iii d
Lyveries for the whole yeare iiii li xiiii s, wherof taken to this [person] xl s
Cariage of x Loade of Sande to the furnes for the same x foundies at vi d the Loade amountes to the Somme v s
Reperacions necesaries bought for inparmentes, Smithes woorke, wast of Iron, wood, Coles and other furnetures, hoyre of waies, rewards trespaces the owners and the Clerkes their charges in Jorneyinge with all other extraordinarie paymentes whatsoever, estimated at C li by the yeare wherof ther is taken to this porcion Somm xxxvii li x s
Hallage and fraight viz at ii d the tonne to the bote xiii s iiii d, fraicte from the Key to the Barke at vi d the tonne xl s, fraicte from Cardiffe to Rie of the saide plates at xx s the Tonne iiii^xx li is in all iiii^xx ii li xiii s
Somma tottalles of the whole charge CCCxxxv li x s iii d
So standith a tonne of plates to the owners after this reconinge in iiii li iii s x d ob
and iii d over in the wh[ole]

[*2r*] Sowes xvi foundies wherin is cast comonlie one foundie with another viii Tonne which amountes in the whole Cxxviii tonnes

whiche

[15]68 Maketh in cleane Iron after ii tonne Iron unto of thre tonne of Sowes iiii^xx v tonne vi^c di xviii^to waight
Coles v^c xii loades accomptinge xxxii loade to every foundie at the price before rehersid in thestimate of the plates which in all Ammountes to Clxviii li x s viii d
Myne CCCiiii^xx iiii loades accomptinge iii loade to every tonne of Sowes at the price mencioned in thestimate of the Plates which in all ammountes to lxvii li iiii s

Marle xl Loade accomptinge ii Loade di to every foundie at the price mentioned in thestimate of the Plates which in all amountes to iii li vi s viiii d

founders wagis for xiii wekes and v daies for the saide xvi foundies vz The Master at ix s vi d the weke vi li xi s v d, his fellow at viii s the weke v li x s viii d, their man at vi s the weke iiii li iii s, more to the Master founder for his wagis, xviii wekes v daies di for digginge of Myne at the Pittes at vii s vii d the weke vii li iii s v d ob, Which in all amountes to xxvii li viii s vi d ob

fyllers wagis for the saide xvi foundies at vi s the foundie iiii li xvi s, washers and burners of myne at iii s the foundie to eche of them duringe the saide tyme iiii li xvi s, which ammountes in all to ix li xii s

Clerkes wagis as for the residue of his whole yeare viz for ii qr di after the rate expressid in thestimate of Plates the Som of xxv li

Rentes as so moche dewe for the residue of the whole yeare for the furnes viz for ii quarters di amountes to the Somme of xv[i] li xiii s x d

Rentes as so moche dew for the whole yeare for the forge Som of iii li vi s ix d

Colliers paide at the forge for theforsaide iiii^{xx}v tonn vi^{C} di xviii lli waight of cleane Iron at xi s the tonne amountes to the Som of xlvi li xviii s viii d

Coles CCCCxxvi loade accomptinge v loade to the makeinge of every tonne of cleane Iron at the price of ii s the Loade viz accomptinge iiii cordes to every lode of Coles the wood standinge at ii d the corde and for cuttinge of every corde iiii d which amountith to in the whole to xlii li xii s

Cariage of the saide Cxxviii tonne of Sowes from the furnes to the forge at v s the Tonne ammountes to xxxii li

Cariage of thesaide iiii^{xx}v tonne vi^{C} di xviii lli waight of wrought Iron from the forge to Cardif at v s the Tonne ammountes to xxi li x s iiii d

Wagis for the whole yeare at the forge viz the hamerman iii li vi s viii d the wood cariar iiii li, the Collier ther iii li, the Cole carier xxiiii li, the Cole bearer xlvi s viii d, in Lyveries there iiii li viii s with Liiii s beinge the residue of the charge of lyveries for the fornes amountes to xliii li xv s iiii d

Repracions with the residew exprest in thestimate of Plates lxii li x s, more in like sorte for the whole yeare at the forge estimated at xl li, whiche in all ammountes to Cii li x s

fyninge and hamerynge of the saide iiii^{xx}v tonn vi C di xviii lli waight of cleane Iron at xx s the tonn iiii^{xx}v li vi s vi d, Hallege of thesame to the Bote at ii d the ton xiiii s ii d be
iiii^{xx}vi li viii d ob

Somma tottalles of the whole charge viCiiii^{xx}xviii li ix s vi d

So standeth a tonne of Iron to the owners after this reckoninge in the Som of viii li iii s viii d
iii s iiii d over in all

[2^v] *blank*

APPENDIX

THE IRON AND STEELWORKS DOCUMENTS

The system of numbering used by the Historical Manuscripts Commission (369–388) is straightforward, apart from minor items within 372 and 375, which were not all clearly marked. Certain documents from outside this main series are included in the list below where relevant to the ironworks. The Kent Archives Office numbering (prefix U 1475) is on an entirely different system. The documents included in this edition are indicated by italic numbering, and their position in the text of this volume is indicated by bold numbers in square brackets.

		H.M.C.	K.A.O. (U 1475)	
	1541	369	B5/1	Complementary summary accounts, covering the first period of building at Robertsbridge
		370	B5/2	
[1]	1541		*E59*	*Lease of Panningridge: Richard Clarke, parson of Penhurst to William Spycer, for construction of a furnace*
	c. 1541	1147	E54/1	Enquiries to be made at Robertsbridge (includes furnace, mining, and wood cutting)
	1542	371	B7/1	Book of payments at Robertsbridge, excluding April–August
		372	B7/2	Detailed account, April–August only
		374	B13	Roll of payments—most totals correspond with 376
		376/2	B6/2	Payments by Horrocke
		375/1	B12	Fragment of Forge Book
		376/1	B6/1	Summary account (omits April–August)
	1541–3	375/4	B12	Money delivered to Horrocke
		375/7	B12	Money delivered to Westall
	1543	379/1	B2/2	Detailed book of receipts and of payments at the forge and the furnace

[2]		*373*	*B9*	Panningridge Furnace *building* and operating account
[3]		*377/1*	*B2/3*	*Summary account, based on details in 379/1 and 373*
	1544	379/2	B7/3	Forge wages
		375/5	B15	Furnace stocks
		375	B1/1	Summary account
		375	B12	Payments to lighterman corresponding with B1/1*
	1545	377/3	B1/3	Summary account
	1546	377/4	B1/4	Summary account
	1547	383/1	B10/1	Furnace Book
[4]		*377/5*	*B1/5*	*Summary account*
	1548	372A	B8/1	Forge Book
		372A	B10/2, 2A	Furnace Book
		375	B2/1	Draft for Furnace Book
		382/1	B10/3	Draft for Furnace Book
[5]		*377/6*	*B1/6*	*Summary account*
	1549	372A	B8/2	Forge Book
		372A	B8/3	Draft for Forge Book
		382/2	B10/3	Furnace Book
		383/2	B11	Incomplete Furnace Book, without totals
		383/4	B11	Furnace payments; only the ore mining and carriage correspond with 377/7
[6]		*377/7*	*B1/7*	*Summary account*
[7]	1550	*383/3*	*B11*	*Furnace Book*
	1551	380/1	B8/4	Forge Book
		382/3	B10/5	Furnace Book
[8]		*378/1*	*B3/1*	*Summary account*
		378/2	B3/2	Draft for summary
	1552	378/3	B3/3	Summary account
	1553	380/2	B8/5	Forge Book
		382/4	B10/6	Furnace Book
[9]		*378/4*	*B3/4*	*Summary account*
		378/5	B3/5	Draft for summary account
	1554	382/9	B8/6	Forge Book
		382/5	B10/7	Furnace Book
		383/5	B11/4	Basis for Furnace Book
[10]		*378/6*	*B3/6*	*Summary account*

* There are two undated fragments relating to carriage of iron to Bodiam and Rye (375/2:B14/2; 375/3:B14/1) which do not seem to relate to 1544.

[11]	1555	*381/1*	*B8/7*	*Forge Book*	
		382/6	B10/8	Furnace Book	
[12]		*378/7*	*B3/7*	*Summary account*	
		375	B1/2	Draft for summary account (incomplete)	
	1556	381/2	B8/8	Forge Book	
		382/7	B10/9	Furnace Book	
[13]		*378/8*	*B3/8*	*Summary account*	
	1558	382/8	B10/10	Furnace Book	
[14]		*378/9*	*B3/9*	*Summary account*	
	1559	378/10–1			
	1560	378/10–2			
	1562	378/10–3			
[15]	1563	*378/10–4*	B3/10	Summary accounts	
	1564	378/10–5			
	1565	378/10–6			
[20]		*386*	*B17/1*	*Glamorgan Ironworks account*	
	1566	378/10–7	B3/10	Robertsbridge summary account	
[18]		*384*	*B4/1*	*General account of the Steelworks*	
	1567	268E	E20/1	Survey of Robertsbridge Demesne, including forgemens' houses	
		378/10–8			
[16]	1568	*378/10–9*	B3/10	Robertsbridge summary account	
[21]		*387*	*B17/2*	*Glamorgan Ironworks account*	
[22]		*388*	*B17/3*	*Glamorgan Ironworks estimates of costs*	
[19]		*385*	*B4/2*	*Summary account of the Steelworks*	
	1569	378/10–10	B3/10	Robertsbridge summary accounts	
	1570	378/10–11			
	c. 1570	268E	E20/2	Survey of Woods at Robertsbridge indicating those 'appointed for the iron forge'	
	1571–2	378/10–12	B3/10	Robertsbridge summary accounts	
[17]	1572–3	*378/10–13*			
	1574	997A	E5	Rental 1574	Refer to rent of ironworks and woods
	1575	273	E6	Valuation 1575	

INDEX